A THEORY OF TORT LIABILITY

This book provides a comprehensive theory of the rights upon which tort law is based and the liability that flows from violating those rights. Inspired by the account of private law contained in Immanuel Kant's *Metaphysics of Morals*, the book shows that Kant's theory elucidates a conception of interpersonal wrongdoing that illuminates the operation of tort law. The book then utilises this conception, applying it to the various areas of tort law, in order to develop an understanding of the particular areas in question and, just as importantly, their relationship to each other. It argues that there are three general kinds of liability found in the law of tort: liability for putting another or another's property to one's purposes directly, liability for doing something to a third party that puts another or another's property to one's purposes, and liability for pursuing purposes in a way that improperly interferes with the ability of another to pursue her legitimate purposes. It terms these forms liability for direct control, liability for indirect control and liability for injury respectively. The result is a coherent, philosophical understanding of the structure of tort liability as an entire system. In developing its position, the book considers the laws of Australia, Canada, England and Wales, New Zealand and the US.

Volume 16 in the series Hart Studies in Private Law

A Theory of Tort Liability

Allan Beever

•HART•
PUBLISHING
OXFORD AND PORTLAND, OREGON
2016

Hart Publishing
An imprint of Bloomsbury Publishing plc

Hart Publishing Ltd
Kemp House
Chawley Park
Cumnor Hill
Oxford OX2 9PH
UK

Bloomsbury Publishing Plc
50 Bedford Square
London
WC1B 3DP
UK

www.hartpub.co.uk
www.bloomsbury.com

Published in North America (US and Canada) by
Hart Publishing
c/o International Specialized Book Services
920 NE 58th Avenue, Suite 300
Portland, OR 97213-3786
USA

www.isbs.com

First published 2016

British Library Cataloguing-in-Publication Data
A catalogue record for this book is available from the British Library.

ISBN: HB: 978-1-50990-318-4
ePDF: 978-1-50990-320-7
ePub: 978-1-50990-319-1

Library of Congress Cataloging-in-Publication Data

Names: Beever, Allan, author.

Title: A theory of tort liability / Allan Beever.

Description: Oxford ; Portland, OR : Hart Publishing, 2016. | Series: Hart studies in private law ; volume 16 | Includes bibliographical references and index.

Identifiers: LCCN 2016015257 (print) | LCCN 2016015646 (ebook) | ISBN 9781509903184 (hardback : alk. paper) | ISBN 9781509903191 (Epub)

Subjects: LCSH: Torts. | Liability (Law)

Classification: LCC K923 .B44 2016 (print) | LCC K923 (ebook) | DDC 346.0301—dc23

LC record available at https://lccn.loc.gov/2016015257

Series: Hart Studies in Private Law, volume 16

Typeset by Compuscript Ltd, Shannon
Printed and bound in Great Britain by
CPI Group (UK) Ltd, Croydon CR0 4YY

To Piri

CONTENTS

It is an ancient wish—who knows how long it will take until perhaps it is fulfilled—that in place of the endless manifold of civil laws, their principles may be sought out; for in this alone can consist the secret, as one says, of simplifying legislation. (Immanuel Kant, *The Critique of Pure Reason*, A301/B358)

Introduction

I. Torts and Wrongs

Tort law is notoriously hard to define. Perhaps the best definition we have is that it is the law of civil wrongs.[1] I do not wish to claim that this definition is particularly illuminating. On the contrary, it is perhaps most useful for revealing a surprising weakness in our understanding of the law. If tort law is a law of wrongs, then our understanding of these wrongs is remarkably weak.

Take a simple case. Imagine that I punch you in the face. We can all agree that this is a wrong. But exactly why is it wrong to punch someone in the face? Tort lawyers label this wrong 'battery' and they are able to tell you what needs to be proven in order to establish a cause of action for battery before a court, what the court's response will be given such proof, the historical development of this action, its economic consequences, its relationship to certain forms of justice and so on. In other words, there exists a wealth of scholarship on the legal structure and consequences of this wrong. But there is little discussion of the wrong itself.

That might seem to be a surprising claim given that there is a standard legal answer to our question. It is that a punch violates the victim's right to bodily integrity. This is often a helpful answer, but at least on its own it is unsatisfactory. Consider the following example.

Imagine that I drive my car carelessly, causing you personal injury. Here also you are able to sue me. In this case, the tort is negligence. Again, the lawyer will be able to detail what must be shown in order to ensure that you succeed in your claim, what the consequence of establishing liability will be, the origins of this action and so on. But our question again is: what is the wrong in this case? 'Negligently injuring you' is an obvious response. But why is it wrong negligently to injure someone?

The answer is again likely to be that my action violated your bodily integrity. And this reveals the inadequacy of both of our answers. If our examples involve the violation of the same right, then why do we have two separate areas of law to deal with them? And, more importantly, why do these areas of the law possess divergent rules? Why, for instance, do you have to prove that you suffered damage in the second case but not in the first, at least not if you are suing in a Commonwealth

[1] See, eg, P Birks, 'The Concept of a Civil Wrong' in D Owen (ed), *Philosophical Foundations of Tort Law* (Oxford, Oxford University Press, 1995).

court?[2] And why do you have to show that I intended to make contact with you in the first case, while you must prove only that I fell below a standard of care in the second? The mere appeal to the right to bodily integrity cannot answer these and like questions, but without these answers we cannot claim to understand the nature of the wrongdoing that these examples involve.

If tort law is a law of wrongs, we might also say that it is a law of remedies. To take our first example, the law conceptualises the punch as a wrong, a battery, and institutes a remedy for that wrong. It was natural, then, for this area of the law to be understood in terms of wrongs and remedies. But a recent trend has been to argue that tort law must also be understood in terms of the primary rights that underlie the wrongs to which it responds.[3] So we have the idea that battery protects the right to bodily integrity, false imprisonment the right to freedom of movement, defamation the right to reputation, trespass to land and goods the right to property and so on. This book accepts that this has been a major step forward in our analysis of the law. But from the perspective relevant here, this approach can be problematic.

As we have noted, it is now common to claim that the rights to bodily integrity, freedom of movement, reputation and property underlie the torts of battery, false imprisonment, defamation and trespass to land and goods respectively. But is this anything more than the production of a list? Are we simply translating the language of wrongs into the language of rights? If so, then the objection is that translation is not explanation.

Prima facie, a list of rights is no more satisfactory than a list of wrongs. Thus, the strategy of translating wrongs to rights aids legal theory only if the posited rights possess greater conceptual unity than the list of wrongs. In other words, from the perspective of the theorist, the translation from wrongs to rights is worth performing only if doing so generates a better understanding of the law. But from this perspective, that seems not to have occurred. For the theorist, our list of rights raises as many questions as the traditional list of wrongs.

Take again the right to bodily integrity. We have seen that this right is said to underlie the law of battery and part of the law of negligence. As we also saw, negligence but not battery requires proof of damage (in the Commonwealth), and while battery requires intention, negligence demands only the failure to live up to a standard of care. The tendency, therefore, is to say that the right to bodily integrity is such that one is entitled not to be touched intentionally, but only not to be injured negligently. That is fine as far as it goes, but there are two problems here. The first is that the shift from wrongs to rights seems to have added only unnecessary complexity. If the right is defined so that it mirrors exactly the wrongs as they

[2] This difference between US and Commonwealth law is examined in Ch 4.

[3] The landmark in this regard is P Benson, 'The Basis for Excluding Liability for Economic Loss in Tort Law' in D Owen (ed), *Philosophical Foundations of Tort Law* (Oxford, Oxford University Press, 1995). This approach was followed in works such as EJ Weinrib, *The Idea of Private Law* (Cambridge, MA, Harvard University Press, 1995); R Stevens, *Torts and Rights* (Oxford, Oxford University Press, 2007); and A Beever, *Rediscovering the Law of Negligence* (Oxford, Hart Publishing, 2007).

are recognised in the law, then the shift is a mere translation that reveals nothing, while adding an extra layer of analysis. The second closely related problem is the propensity to the ad hoc in this strategy. Instead of explaining the action it is said to underlie, the right in question is constantly redefined to match the contours, the sometimes changing contours, of the relevant action or actions.

In short, the difficulty is that this strategy seems inherently unsatisfactory from a theoretical point of view, however useful it may be in terms of substantive legal analysis. Theory is not satisfied by translating one list into another. Translation must not be allowed to pose as explanation.

There is also a different and perhaps even more important problem. The following chapter argues that thinking about tort law is dominated by a conceptual model inadequate to its subject matter. This model causes us to misunderstand the law, blinding us to the structure present within it. The problem here is that this model also influences our understanding of the rights thought to underlie the law. It is this model that has produced the idea that we possess rights to bodily integrity, freedom of movement and reputation, for example. A proper understanding of the law would reveal that these are not the bases of liability. In some cases, there are no such rights. In some cases, there could not be.

It is important, then, to start again. As noted, I regard the shift in focus from wrongs to rights as a major step forward; a step on the road to our destination. But to arrive there, we must do more than postulate a set of rights; we must show how those rights relate to each other and ground a systematic form of liability. That is the task undertaken here.

II. The Theory of Tort Law

Why might we want a systematic understanding of the law? Two interrelated reasons stand out. They are understanding and justification. I deal briefly with these in turn, mainly in order to avert potential misunderstandings.

It is a general principle of enquiry that, all other things being equal, more highly unified accounts of phenomena are to be preferred to the less unified. To put this another way, one way to assess a theory is to examine its explanatory power. So, for instance, while it would be possible to present one theory to explain the orbits of the planets of the inner solar system and a quite different theory to account for the orbits of the planets of the outer solar system, we recognise that this is not desirable.[4] The theory of gravitational attraction is appealing in part because

[4] Note that there would be nothing strictly illogical in such an approach. There is no reason to think a priori that the planets of the inner solar system do not orbit the sun for reasons different from those of the planets of the outer solar system. In fact (in the spirit of some legal anti-theorists), one might ask oneself whether one is not perhaps assuming too much by describing all of these behaviours with the one word: 'orbit'. And, after all, the only gravity one ever actually experiences or strictly observes is the gravity pulling on one—it is not experience that teaches me that Jupiter orbits for the same reason as Mercury. Yet these facts do not at all incline us to posit a view of the kind presented in the text.

it provides a unified account of the behaviour of all such bodies. Accordingly, it is a theory that possesses great explanatory power. The desire is to present such a theory of tort law. With explanatory power comes understanding.

The goal of scientific theory is to provide an accurate account of what exists. The job of physics is to describe the fundamental structure of physical reality, the role of chemistry is to explain the nature and behaviour of the matter constituted by that reality, and so on. Legal theory is also scientific in this sense. It is the attempt to explain a subset of what exists, in this case legal reality. But it is at this point that we may encounter difficulty. What is legal reality? With respect to law, what is it that actually exists?

It is important to acknowledge that there are different ways of answering this question. Just as a neuron in the human brain can be studied from the perspectives of physics, chemistry, biology, physical anthropology and so on, examination of law can take different points of view. For instance, one might start with the observation that the deeds of legal actors through history exist (or existed) and focus one's account on these, thereby providing an historical account of the law. Alternatively, one might note that the actions of contemporaries exist and concentrate specifically on those. This approach would emphasise the concepts utilised by present-day legal actors such as legislators, judges and barristers, and explore how those concepts are employed in today's legal decision making. Let us call this a practical approach. A third possibility would be to focus on the effects of law on society generally, exploring, say, the incentive structures produced by the law or the law's impact on matters of social justice. We might call this approach pragmatic. There are other possibilities.

One such possibility is to begin with a peculiar feature of law not found in the subject matter of the natural sciences: to begin with the fact that law is a normative enterprise. Unlike nature, law is concerned with entities such as rights, duties, permissions, liberties, obligations, powers and so on. These too exist. And so one may approach the law in an attempt to understand this normativity. Let us call this approach theoretical.[5] If one adopts this methodology, then the task is the same as it always is: to present as unified an understanding of the relevant phenomenon as possible, the phenomenon here being the law qua normative phenomenon.

This also relates to justification. If law is a normative enterprise, if law is concerned with rights, duties, permissions, liberties, obligations, powers and the like, then it must be possible in principle to explain to individuals why these norms apply—ie, there must be a sufficient reason for the existence of the norms. And in the absence of a certain degree of unity, that is not possible.[6] One cannot, for

[5] Of course, all approaches are in some way theoretical, but if we are to reserve the term for one kind of approach, this seems the most appropriate.

[6] See also GJ Postema, 'Law's System: The Necessity of System in Common Law' [2014] *New Zealand Law Review* 69. A comment about Postema's important position is in order at this point. Postema takes himself to defend what he calls the common law conception of system, which he associates with common law tradition, against alternative views, including the 'cartographic' position adopted by Peter Birks. Though Postema's analysis is outstanding, there are two related difficulties with it. First, he takes

instance, explain to one person why he has a certain obligation if the law also maintains that another person, who seems for all the world to be identically situated in the relevant respects, does not have that obligation.[7]

This type of approach is interpretive rather than descriptive or prescriptive.[8] Like descriptive accounts, the theoretical begins with the positive law, but it does not rest there. It attempts to provide the most conceptually satisfying account of the norms found in that law. Importantly, this may mean deciding that certain elements of the positive law are defective (eg, that a case is wrongly decided) because they cannot be accommodated from within the relevant system of norms set out by the law itself. On the other hand, though the theory is prepared to jettison some elements of the positive law, it is not prescriptive. It is not an account of how the law ought to be in some ideal, or even non-ideal, state. Its aim is to provide the best account of the normative structure of the law as that law is found in the actual jurisdictions in which we live. It does not therefore provide a *political* justification of tort law.[9]

One possible source of confusion in this regard is that interpretive theorists tend to use the term 'law' to apply not only to the positive law, but also to the principles discovered by interpretive legal theory—whether by one's own theory or by the theories presented in the positive law itself.[10] In this book, that approach has already been adopted. Others, however, restrict the term 'law' to only the positive law. It is important to keep this in mind.

One of the most unfortunate features of modern legal scholarship is the degree of unnecessary hostility that exists between proponents of the different

the writings of Birks' sympathisers—specifically Stephen Smith—out of context. Birks' opponents presented arguments against the 'cartographic' analysis of the law. Smith and others found those arguments unpersuasive and responded accordingly. But there is an important difference between showing an argument to be unpersuasive and presenting one's own position. Postema is insufficiently sensitive to this. For my own part, I would argue that the mainstream criticisms of Birks are uncompelling, but that does not mean that I should be categorised as a 'cartographer'. Second, the attacks on Birks advanced by those Postema mentions were not consistent with Postema's own view. Certainly, these theorists claimed to be supporting the common law tradition against Birks' innovations, but they did not share Postema's understanding of that tradition. Postema's general point is that legal analysis can be theoretical without being 'cartographic', but many of Birks' critics are indeed asserting that legal analysis cannot and/or should not be theoretical. This book is theoretical but not 'cartographic'. I regard its thesis as at least broadly consistent with Postema's position.

[7] Legal theorists are sometimes accused of being 'system builders', but the criticism is misplaced. The system is a consequence of the normative character of the law itself. The theorist is not a builder; she is a discoverer. Moreover, it is worth considering how it can be thought appropriate to criticise a legal theorist as a 'system builder' when that criticism would be laughable when applied to a natural scientist, even to one who built a system of far greater extent. Who would think of insulting Newton, Darwin or Einstein in this fashion? And there is surely more reason to think that system will be found in law than in nature. The latter is merely 'given' to us while the former is created by people trying to be systematic. On system in the common law, see also ibid.

[8] See also SA Smith, *Contract Theory* (Oxford, Clarendon Press, 2004) ch 1; A Beever and C Rickett, 'Interpretive Legal Theory and the Academic Lawyer' (2005) 68 *Modern Law Review* 320; A Beever, *Rediscovering the Law of Negligence* (Oxford, Hart Publishing, 2007) ch 2.

[9] See also section III in Ch 1.

[10] A leading example being the theory of negligence presented by Lord Atkin in *M'Alister (or Donoghue) (Pauper) v Stevenson* [1932] AC 562 (HL Sc).

approaches. It is often wrongly thought that they are incompatible. In particular, it is frequently supposed that historical, practical and pragmatic approaches are inconsistent with the theoretical. Perhaps even more unfortunately, because of this assumption, it is often taken for granted that those who advance theoretical approaches intend thereby to attack the historical, practical and pragmatic. That is a mistake. This book presents a theoretical account of tort liability. It is intended as an attack on historical, practical or pragmatic accounts of the law only to the extent that those accounts claim to close off the possibility of the theoretical.

It is sometimes said that the actual practice of law is too complicated and its practitioners too diverse to expect systematicity. If this means that it is unrealistic to imagine that the positive law and day-to-day legal decision making will exhibit a high degree of unity, then one can only agree. In fact, this complexity is usually explicitly acknowledged, even emphasised, by legal theorists and it is in part in order to remove the difficulties produced by this complexity that the theorist writes. But if one means that it follows that the normative structure of the law cannot possess systematicity, then the argument is a curious *non sequitur.*

We ought to consider that academia is full of systematic accounts of phenomena that, at the level of the phenomena, seem far more complex and diverse than legal practice—consider, for instance, the study of sociology, economics and botany to name but a few subjects. A single neuron in the human brain is probably more complex than the common law throughout its entire history and yet, thankfully, this does not prevent neurologists developing theories of the brain. Why not? Part of the answer is that these disciplines do not try to understand phenomena at the level of the phenomena. Sociologists do not try to explain why Allan Beever just pressed the 'k' key on his laptop at 11 am on the 9th day of January while sitting in his garden in Auckland while, on the other side of the world, some other hardworking academic pressed the 'l' key. Nor do botanists attempt to explain why the daisy closest to that 'k' key on that lawn in Auckland had leaves of the precise contours it possessed. The approach is more abstract and general. And that is true of legal theory as well. The theorist is not trying to capture every element of the positive law, still less the daily grind of legal practice. She is trying to capture the law qua normative enterprise.[11]

It is entirely undisputed that the positive law and legal practice is less 'tidy' than the theory presented here and that elements of these are in tension with, or even inconsistent with, the theory. Some of these elements are examined in the following. This is a theory of the bones of tort law, not of all of its flesh, still less of its malignant growths. As science can accommodate departures from the normal, a legal theory is not disproved by variations from the norm. It is just that, in the legal

[11] It is particularly important to stress that we are not trying to predict what will happen in the future. Compare B Leiter, *Naturalizing Jurisprudence: Essays on American Legal Realism and Naturalism in Legal Philosophy* (New York, Oxford University Press, 2007) 30–31, 50–52, 184. It may well be that even a perfect account of the law's normative structure provides poor tools for prediction.

context, this divergence is not merely abnormal but also deviant—a departure from the law qua normative system.[12]

It is of course possible that, even at this level, the law is too conflicted to possess anything that could be called a structure. But there is only one way to find out: to look. And that means developing theories and seeing how successful they are.

Having said that, theoretical accounts of law can rightly influence future legal practice. This is because they can provide utile methods for understanding the law. The basic theme of this book is that today's dominant model for comprehending tort law—what the following chapter labels the 'conventional view'—has enormous difficulty grasping the operation of that law and that an alternative model does far better. If this is so, then that model ought to have practical legal influence.

It may help to elucidate the relevant issues in the following manner. Imagine a conversation between a judge and a legal theorist concerning an important decision that the judge recently handed down. The theorist explains the decision in terms of a set of reasons, *x*. But the judge responds that these reasons never crossed her mind and that the real reasons for her decision were an alternative set, *y*. Here we seem to have a disagreement. In particular, to the judge, it will seem that the theorist is inventing a fantasy. That, however, is the illusion. The theorist might respond as follows. 'If the question is, "What motivated you to make the decision you made?", then I accept that *x* is the wrong answer. But I did not intend *x* as an answer to that question. What I am saying is this. If the question is, "Taking into account the fact that the reasons for your decision must justify that decision and do so from within the existing system of law, what is the best explanation for the decision that you made?", then *x* is the best answer.' Notice that *x* is not a descriptive claim about the law or the judge's psychology, but nor is it prescriptive. It is not an account of how the law should ideally be, but an analysis of how the extant law is best explained and justified. And the crucial point for now is that if *x* is indeed the best account of the judge's decision in this regard, then it would make sense for the judge to base future decisions of a relevantly similar kind on *x* and not on *y*. Moreover, if the decision in question is to serve as a point of development for the law, then that development ought to be guided by reasons *x* and not by reasons *y*. And so on. Theory starts with the practice of the law and feeds back into that practice without being a description of that practice.

[12] If only it were possible to insist that those who fail to see the fundamental good sense in the following passage are prohibited from writing on the subject of theory: 'Scientific understanding proceeds by way of constructing and analyzing "models" of the segments or aspects of reality under study. The purpose of these models is not to give a mirror image of reality, not to include all its elements in their exact sizes and proportions, but rather to single out and make available for intensive investigation those elements which are decisive. We abstract from nonessentials, we blot out the unimportant to get an unobstructed view of the important, we magnify in order to improve the range and accuracy of our observation. A model is, and must be, unrealistic in the sense in which the word is most commonly used. Nevertheless, and in a sense paradoxically, if it is a good model it provides the key to understanding reality.' PA Baran and PM Sweezy, *Monopoly Capital: An Essay on the American Economic and Social Order* (New York, Monthly Review Press, 1966) 14.

That said, the aim of this book is not to legislate how judges, textbook writers and the like describe the law of tort. Theory should influence practice, but theory and practice ought to exist in a reflective equilibrium. Again, an example should help to explain the relevance of this idea. Chapter 12 argues that the law of negligence is best conceptualised as dealing with cases in which the defendant has pursued her purposes in ways that wrongly interfere with the plaintiff's ability to pursue his purposes. This is a *theoretical* suggestion. It is submitted that seeing the law in this way will make it more comprehensible than viewing it through the lens of alternative models. This does not entail that judges or textbook writers must begin to use the language employed in that chapter—that they must abandon their talk of duties of care and begin to speak of conflicting purposes, for example. On the contrary, as that chapter presents an explanation of the extant doctrines of negligence law, it implicitly invites judges to continue to utilise these doctrines. I am not trying to rewrite the law of tort, but to explain it.

Most significantly, though this book argues that the law of tort has a unified conceptual basis, that claim is again made at the level of theory. This does not imply that the law of tort in practice should be unified, so that, for example, the individual torts should be abolished and combined into one overarching tort. There is no reason to think that unified moral concepts cannot best be implemented in practice through separate institutions.[13] In fact, the argument that follows suggests just this approach for tort law.[14]

Of course, I am not naïve enough to think that any lawyer armed only with the arguments presented in this book would have a hope in hell of succeeding as a tort lawyer. But I hope that, in conjunction with her knowledge of the positive law and day-to-day legal practice, she will find this material valuable for developing her understanding of the law, a development that will lead to greater success. And perhaps one day, if these ideas are found to be useful, they will influence that practice more directly and some of them will be found on the lips of judges, barristers and the like. Perhaps.

But it is also important to recognise that utility is not a truth condition of any theory. Ultimately, theory must aspire to truth rather than usefulness. And in this

[13] I take Kant's moral theory to be an exemplar in this regard. The unified moral concept is examined in I Kant, *Groundwork of the Metaphysics of Morals*, M Gregor (trans) (Cambridge, Cambridge University Press, 1996). It is applied to general areas of human endeavour in I Kant, *The Metaphysics of Morals*, M Gregor (trans) (Cambridge, Cambridge University Press, 1996) and to more specific ones in I Kant, *Anthropology from a Pragmantic Point of View*, RB Louden (trans) (Cambridge, Cambridge University Press, 2007).

[14] To employ language that has become fashionable recently: the study of law will be healthy only if it is pursued by both foxes and hedgehogs. It may be best for courts and for those focused on the operation of courts to be relatively foxy. But this in no way undermines the scholarship of the hedgehog or the need for that scholarship. It is useful to compare this view with that advanced in L Smith, 'The State of the Law of Unjust Enrichment in Common Law Canada' (2015) 57 *Canadian Business Law Journal* 39. Smith concludes his thought-provoking paper (at 57) by remarking 'By nature, I am a hedgehog, but sometimes it is necessary to adapt. In this field, it seems to me that the future belongs to the foxes.' But nature needs both foxes and hedgehogs. The more foxes there are, the more need for the work of the hedgehog (and vice versa, though in the common law, foxes have never been in short supply).

context, it is not impossible that the correct theory of the law's normative structure will prove difficult to use. Thankfully, however, I think that this is not the case.

III. Scope

This book examines the laws of Australia, Canada, England and Wales, New Zealand and the US. Because these fall into two sub-families, it is convenient to have a term to refer to the first four jurisdictions. Though it is somewhat erroneous, I use the usual term: Commonwealth. It must be said that the approach to US law is very much that of an outsider looking in, though to an extent that is true with respect to Commonwealth law as well. It is my hope that the thesis of this book will prove all the more utile because of this.

Part I

Foundations

The following three chapters present the foundations of the theory examined in the remainder of this book. The first sets out the fundamental moral conception upon which this material is based. The second presents a general theory of tortious liability based on that conception. The final chapter in this part explores the form of liability found in tort law and its relation to the moral theory examined earlier.

1

Moral Foundations

This book is inspired by Immanuel Kant's *Rechtslehre*. Its thesis is a reflection of the legal theory developed in that work. But the book is not a presentation of Kant's theory of tort law. It could not be. As Kant had nothing to say about tort law, there is no such theory.[1] What, then, is the nature of this inspiration? The answer is that the *Rechtslehre* presents a framework for thinking about legal issues that can be applied to any legal subject. This scaffolding is erected in this chapter and utilised throughout the book. It is particularly useful in this context because the framework contrasts strongly with the dominant model from which tort law is today understood. It will be well to examine that now.

I. The Conventional View

One way to approach this model is to notice the manner in which the third *Restatement of the Law of Tort* is progressing. Note particularly the following titles of what we already have: *Liability for Physical and Emotional Harm* and *Liability for Economic Harm (Tentative Drafts)*. Consider also the following from the former of these, the first passages to deal with liability. 'An actor who intentionally causes physical harm is subject to liability for that harm.'[2] 'An actor whose negligence is a factual cause of physical harm is subject to liability for any such harm.'[3] Impossible to miss here is the notion that tort law is fundamentally about responding to harm. Harm in this theory is never clearly defined, but the basic idea is plain. Tort law is the common law's mechanism for dealing with loss.

In the Commonwealth, this view has been usefully summarised by Robert Stevens:

> On this conception 'the overall object of tort law is to define cases in which the law may justly hold one party liable to compensate another'.[4] Within liability for negligence

[1] This is because, as Jacob Weinrib has reminded me, Kant's focus is on primary and fundamental rights rather than on wrongs or remedies.

[2] *Restatement (Third) of Torts: Physical and Emotional Harm* (St Paul, MN, American Law Institute Publishers, 2010) §5.

[3] ibid §6.

[4] *Fairchild v Glenhaven Funeral Services Ltd* [2002] UKHL 22, [2003] 1 AC 32 [9].

> 'damage is the gist',[5] and where there is no recovery for negligently inflicted loss it needs justification. Under this model, the role of the 'duty of care' in liability for negligence is as a 'control device,' primarily concerned with the diverse reasons why a particular defendant has an immunity from being liable for carelessly causing loss. This conception of the law of torts I shall call the 'loss model'.[6]

The debate over the loss model and its alternatives is alight in theoretical discussion of the law. It has raged over a natural battleground: whether the loss model provides a satisfactory understanding of the law. Unsurprisingly, the argument against the loss model is that it does not. In fact, the argument goes, the model provides so poor an analysis that it must routinely appeal to policy arguments in order to keep liability within sensible limits. The reason for this is clear. There is simply too much loss in the world for it always to attract liability. Thus, 'control mechanisms' must be introduced to keep liability in check.

As Stevens notes, this feature of the loss model is most obvious in the law of negligence. Thus, speaking from the perspective of the conventional view, Stephen Todd has noted that:

> The duty requirement exists because the potential scope of negligence as a basis for legal liability is virtually unlimited. On its face 'negligence' looks only to the quality of the defendant's conduct and not to factors such as the likely or possible number of plaintiffs, the likelihood that loss would be caused, the nature and extent of particular loss and the circumstances in which the loss came to be inflicted. Thus the courts have had to devise principles to delimit the boundaries of liability. To this end they have instituted a requirement in every case of foreseeability of damage to the person bringing the action, and have also taken account of these other factors in deciding whether, for reasons of policy, liability ought to be especially restricted or denied altogether. The language of duty provides the formula for expressing these conclusions of policy. It operates as a 'control device' or filter through which any particular claim must pass. It is apparent, then, that the function of the duty of care is not so much to identify cases where liability is imposed as to identify those where it is not.[7]

The upshot of this is that the law tends to be analysed in the following way. First, one or more principles are identified. In the law of negligence, the fundamental principle is said to be that individuals are responsible for the losses caused by their negligent behaviour—the view witnessed in the third *Restatement* above. Second, an enormous raft of exceptions are listed to the principle, exceptions that are said to be justified on policy grounds—ie, grounds other than, and often inconsistent

[5] *Gregg v Scott* [2005] UKHL 2, [2005] 2 AC 176 [99].

[6] R Stevens, *Torts and Rights* (Oxford, Oxford University Press, 2007) 2 (some citations omitted).

[7] S Todd, 'Negligence: The Duty of Care' in S Todd (ed), *The Law of Torts in New Zealand*, 6th edn (Wellington, Thompson Reuters, 2013) 147 (citation omitted), quotation from *Smith v Littlewoods Organisation Ltd* [1987] 1 AC 241 (HL), 280. See also, eg, P Cane, *The Anatomy of Tort Law* (Oxford, Hart Publishing, 1997) 10; J Fleming, *The Law of Torts*, 9th edn (Sydney, LBC Information Services, 1998) 115; WP Keeton et al, *Prosser and Keeton on the Law of Torts*, 5th edn (St Paul, MN, West Group, 1984) 358; WE Peel and J Goudkamp, *Winfield and Jolowicz on Tort*, 19th edn (London, Sweet & Maxwell, 2013) 81.

with, the general principle. This too is neatly captured by the summary of negligence in the *Restatement*: 'An actor whose negligence is a factual cause of physical harm is subject to liability for any such harm within the scope of liability, *unless the court determines that the ordinary duty of reasonable care is inapplicable*.'[8] The unless clause is of considerable practical importance.

As a descriptive matter, the conventional view is of course impeccable.[9] It is, after all, the conventional view, the view utilised by the vast majority of lawyers. But our focus is theoretical. And at that level, it is clear that the model is inadequate. An understanding that presents a principle with exceptions is faulty. An understanding that presents a principle with so vast a list of exceptions is no understanding at all. Imagine a chemist who maintained that all elements were metals, but then catalogued the 26 non-metals as exceptions.[10] We would be right to conclude that this chemist did not understand what an element was. For just the same reason, we must conclude that the loss model cannot comprehend the law of tort. In fact, it is worse than this, because at least in many areas of the law, the exceptions are both more important and the potential cases that fit them far more numerous than the rule. That is more like a zoologist stating that all felidae are lions and then listing tigers, jaguars, leopards, cougars, cheetahs, lynxes, ocelots, domestic cats etc as exceptions. Here, we would rightly conclude that this zoologist did not know what felidae were and did not seem concerned to find out. If our conception of the law of negligence leads to the conclusion that 'the potential scope of negligence as a basis for legal liability is virtually unlimited'[11] and we are thus forced to introduce a host of control mechanisms, then we need a new conception.

In the end, then, history itself is sufficient to reveal that the loss model is a failure. That model was invented in the belief that it would provide a utile starting point for developing a conceptually adequate understanding of the law of tort.[12] No objective observer could resist the conclusion that it has failed. The lists of exceptions to its general principles have grown well beyond breaking point. In fact, it is arguable that the reason it is not more widely appreciated that the conventional view has broken down is that lawyers have simply got used to dealing with the near-chaos that the view has created. That says a great deal for their resourcefulness, but not much for the law itself. And that is not the end of the matter. These are only the general problems with the conventional view. The case against the conventional view has really only begun. Other, more specific, problems are examined throughout this book. But these problems too manifest themselves in the same general way: they show that the conventional view cannot comfortably

[8] *Restatement (Third) of Torts* (n 2) §6 (emphasis added).

[9] However, though this is not the place to discuss this matter, it is highly unlikely that the loss model was the conventional view throughout the law's history. On the contrary, it is, I think, a creature of the twentieth century.

[10] Here, I am including in the set of non-metals the nonmetals and the metalloids.

[11] Todd, 'Negligence: The Duty of Care' (n 7) 147.

[12] It reaches its zenith in great works such as J Fleming, *The Law of Torts*, 9th edn (Sydney, LBC Information Services, 1998).

explain the working of the law in practice and so must continually have resort to policy-based exceptions. The unfortunate result is increasingly obscure and arbitrary legal decision making.

In the US, matters have taken a somewhat different turn. There, theorists have not been content with principles and lists of exceptions. On the contrary, a powerful theory has been developed that attempts to explain the principles and the apparent exceptions in a unified and theoretically satisfactory fashion. I refer, of course, to the school of thought known as law and economics.

This is certainly a view worthy of respect—a genuine theory that provides genuine analysis. The problem is that if it intends directly to explain the practice of the law of tort,[13] then it fails because it is structurally inconsistent with structural features of that law. This argument has been pursued by others and so need not be examined here in detail.[14] I give only the flavour of the argument by examining two examples.

Some torts demand that a defendant can be liable to a plaintiff only if he caused injury to that person. This is known as factual causation or cause-in-fact. On the face of it, this has nothing to do with economics. Thus, it has been claimed by law and economics scholars that 'the idea of causation can largely be dispensed with in an economic analysis of torts'.[15] This reveals the gulf between economic and legal analysis and the fact that, despite the claim that economics reveals the implicit logic of the common law, the logic of economics and the logic of law are very different.[16]

Similarly, some torts require the defendant to have intended harm to the plaintiff. Economic explanations can be attempted of this feature of the law, but they too seem to depart from the law itself. For instance, it might be claimed that the law is particularly concerned with intention because a defendant who intends to cause harm is more likely to bring that harm about than one acting merely carelessly. The problem is that it is easy to invent examples in which this is not the case. Imagine a man who wants to kill another who is in a hall of mirrors, where having the intention to shoot the desired victim virtually guarantees that he will miss. Here, the intention makes the man less likely to cause harm, but if he nevertheless shoots the plaintiff, the legal rules concerning intention will apply. Again, this suggests that the concerns of the law are not economic.

[13] It is important to recognise that much law and economics does not have this aim and so is not subject to this criticism. Nevertheless, this type of analysis is not a rival for the one presented here, however useful it is in other contexts.

[14] eg, EJ Weinrib, *The Idea of Private Law* (Cambridge, MA, Harvard University Press, 1995) 1–21, 36–38, 46–50; J Coleman, *The Practice of Principle* (Oxford, Oxford University Press, 2001) 1–64.

[15] W Landes and R Posner, *The Economic Structure of Tort Law* (Cambridge, MA, Harvard University Press, 1987) 229.

[16] Curiously, this is often admitted by law and economics scholars. See, for instance, the claim in W Landes and RA Posner, 'Causation in Tort Law: An Economic Approach' (1983) 12 *Journal of Legal Studies* 109, 134 that: 'In so analyzing the causation cases we are admittedly far from the language and concepts with which the courts analyze these cases.'

The point is not that the law is economically inefficient. It may be that it is highly efficient. Indeed, the law may mirror the outcomes called for by economics closely. If that is so, then economics will usefully describe the incentive structures produced by the law etc. The claim is not that economics cannot fruitfully be used to analyse the law. The point is that the *reasons* given in the law and by economics differ. Thus, even when economics and law argue for the same outcomes—as *arguendo* they may always do—the content of their arguments are very different. Hence, economics cannot explain or justify the law in the sense that it cannot support the reasons given in law for legal decisions.

It is important to stress that I do not mean to reject economics *tout court*, even in the quite narrow sphere in which I question it at all. Some years ago, I attended a seminar given by a prestigious American academic in Hamburg considering the economic analysis of the law. One of the German economists in the room asked the presenter why he had considered only economics that focused on material social cost and ignored the kind of economics that begins with the Kantian notion that the fundamental human entitlement is not to welfare, but to equal freedom. The presenter's response was that this form of economics was not influential in the US. I do not doubt that the response was right, but these thoughts nevertheless raise the possibility that contemporary examples of law and economics scholarship fail directly to latch onto law, not because economics and law are analytically forever distinct, but because these examples of law and economics involve bad economics and the study of law is one of the ways in which this can be brought home.

Whatever the truth of that, it seems clear that US-style law and economics also takes its cue from the loss model. It holds that it is with loss or harm that tort law is most deeply concerned. Hence, we have the idea that the aim of the law of negligence is to find the lowest cost avoider and that it is deeply concerned with loss spreading. And most fundamentally, it is the commitment to the loss model that cannot be accepted, whatever particular form that commitment takes.

What could the relationship between tort law and loss be? One answer—the one suggested by law and economics—is that tort law is designed to minimise loss. The problem with that answer is that it is flatly inconsistent with the law as it presents itself. As we have said, tort law is a law of wrongs. A defendant who batters, falsely imprisons or negligently injures another is conceptualised as a wrongdoer. It is not in the nature of the law to regard this person as a mere loss non-minimiser, as an agent acting merely inefficiently. This does not prove that loss minimisation is not what tort law is really all about, but the law does not seem to be about this. It seems to be about wrongdoing of some kind, and it is with this notion that the theory of tort law ought to begin.[17]

[17] In the end, everything is up for grabs, so it is possible that the best theory of tort law will leave the notion of wrongdoing behind. But wherever it ends up, legal theory must begin with the law's most salient features, and the notion of wrongdoing is one of them.

This leads the loss model to the notion that the causing of loss is wrongful, at least prima facie, and that is how the model operates in the Commonwealth. Recall that the model maintains that tort law is most fundamentally concerned with loss. The model therefore sees loss as the basic evil to be alleviated. Of course, however, practicalities demand that not all losses can be compensated. Thus, control mechanisms must be introduced to constrain liability.[18]

There is a deep problem with this view, far deeper than its inability to provide an adequate account of the law, which inability is a mere symptom of this problem. The problem is that the loss model is based on notions inconsistent with the reality of the human condition.

Given human nature and the world in which we find ourselves, causing loss to others is a fact of life. To take just a miniscule set of examples, I obtained a place at university that would have profited other potential students, a scholarship that others could have used, acquired a job that others want, live in a house that others prefer, am married to a woman who could make others happy, have friends who could devote themselves to other people and so on. I cause loss to people when I enter a queue ahead of them or press the button at traffic lights to cross the road. I say things that people would prefer me not to say, think things that people would prefer me not to think, and so on and on. I cause people loss all the time. We all do. It is part of life. How, then, could it be appropriate to regard causing loss as even prima facie wrongful?[19]

I do not mean to deny that this feature of the human condition is a source of sadness and regret. On the contrary, naturally, it would be better were things otherwise. But building into one's understanding of law the notion that things are even prima facie unjust unless they are otherwise is, frankly, otherworldly. It is reality denyingly utopian; the result of failing to look the human condition in the eye. It is an understanding fit only for the law of the kingdom of heaven.

If loss is an evil, then life itself is evil and living a life with one's eyes open to the consequences is an act of intentional evil. I cannot believe any of this. The loss model is not merely wrong, it is pathology. It is interesting to consider what it is about the modern world that makes it seem attractive to so many. It is impossible to imagine it thriving in, say, ancient Greece or the medieval Europe in which our law grew up. But I will not pursue that issue here. Our focus is on providing an alternative understanding of the law.

[18] Note that if loss was not seen as prima facie wrongful, then it would be odd to refer to these features of the law as 'control mechanisms'. They are seen to be control mechanisms because they prevent liability from falling where it would otherwise fall.

[19] Note that it is no reply to say that modern lawyers all accept that these losses are not actionable. Of course, that is true. The point is that, on the loss model, that is because of some policy concern favouring an exception to a general principle. And that is entirely implausible.

II. A Kantian Understanding

If tort law is not most fundamentally concerned with loss, then what is it concerned with? The Kantian answer is that it is concerned with freedom. Thus, we have Kant's fundamental principle of law:

> Any action is *lawful* if it can coexist with everyone's freedom in accordance with a universal law, or if on its maxim the freedom of choice of each can coexist with everyone's freedom in accordance with a universal law.[20]

For our purposes, the most important feature of this principle is its commitment to equal maximum freedom. Individuals are entitled to the maximum amount of freedom possible consistent with the recognition of the same freedom in others.

Kant maintains that this principle generates a single innate right:

> *Freedom* (independence from being constrained by another's choice), insofar as it can coexist with the freedom of every other in accordance with a universal law, is the only original right belonging to every man by virtue of his humanity.[21]

So, freedom is defined as independence from constraint imposed by others' choices. We must pause to examine this important idea.

The innate right generates an entitlement to be free of constraint imposed by the choices of others. A direct consequence of this principle is that constraint not imposed by others does not violate the innate right. We are constrained to walk on the earth, unable to flap our arms and take to the sky. But that is no encroachment on our freedom. The inability to fly is not imposed on us by others. Importantly, the same is true when we are constrained in ways that are not the result of others' choices. The fact that I was born means that there are fewer resources available for you, but that cannot be regarded as a violation of your freedom by me as it did not result from any choice of mine. In general, one is responsible only for one's actions, and actions are behaviours that can be imputed to an agent.[22]

We might make this point by distinguishing between moral and merely factual constraint. An individual is factually constrained if there is some impediment to her will. Moral constraint, on the other hand, is factual constraint that is the result of the action of another. In the following, 'constraint' is used only in this latter sense. For us, then, a constraint is an interference with freedom in terms of another's choice.

Moreover, both of the principles examined above demonstrate Kant's commitment to the protection of what is often referred to as external freedom,[23] here

[20] I Kant, *The Metaphysics of Morals*, M Gregor (trans) (Cambridge, Cambridge University Press, 1996) 6:230. For reasons that cannot be elucidated here, I generally translate 'Das Recht' as 'law', not as 'right', and the cognates of 'Recht' accordingly.

[21] ibid 6:237.

[22] ibid 6:223.

[23] The term 'external freedom' is designed clearly to distinguish the notion to which it refers from that denoted by 'autonomy' examined in the *Groundwork*, which is a more positive account of freedom

specifically conceptualised as the ability to live independently of the choices of others. This too must be stressed. The formulation of the innate right not only elucidates the content of that right, it also defines the operative conception of freedom. According to this understanding, freedom *is* independence from the constraint of others' choices.

Kant's position is not that human life should be lived in splendid isolation from others or that the law should encourage this. It is that respect for individual freedom entails that individuals must be able to insist on independence if and when they choose. So, while one can accept that individuals must form associations if they are to live well, the point is that they must also be free to make their own decision to associate and leave entered associations if they choose to do so. On the Kantian understanding, the job of legal theory is not to paint a picture of the good life and the job of law is not to push people towards it. Rather, the task is to elucidate and insist on the freedom that makes human flourishing even a possibility.

It is important to elucidate one further implication of the innate right: one is free to do anything that does not violate a right in another. Kant identifies this with a specific principle, that of being beyond reproach.[24] I label it the *principle of innocence*.[25] This can be illustrated by imagining that you and I are alone in the state of nature. In this condition, I am entitled to do as I will unless my action will violate the same entitlement in you. This entitlement is a product of my innate right. The restriction on my entitlement is a product of your innate right. Thus, if I perform an action that violates your freedom, that must *ipso facto* be a violation of your innate right. To put this negatively, if I do not violate your innate right in these circumstances, then I cannot have violated your freedom and thus cannot have wronged you.

Kant also accepts that human beings can acquire rights, eg, proprietary and contractual rights. Though we will not examine these aspects of his theory here, suffice it to say that I also violate your freedom if I violate your acquired rights. The central point at the moment is the negative one: if I do not violate your rights, I cannot have violated your freedom. The crucial upshot of this is that this legal theory is—at least at this point[26]—unconcerned with human needs and desires.[27] Consequently, the theory of tort law based on this account is also indifferent to need and desire.

If that sounds unacceptably harsh, the following comments are in order. First, the position is not that the law as a whole, still less politics in general, should

in Isaiah Berlin's sense. I Kant, *Groundwork of the Metaphysics of Morals*, M Gregor (trans) (Cambridge, Cambridge University Press, 1996) 4:440; I Berlin, *Two Concepts of Liberty* (Oxford, Oxford University Press, 1958).

[24] I Kant, *The Metaphysics of Morals*, M Gregor (trans) (Cambridge, Cambridge University Press, 1996) 6:237–38.

[25] In passing, one might note that the loss model is inconsistent with the principle of innocence. It holds that liability is based on a principle, where one cannot live a life without breaking that principle.

[26] *cf* Kant (n 24) 6:325–28.

[27] The innate right is an entitlement to be free based on the fact that human beings possess rationality. It does not receive justification from the fact, to the extent that it is a fact, that human beings need or want to be free.

ignore need and desire. The claim is only that these are not appropriate subjects for tort law. Second, the theory holds this view not out of a callous disregard for human need and desire, but out of respect for human freedom. Its thesis is that justice requires areas of law—of which tort law is one—focused on human freedom. Its thesis is not that human need and want ought everywhere to be ignored.

This is only the briefest outline of Kant's legal theory, but it will suffice. It is not intended to provide a list of the rights we find in tort law. Nor is it proposed as a set of first principles from which tort law is to be derived. Rather, its chief importance is to reorient our thinking about tort law. For decades, we have been attempting to understand that law as society's response to loss. That attempt has failed. This book adopts a different perspective and seeks to show that it provides a considerably more powerful picture of the law of tort.

III. The Scope of Analysis and the Criticism of Tort Law

This book is an analysis of the principles of tort *liability*. It maintains that those principles are better understood as protecting freedom than as responding to loss. This book is not an examination of tort law *tout court*. Thus, it does not argue (though it does not deny) that tort law actually succeeds in protecting freedom. Whether it does so depends not only on the shape of its liability rules but also on the adequacy of its remedies. In that regard, there is a great deal of evidence to suggest that tort law is (or at least parts of tort law are) a disaster in this regard.[28] Though this book does not focus on these issues, some brief comments are in order.

At heart, this criticism of tort law is concerned to show that the law fails to provide an adequate social response to what we might call the problem of incapacity.[29] It must be understood that the argument of this book is entirely consistent with this criticism. In particular, the following points should be made.

The criticism under consideration holds that tort law provides the most important social response to incapacity, but that this response is inadequate. Though some have thought that positions of the kind advanced here are in tension with this view,[30] on the face of it, the reverse is the case.[31] To put this into the language

[28] In the English context, see, eg, D Harris, *Compensation and Support for Illness and Injury* (Oxford, Clarendon Press, 1984); H Genn, *Hard Bargaining: Out of Court Settlement in Personal Injury Actions* (Oxford, Clarendon Press, 1987); T Baker, 'Blood Money, New Money, and the Moral Economy of Tort Law in Action' (2001) 35 *Law and Society Review* 275.

[29] D Campbell, 'The Damages System in Practice' in D Harris, D Campbell and R Halson (eds), *Remedies in Tort and Contract* (Cambridge, Cambridge University Press, 2002).

[30] See, eg, ibid 440.

[31] At this point, the differences between positions such as those advanced in A Burrows, 'In Defence of Tort' in *Understanding the Law of Obligations* (Oxford, Oxford University Press, 1998) and R Stevens, *Torts and Rights* (Oxford, Oxford University Press, 2007) ch 15 from the position advanced here must

adopted here, tort law is a poor vehicle for responding to incapacity not only because of problems with the law's remedial facility, but most fundamentally because it is not an attempt to deal with incapacity at all. On this view, then, the criticism of the status quo is in fact deepened as a result of the thesis advanced here, though that criticism is not now directed at tort law per se.

David Campbell has argued that perhaps the most objectionable feature of tort law is that it '*prevents* general reform [of social response to incapacity], and it is highly arguable that tort should be abolished for just that reason'.[32] This, I think, is wrong. But it is important to see just why that is so.

Currently, tort law prevents reform. It does so because it is regarded as providing a more or less comprehensive response to incapacity and, despite widespread acknowledgement of tort law's failures in this regard, alternative responses seem to many to be undesirable or impractical.[33] In these circumstances, despite the fact that tort law is the worst solution to the problem of incapacity of all the alternatives, that it does not fail entirely to compensate for incapacity can appear to justify delaying necessary but controversial and difficult reform. Yet what is the fundamental problem here? For Campbell, it is tort law itself. According to the position advanced here, however, it is the false belief that tort law is properly regarded as a response to incapacity.

If the view advanced in this book were to be accepted, one consequence would be that tort law would no longer be viewed as society's inadequate response to incapacity. That is not because the law would be viewed as an adequate response to incapacity; it is because it would be viewed as no response to incapacity whatsoever. Consequently, we would not view society as possessing a more or less comprehensive though poorly functioning mechanism for dealing with incapacity; we would view society as possessing no such (general) mechanism at all. This would achieve precisely what Campbell wishes the abolition of tort law to achieve.

That might appear to raise the following question: what, then, is the point of tort law? This book, of course, is an answer to that question. It should also be noted that moving away from the loss model and the idea that tort is to be viewed as society's response to incapacity is likely dramatically to reduce the burdens placed on tort law in general, including on its remedies. This may be another area, then, in which the best way to save a phenomena is to shrink it[34] (here, though, the necessary shrinking is mainly conceptual). Ironically, then, the general reluctance of these critics of tort law to entertain views of the kind advanced here is an

be stressed. I have explained some of these differences in A Beever, 'Corrective Justice and Personal Responsibility in Tort Law' (2008) 28 *Oxford Journal of Legal Studies* 475.

[32] D Campbell, 'The Damages System in Practice' in D Harris, D Campbell and R Halson (eds), *Remedies in Tort and Contract* (Cambridge, Cambridge University Press, 2002) 457.

[33] ibid 453–61.

[34] *cf* D Campbell, 'Gathering the Water: Abuse of Rights after the Recognition of Government Failure' (2010) 6 *Journal of Jurisprudence* 487, 533.

obstacle to the reform they ultimately seek.[35] Because they insist that tort law must be understood as a response to loss, closing their ears to legal theory that suggests the contrary, they perpetuate the damaging myth that society has such a response, albeit a poor one, when in fact it has none.[36]

In short, these critics insist on interpreting tort law as an arm of the welfare state. This book argues that this is the wrong analysis. That argument says nothing itself about the welfare state. Naturally, there is far more to say on this issue, but that is not the subject matter of this book. It is time to begin our examination of tort liability.

IV. Three Foundational Principles

This chapter has presented three central principles. As noted, their chief importance is to reorient our thought regarding tort law. Because they will make appearances in the chapters that follow, it will help to present them formally here:

Equal maximum freedom: individuals are entitled to the maximum amount of freedom possible consistent with the recognition of the same freedom in others.
Innate right: individuals are entitled to independence from others, specifically not to be subject to constraint.
Innocence: individuals commit wrongs—ie, act illegally—only if they violate the rights of others.

These are the building blocks of the theory of tort law that follows.

[35] Here I wish explicitly to exclude David Campbell from these comments, whose work and advice has been extremely important in the formation of my own views.

[36] I hope that this brief discussion will have done something to undercut the unfortunate assumption that positions of the kind advanced in this book are necessarily wedded to a particular political ideology, let alone the claim that they are essentially covert attempts to implement such ideologies. The world and, thankfully, my mind are more complicated places than these criticisms suggest.

2

The General Theory of Liability

This chapter provides a general theory of tort liability, a framework or structure within which the specific torts are analysed in following chapters. Its primary task is to elucidate the conception of wrongdoing implied by the theory outlined in the previous chapter.

I. Influence, Constraint and Coercion

As discussed in Chapter 1, the individual's fundamental legal entitlement is to freedom understood as independence from constraint imposed by others' choices. It follows that in order to be constraining, an action must interfere with another's freedom and this means that the action must violate another's innate or acquired rights.

It is also important to recognise that though the innate right is absolute, neither it nor any other right generates any absolute entitlement to any subject matter, not even to freedom. This is built into the innate right itself, which guarantees freedom 'insofar as it can coexist with the freedom of every other in accordance with a universal law'.[1] There is no right to freedom *simpliciter*. Rather, the right is to what we are calling equal maximum freedom. Thus, I am entitled to be independent of you, but not in ways that will make you dependent on me. The level of my entitlement to independence is set at the highest point consistent with an equal level being set for all.

This general point can usefully be illustrated by the following example. Imagine that you and I are neighbours and you mow your lawn once a month. Your action creates noise and smell that annoys me. As a result, you constrain me. You use your property in a way that prevents me using my property as I would wish.[2] However, a law that prevented you from mowing your lawn to avert your constraining me

[1] I Kant, *The Metaphysics of Morals*, M Gregor (trans) (Cambridge, Cambridge University Press, 1996) 6:237.

[2] Note that it is the potential use of the property that is relevant here, not the wish per se. The thwarting of a wish is negative influence (defined below). The interference with the enjoyment of a property right is constraint.

would constrain you, because it would prevent you using your property as you wish. Hence, this difficulty cannot be resolved by insisting that we each refrain from constraining the other. But that does not mean that appeal to freedom is unhelpful. On the contrary, the issue is appropriately settled by establishing a regime of equal maximum freedom. In effect, the person who should win this dispute is the one whose action, when universalised, is the least constraining. That issue must be determined qualitatively. The task is to determine whose freedom is the most fundamental.[3] In our example, the dispute should be settled by considering whose freedom is the most basic: yours to mow your lawn or mine to be free of the noise and to realise my ideal home environment. In the abstract, this may seem to be a hopeless task, but, as I have argued elsewhere, the common law has worked out an eminently plausible way of doing this.[4] Equal maximum freedom, then, means equal maximally fundamental freedom.

As a consequence of the above, an action that constrains is not necessarily wrongful. In fact, constraint and the threat of constraint are necessary features of a society that protects equal maximum freedom. To take an obvious example, a law against murder is constraining, in that it limits freedom of action, but it is justified because it prevents a more fundamental form of constraint. The law constrains but provides for equal maximum freedom.

The obvious upshot of this is that there can be no right to be free of constraint *simpliciter*. Instead, one has a right to be free of constraint unnecessary for the provision of equal maximum freedom. Likewise, constraint is not necessarily wrongful; it is not wrongful when it is necessary to protect equal maximum freedom.

We need a convenient way to express these notions. I have referred already to constraint and will continue to use that term as defined in the previous chapter. We additionally need a term to pick out unjustified constraint—constraint that cannot be justified on the ground that it is necessary to protect equal maximum freedom. Following suggestions in the *Rechtslehre*, I have chosen 'coercion'.[5] We also need a term to refer to loss. Naturally, 'loss' suggests itself, but it will not do. This is because while the thesis advanced here is opposed to the notion that tort law is fundamentally concerned with loss, it of course accepts that one can be compensated for loss in tort and that this is characteristically of great importance to the litigants. The objection is not to recovery for loss, but to the idea that loss is the key to understanding tort liability. In order to avoid confusion, therefore, an

[3] Kant (n 1) 6:224.

[4] A Beever, *The Law of Private Nuisance* (Oxford, Hart Publishing, 2013).

[5] Kant (n 1) 6:231. In philosophical discussion, 'coercion' has a narrow and a wide meaning. According to the former, coercion occurs when one person gets another to do something that he would not otherwise have done through some sort of illegitimate pressure (eg, R Nozick, 'Coercion' in S Morgenbesser, P Suppes and M White (eds), *Philosophy, Science, and Method: Essays in Honor of Ernest Nagel* (New York, St Martin's Press, 1969)). According to the latter, coercion is about force (eg, Kant (n 1) 6:231; A Ripstein, 'Authority and Coercion' (2004) 32 *Philosophy and Public Affairs* 2). A version of this second understanding is in operation here.

alternative term is desirable. I have chosen 'negative influence'. Because the argument of this book relies on these terms, it will help to define them formally now:

Negative influence: A negatively influences *B* if *A*'s actions have a deleterious effect on *B*.
Constraint: A constrains *B* if *A* interferes with *B*'s freedom, as defined in accordance with *B*'s innate and acquired rights.
Coercion: A coerces *B* if he constrains *B* and that constraint is not consistent with equal maximum freedom.

The position advanced in this book is the following. First, as far as liability is concerned, the law is not concerned with negative influence, at least not for its own sake. As we might say, then, the modern focus on loss is a loss of focus. The law is interested only in constraint. An action is even prima facie available only when a defendant has constrained a plaintiff. What is more, the law imposes liability only in response to that form of constraint we have labelled coercion. A defendant is found liable only when he has coerced the plaintiff. It is the aim of this book as a whole to make good these claims and to show that they provide the key to understanding tort law. However, one important consequence of this notion must be examined now.

When determining whether a defendant has acted illegally with respect to a plaintiff, the issue is whether the defendant coerced the plaintiff. The defendant will have done so if and only if his action constrained the plaintiff inconsistently with equal maximum freedom. The important point now is a negative one. The issue is not whether the defendant acted immorally in some non-legal sense. In particular, the ethical status of the defendant's behaviour or character is irrelevant.

For instance, if I set up in business to destroy the business that you have created through years of hard work, then I act unethically (we can accept at least *arguendo*). We can tell this by looking solely at me and examining my motivations. But in order to show that my action is illegal, it is necessary to show that it constrains you and that this constraint amounts to coercion. The focus therefore must be on the quality of my action vis-a-vis you and not on my ethical status in performing it.

That does not entail that a defendant's state of mind is necessarily irrelevant. It may be that certain forms of constraint or coercion occur only when an agent has particular intentions or purposes. But the point remains that it is impossible to determine whether a defendant has acted illegally by focusing only on that person. Only ethical judgements can be made in that way.

Moreover, the demand to realise equal maximum freedom in this context requires comparing the freedom of the defendant with the freedom of the plaintiff. This requires interpersonal judgement. Let us return to the example in which you and I are engaged in a dispute about lawn mowing. Because this is a dispute between you and me, because it involves our rights and obligations inter se, it is to be settled by asking whether your actions constrain me and, if they do, whether that is consistent with equal maximum freedom. The issue cannot be settled by focusing on either of us in isolation. Examining only you will fail to reveal whether I am constrained. It could result only in an ethical judgement. Examining only me will show whether I am constrained, but will not allow us to determine whether that constraint was consistent with equal maximum freedom. Focusing on the demands of society can respect equal maximum freedom, but not equal maximum freedom as between you and I, the actual disputants. The focus therefore must be on both of us together as a unity. My complaint is about the effect of your action on me. A just and lawful resolution of that dispute must consider the freedom of both of us and of no one else. As we will see, this point is of great importance.

II. The Forms of Constraint

It is also important to see that constraint can take two general forms. First, one constrains another by putting that person to one's purposes.[6] We can call this *control*. Second, one constrains another if one acts so as to damage the means, rightly possessed by the other, to realise her purposes. We can call this *injury*. These concepts also apply to property. You can constrain me by putting my property to your purposes (control) or by damaging my property in a way that prevents me being able to use it for my purposes (injury).

Again, it is useful to provide formal definitions:

Control: putting the plaintiff or the plaintiff's to one's purposes.
Injury: damaging the means, to which the plaintiff has a right, to realise her purposes.

These terms, as well as those outlined above, will be relied on in the following to develop a theory of tortious liability.

[6] See, eg, Kant (n 1) 6:203, 237.

3

The Form of Liability in Tort Law

The previous chapter presented a general theory of liability. This chapter begins to relate that theory to the positive law. It is specifically concerned to show that, substantively speaking, though liability could take three possible forms, only one of these is found in the law of tort. It also demonstrates that this is fitting, as the two forms of liability not found in the law are morally inappropriate to it.

I. The Forms of Liability

It is generally agreed that tortious liability falls into two general classes: strict and fault-based. It is also thought that there is general agreement as to the meanings of those terms. In fact, as we will see, the first claim is questionable and the second is wrong. The terms 'strict liability' and 'fault-based liability' are frequently used equivocally, generating considerable confusion. And because of this, it is not entirely clear what it means to say that tortious liability can be either strict or fault-based. The final section of this chapter examines and suggests a way out of this confusion.

One way to reveal the problem is to witness the existence of a debate that could not have occurred without the equivocation. The debate is conducted by two rival camps. On the one side stand a group who deny that the law of tort contains any strict liability.[1] Opposed to them is arranged a company who respond that it very definitely does, pointing with frustration to what seem to them to be obvious examples.[2]

Debates—if that is the right word—of this kind are almost never genuine. Rather, they are practically certain to be the result of equivocation in terminology. That is the case here. Those who argue that strict liability does not exist are not blind to the large areas of the law that seem to their opponents so obviously to be strict. Naturally, they are intimately familiar with all areas of tort law. But they use the term 'strict liability' in such a way that it does not correctly apply to those

[1] eg, OW Holmes, *The Common Law* (New York, Dover Publications, 1881) lectures 3–4; EJ Weinrib, *The Idea of Private Law* (Cambridge, MA, Harvard University Press, 1995) ch 7.

[2] eg, P Cane, 'Corrective Justice and Correlativity in Private Law' (1996) 16 *Oxford Journal of Legal Studies* 471, 485–87.

areas. Hence, when their opponents respond by pointing to those areas of the law, the response seems irrelevant. The camps are talking past each other. How have we come to this state of affairs?

A. Holmes' Analysis of Strict and Fault-Based Liability

The seminal discussion of the distinction between strict and fault-based liability is found in Oliver Wendell Holmes' *The Common Law*. Because of its importance, I quote from it in some detail:

> [T]here are two theories of the common-law liability for unintentional harm. Both of them seem to receive the implied assent of popular textbooks, and neither of them is wanting in plausibility and the semblance of authority.
>
> The first is that of [John] Austin, which is essentially the theory of a criminalist. According to him, the characteristic feature of law, properly so called, is a sanction or detriment threatened and imposed by the sovereign for disobedience to the sovereign's commands. As the greater part of the law only makes a man civilly answerable for breaking it, Austin is compelled to regard the liability to an action as a sanction, or, in other words, as a penalty for disobedience. It follows from this, according to the prevailing views of penal law, that such liability ought only to be based upon personal fault; and Austin accepts that conclusion, with its corollaries, one of which is that negligence means a state of the party's mind …
>
> The other theory is directly opposed to the foregoing … According to this view, broadly stated, under the common law a man acts at his peril … [T]he whole and sufficient ground for such liabilities … is supposed to be that he has voluntarily acted, and that damage has ensued. If the act was voluntary, it is totally immaterial that the detriment which followed from it was neither intended nor due to the negligence of the actor.[3]

There is no difficulty recognising the first of these two theories as arguing for fault-based liability and the second for strict liability. But Holmes insists that neither of these views is morally appropriate to or reflected in the law of tort. I begin by examining Holmes' treatment of the second theory.

In opposition to that theory, Holmes insists that fault cannot be irrelevant to liability in tort. This is because strict liability is inconsistent with the notion, generally accepted throughout the law, that liability can attach only to voluntary action:

> 'All the cases concede that an injury arising from inevitable accident, or, which in law or reason is the same thing, from an act that ordinary human care and foresight are unable to guard against, is but the misfortune of the sufferer, and lays no foundation for legal responsibility.' If this were not so, any act would be sufficient, however remote, which set in motion or opened the door for a series of physical sequences ending in damage; such as riding the horse, in the case of the runaway, or even coming to a place where one is seized with a fit and strikes the plaintiff in an unconscious spasm. Nay, why need the defendant have acted at all, and why is it not enough that his existence has been at the

[3] Holmes (n 1) 81–82.

> expense of the plaintiff? The requirement of an act is the requirement that the defendant should have made a choice. But the only possible purpose of introducing this moral element is to make the power of avoiding the evil complained of a condition of liability. There is no such power where the evil cannot be foreseen.[4]

According to this argument, the demand that liability arise in the absence of fault entails that it arise for all the negative consequences of a person's existence. That is not the position taken by the law, however. The law insists that a person can be responsible only for the consequences of her voluntary actions.

It seems possible to respond that defendants should be liable even in the absence of fault only for their voluntary actions, but Holmes argues against this view too. He maintains that there can be no justification for restricting liability to voluntary action that does not also demand restricting liability to faulty action:

> Unless my act is of a nature to threaten others … it is no more justifiable to make me indemnify my neighbor against the consequences, than to make me do the same thing if I had fallen upon him in a fit, or to compel me to insure him against lightning.[5]

If a person struck by lightning sues another for his injury, the defendant is entitled to reply that she is not responsible. The position is morally identical if the defendant injures the plaintiff while having an epileptic seizure. But it is also identical, Holmes maintains, if a person causes an unforeseeable injury. Hence, Holmes concludes that strict liability must be rejected.

One might question the soundness of Holmes' arguments, but that is not our task now. We are focused on understanding the terminology Holmes employs. In particular, when Holmes rejects strict liability, what exactly is he rejecting? The answer is liability based on the causation of injury *simpliciter*.

What, then, is to be said for the other theory Holmes examines in the first passage quoted above, the theory associated with Austin according to which 'liability ought only to be based upon personal fault'?[6] The following passage does three things: it argues against the form of liability supported by Austin, it describes the law, revealing it to contain an alternative form of liability, and it supports that alternative:

> The standards of the law are standards of general application. The law takes no account of the infinite varieties of temperament, intellect, and education which make the internal character of a given act so different in different men. It does not attempt to see men as God sees them, for more than one sufficient reason. In the first place, the impossibility of nicely measuring a man's powers and limitations is far clearer than that of ascertaining his knowledge of law, which has been thought to account for what is called the presumption that every man knows the law. But a more satisfactory explanation is that, when men live in society, a certain average of conduct, a sacrifice of individual peculiarities going beyond a certain point, is necessary to the general welfare. If, for instance, a man is born hasty and awkward, is always having accidents and hurting himself or his neighbors, no

[4] ibid 95 (citation omitted). Quotation from *Harvey v Dunlop* Hill & Denio (Lalor) 193.

[5] ibid 96.

[6] ibid 82.

> doubt his congenital defects will be allowed for in the courts of Heaven, but his slips are no less troublesome to his neighbors than if they sprang from guilty neglect. His neighbors accordingly require him, at his proper peril, to come up to their standard, and the courts which they establish decline to take his personal equation into account.[7]

Unlike Austin's view, this account of liability does not concern itself with the defendant's personal fault. Rather, it operates in accordance with general standards of behaviour, stipulating as candidates for liability those who fall below those standards. Similarly, with respect to the torts of trespass to property, Holmes writes:

> One who diminishes the value of property by intentional damage knows it belongs to somebody. If he thinks it belongs to himself, he expects whatever harm he may do to come out of his own pocket. It would be odd if he were to get rid of the burden by discovering that it belonged to his neighbor.[8]

Again, this is not because the defendant was personally at fault, but because of the operation of general standards, here property rights.

Despite his rejection of Austin's theory, Holmes nevertheless accepts that liability in tort is properly described as fault-based.[9] This fault, however, is not personal fault. It is rather the fault of falling below a general standard, even if one could not help doing so. We find this understanding of fault in the law of negligence with its objective standard of care. And Holmes claims that we find it in trespass and other torts too.

Accordingly, Holmes' discussion reveals three potential forms of liability: liability based on causation alone, liability based on personal fault and liability for failing to observe general standards. Only the first is labelled strict.

B. Two Alternative Accounts

Holmes' distinction between strict and fault-based liability is by no means the only one. An alternative account defines strict liability as 'liability regardless of fault',[10] where fault is identified as personal fault.[11] Theorists of this stripe tend to say little about the nature of personal fault, because it does not relate to their interest in law. Instead, they are inclined to develop alternative accounts of personal responsibility thought to be more relevant to legal analysis.[12] It must suffice to say that personal fault is thought to connect to familiar moral concepts such as blame, desert and discredit.[13] Nevertheless, even this quick sketch is sufficient to enable us

[7] ibid 108.
[8] ibid 97.
[9] ibid 107.
[10] P Cane, *Responsibility in Law and Morality* (Oxford, Hart Publishing, 2002) 82.
[11] eg, ibid 66–78; T Honoré, *Responsibility and Fault* (Oxford, Hart Publishing, 1999) ch 2.
[12] Again, prominent examples are Cane (n 10) 66–78; Honoré (n 11) ch 2.
[13] Honoré (n 11) 14, 30–31.

to see why the view's leading proponent claims that the law of negligence imposes strict liability.[14] As this law determines liability in accordance with an objective standard of care, liability can fall on defendants not personally at fault. On this view, perhaps all liability in private law is strict.

A third understanding, different yet again, is probably the most prevalent. Found most often in non-theoretical discussion of the substantive law, this view holds that a tort is fault-based if it contains a specific element that refers to fault, and strict if it does not.[15] On this view, it is said that the law of defamation is strict because there is no element in the action for defamation labelled 'fault', while negligence is said to be fault-based because one element in the negligence enquiry is the standard of care, which is understood to be concerned with legal fault.

This conceptualisation of the distinction is formal rather than substantive. It would label defamation strict even if, because of the operation of the elements of the action, only defendants at fault could be liable, simply because there is no specific element in the defamation enquiry that explicitly refers to fault. And it would label negligence fault-based even if it were possible to be liable in negligence without being at fault, because the negligence enquiry does so refer.

Consequently, three different distinctions between strict and fault-based liability can be found in the literature. It may help to capture these ideas in the following table.

Table 1.1: Definitions of the Forms of Liability

	Strict Liability	**Fault-Based Liability**
The First View	Liability based on causation alone.	Liability based on the failure to live up to general standards.
The Second View	Liability that arises regardless of whether the defendant was personally at fault.	Liability that requires the defendant to have been personally at fault.
The Third View	Liability that does not specifically call for proof of fault (however defined).	Liability that specifically calls for proof of fault (however defined).

The result of this equivocation is confusion. Consider, for instance, the law of negligence. On the first and third views, negligence is a form of fault-based liability, but on the second view, it is a form of strict liability. Moreover, as I shall argue

[14] ibid 14.

[15] For instance, WE Peel and J Goudkamp, *Winfield and Jolowicz on Tort*, 19th edn (London, Sweet & Maxwell, 2013) 495 claim that the action based on *Rylands v Fletcher* (1868) LR 3 HL 330 is strict *because* the plaintiff need not prove fault.

in effect in Chapter 4, the law of trespass is strict on the second and third views, but fault-based on the first.

Commentators have frequently overlooked the differences between these understandings. We have already witnessed an example of this. The theorists who deny that any tortious liability is strict have operated with the first sense of the term in mind. Unaware of this, their opponents have pointed to examples of strict liability in the second or third senses of that term. There is no genuine disagreement here.

Obviously, the terminology is problematic as it stands. It seems that the only solution is to introduce new terms. These are my suggestions. First, I refer to what Holmes called 'strict liability' as absolute liability and to fault-based liability as liability based on wrongdoing. Second, I translate 'fault-based liability' and 'strict liability' in the eyes of the second view as 'liability based on personal fault' and 'liability independent of personal fault' respectively. Finally, because of their prevalence, I keep the terms as defined according to the third view. Hence, the distinction between strict liability and fault-based liability as defined herein turns on the elements of a tort that require proof. This is captured in the following table.

Table 1.2: Definitions of the Forms of Liability

Substantive	Absolute Liability	Liability based on causation alone.
	Liability Based on Wrongdoing	Liability that requires wrongdoing on the part of the defendant (though not necessarily personal fault).
	Liability Independent of Personal Fault	Liability that does not require the defendant to have been personally at fault.
	Liability Based on Personal Fault	Liability that requires the defendant to have been personally at fault.
Formal	Strict Liability	Liability that contains no explicit fault element (however defined).
	Fault-Based Liability	Liability that contains an explicit fault element (however defined).

It is important to stress the distinction between the substantive and the formal definitions. As indicated above, any substantive definition can couple with any formal definition. There could, for instance, be a substantive liability based on personal fault instantiated in a tort that was formally strict. It is also important to note that liability based on wrongdoing and liability independent of personal fault are consistent with each other. This is significant as I will argue that all tort liability is of this kind.

That task is taken up in detail in the following chapters. The remainder of this chapter examines the two substantive forms of liability not found in the law: liability based on personal fault and absolute liability.

II. The Rejection of Liability Based on Personal Fault

The defendant in *Vaughan v Menlove*[16] built a haystack next to the plaintiff's barn. The hay caught fire, which spread to and destroyed the barn. The plaintiff sued. At trial, the judge instructed the jury that they were to find the defendant negligent if in building the haystack, the defendant had failed 'to proceed with such reasonable caution as a prudent man would have exercised under such circumstances'.[17] Apparently, in nineteenth-century England, it was common knowledge that haystacks are prone to catch fire and so should not be placed next to things such as barns. Accordingly, the jury found that the defendant had been negligent. On appeal, the defendant accepted that an ordinary man would have known of the risk of fire and would have built the haystack elsewhere. However, he maintained that he could not have been expected to have been aware of that risk, due to the fact that he was exceptionally stupid. He insisted that liability should be decided by looking at his personal circumstances, the issue being whether he had 'acted bonâ fide to the best of his judgment'.[18] The Court of Common Pleas rejected this view.

Tindal CJ ruled that the question was not what could have been expected of the defendant personally, but what could have been expected of 'a man of ordinary prudence'.[19] In other words, the defendant was judged by the standard of the ordinary reasonable person, not by a standard peculiar to himself. In Chapter 12, we explore the positive position taken by the Court. Here, we are interested solely in the Court's rejection of the idea that liability should be determined in accordance with the defendant's personal characteristics. In other words, we are focused on the Court's rejection of liability based on personal fault.

In that regard, Tindal CJ maintained that the defendant's suggestion 'would leave so vague a line as to afford no rule at all, the degree of judgment belonging to each individual being infinitely various'.[20] At least through modern eyes, it is perhaps natural to interpret this as saying that liability should not be based on the defendant's personal fault because that standard is too difficult to apply in practice. If that were Tindal CJ's suggestion, then his argument is weak. Though applying a subjective standard is not without difficulty, criminal lawyers apply it routinely. Moreover, there seems no reason to think that the defendant's suggested approach is any more difficult to apply than the one the Court preferred. After all, as counsel for the defendant argued, and to this the Court offered no reply, on the face of it, one might well think that the objective standard is also 'too uncertain to afford any criterion'.[21]

[16] *Vaughan v Menlove* (1837) 3 Hodges 51, 132 ER 490.
[17] ibid 492.
[18] ibid.
[19] ibid 493.
[20] ibid.
[21] ibid 492.

But this reading seems unfair to Tindal CJ. His claim was not that the defendant's suggestion would result in an approach that was merely vague, but that it would result in a rule that was so vague as not to be a genuine rule. Similarly, he later remarked that the rejected approach 'would be as variable as the length of the foot of each individual'.[22] This must call to mind the famous criticism of equity as varying according to the length of the Chancellor's foot.[23] This implies that the problem with the defendant's suggestion is not that it is inefficient, but that it is unjust.

If that were Tindal CJ's intention, then our theory allows us to see why he was right. If the question is whether the defendant 'acted bonâ fide to the best of his judgment',[24] then the approach is focused on the defendant, ignoring the plaintiff entirely. Given that the issue is whether the defendant's interaction with the plaintiff was legal, that cannot be appropriate. The defendant, then, was attempting to privilege his position in the enquiry, an argument that does not respect justice as between the parties.

In our language, the defendant's suggestion amounted to an insistence that he be judged from the perspective of ethics. This is plain in the argument of his counsel, according to which the defendant:

> [C]an only be called on to act bonâ fide to the best of his judgment: if he has done that, it is a contradiction in terms, to inquire whether or not he has been guilty of gross negligence. At all events what would have been gross negligence ought to be estimated by the faculties of the individual, and not by those of other men.[25]

But it is not appropriate to determine the legality of the interaction between the defendant and the plaintiff in this fashion. The issue is not whether the defendant acted unethically; it is whether he constrained and coerced the plaintiff. That requires a judgement that takes the position of both parties into account.

III. The Rejection of Absolute Liability

The plaintiff in *Buckley and The Toronto Transportation Commission v Smith Transport Ltd*[26] was injured when a truck crashed into the vehicle in which he

[22] ibid 493.

[23] 'Equity is a roguish thing: for law we have a measure, know what to trust to; equity is according to the conscience of him that is Chancellor, and as that is larger or narrower, so is equity.' Tis all one as if they should make the standard for the measure we call a foot, a Chancellor's foot; what an uncertain measure would this be? One Chancellor has a long foot, another a short foot, a third an indifferent foot: 'tis the same thing in a Chancellor's conscience.' John Selden, *Table Talk*, quoted in MB Evans and RI Jack (eds), *Sources of English Legal and Constitutional History* (Sydney, Butterworths, 1984) 223–24.

[24] *Vaughan v Menlove* (n 16) 492.

[25] ibid.

[26] *Buckley and The Toronto Transportation Commission v Smith Transport Ltd* [1946] OR 798 (Ont CA). See also *Slattery v Haley* [1923] 3 DLR 156 (Ont SC App Div). This case was brought in negligence,

was riding. The truck was 'driven' by a man named Taylor, and the defendant was responsible for the actions of this man.[27] This means that, had Taylor committed a tort, the defendant would have been liable. The question for the Ontario Court of Appeal was whether Taylor had committed a tort. The Court found that Taylor had been 'driving' too fast for the conditions and had failed to give way. In other words, Taylor had fallen below the standard of the ordinary reasonable driver. However, the Court also held that Taylor was suffering from syphilis of the brain and was under the delusion that he was not driving, but that the truck was being driven by remote control from head office. The disease was so advanced that he died one month after the accident occurred.

The Court ruled that Taylor had not committed a tort because he 'suddenly and without warning, had become insane'.[28] It is true, of course, that drivers owe a duty to other users of the road to take care not to cause injury, but Taylor's insanity made him incapable of carrying out this duty. In the eyes of the law, then, Taylor was an automaton and his behaviour was incapable of giving rise to liability. Similarly, a person pushed onto another person's land is not a trespasser, even though trespass to land is a tort of strict liability.[29]

The justification for this position is that the alternative would violate the principle of innocence. That principle demands that one can be liable only for the consequences of one's *actions*. This is because non-volitional behaviour cannot be imputed to a person, as the person was not the free cause of the behaviour.[30] Morally speaking, then, there can be no more reason to believe that Taylor committed a tort than to think that anyone else did in that case. Holding a person liable for the results of her non-volitional behaviour is no more justifiable than finding her liable for an event on the other side of the world with which she was uninvolved. Nor is it any more rational than finding liable a tree that had damaged property or a bull that had charged someone, as our ancestors sometimes did.[31] Or as Oliver Wendell Holmes expressed the idea, in a passage we have already encountered:

but as Taylor did not act, if the Court had found the defendant liable, it would have imposed absolute liability. Compare *Restatement (Second) of Torts* (St Paul, MN, American Law Institute Publishers, 1965) §283B; *Restatement (Third) of Torts: Physical and Emotional Harm* (St Paul, MN, American Law Institute Publishers, 2010) §11.

[27] This is because the 'driver' was an employee of the defendant and was 'acting' in the course of his employment. In these circumstances, the employer is liable for the torts committed by the employee. This is known as vicarious liability. Note also that the employee remains liable (ie, both the employer and employee are liable) and, as a matter of law, though this is not enforced, the employee is contractually liable to the employer to indemnify the employer for damages that the employer must pay. For discussion of vicarious liability, see A Ripstein, *Force and Freedom: Kant's Legal and Political Philosophy* (Cambridge, MA, Harvard University Press, 2009) 84, and for a developed analysis of this doctrine that fits Kantian theory (though it is not presented in that way), see R Stevens, *Torts and Rights* (Oxford, Oxford University Press, 2007) 257–74.

[28] *Buckley and The Toronto Transportation Commission v Smith Transport Ltd* (n 26) 800.

[29] This matter is examined in Ch 4.

[30] I Kant, *The Metaphysics of Morals*, M Gregor (trans) (Cambridge, Cambridge University Press, 1996) 6:223.

[31] However, they may not have been as irrational as we think them. See A Watson, *Legal History and a Common Law for Europe* (Stockholm, Institutet för Rättshistorisk Forskning, 2001) 142–49.

> Unless my act is of a nature to threaten others ... it is no more justifiable to make me indemnify my neighbor against the consequences, than to make me do the same thing if I had fallen upon him in a fit, or to compel me to insure him against lightning.[32]

Absolute liability implies liability for non-volitional behaviour. But finding a person liable for non-volitional behaviour implies that the person was guilty of wrongdoing (though not necessarily personal wrongdoing) without choosing to do anything. In other words, it is to hold that wrongdoing can correctly be attributed to a person, though it attaches in no way to that person's agency.[33] But this is to violate the principle of innocence and thus the innate right which generates that principle. It cannot therefore respect equal maximum freedom.

IV. Conclusion

In conclusion, neither absolute liability nor liability based on personal fault is reflected in the law of tort or justifiable in that context. That, of course, is a negative conclusion. Of more interest is the justification and analysis of the form of liability that is found in the law. We are now in a position to turn to that matter.

[32] Holmes (n 1) 96.

[33] Weinrib (n 1) 179–83. Here one can see the connection between absolute liability and the loss model. Because it holds that loss is an evil, it holds that causing loss is an evil even when that loss is not caused by action. It is a small step from there to the notion that the causer should be liable for that loss.

Part II

Direct Control

The following four chapters consider forms of liability that respond to coercion that occurs directly between the plaintiff and the defendant. By 'directly', I mean that, except in unusual cases,[1] the coercion is the result of the defendant acting on the plaintiff or on objects over which the plaintiff has a right that ought to exclude the defendant. The result is that the defendant can be said to have put the plaintiff or the plaintiff's property to her purposes, and thus directly to have exercised control over the plaintiff.

Chapter 4 sets the scene by examining the two areas of the law that most clearly illustrate this analysis: the laws of battery and trespass to property. Chapter 5 expands this analysis to cover the law of trespass more generally. Chapter 6 examines the defences to an action for trespass. Finally, Chapter 7 examines the tort of deceit, here also conceptualised as an action that responds to direct control.

[1] These are cases in which, if the defendant is liable, that liability is secondary. I hire a thug to beat you up, for example. Here, in principle it seems that I ought to be liable in the tort of battery because I procured the battery. Importantly, this reveals that it is not part of the *definitions* of the torts that follow that they involve direct control. The distinction between direct and indirect control is of much analytic convenience because it allows the nature of the actions to come into focus, but the distinction does not play a role in defining the actions themselves.

4

Battery and Trespass to Property

We begin our investigation of tort law with paradigm cases of control: the intentional and unconsented to touching of the plaintiff or the plaintiff's property. These correspond to the torts of battery and trespass to property respectively.

Three key aspects of these torts must be examined here. The first concerns the form of liability that they employ. Are the torts strict or fault-based? As we will see, the answer to this question is remarkably difficult to produce. The second issue concerns harm. In the Commonwealth, it is trite that these torts are actionable per se, meaning that proof of harm is unnecessary.[1] In the US, however, despite first impressions, the law on this matter is unclear. The third issue involves Commonwealth law's insistence that the contact between the parties or between the defendant and the plaintiff's property be direct, an insistence that has been dropped in the US. Let us begin at the top.

I. The Form of Liability

The torts of trespass contain an intention requirement. For this reason, they are often referred to as intentional torts. This appears to imply that the torts are forms of fault-based liability, the idea being that intention is a necessary condition for liability because it indicates that the defendant was at fault in a way that justifies the imposition of this form of liability.[2] This notion is reinforced by analogy with other areas of the law. For instance, the intention requirement is seen as the parallel of the standard of care in the law of negligence, the latter conceptualised as a fault requirement. Similarly, the intention requirement in the law of trespass is

[1] Of course, such proof is relevant to the damages stage of the enquiry, but it is irrelevant to liability. An unharmed plaintiff is able to establish a cause of action against a defendant.

[2] See, eg, S Deakin, A Johnston and B Markesinis, *Markesinis and Deakin's Tort Law*, 6th edn (Oxford, Clarendon Press, 2008) 451–52 (compare S Deakin, A Johnston and B Markesinis, *Markesinis and Deakin's Tort Law*, 7th edn (Oxford, Clarendon Press, 2013) 401–11); J Fleming, *The Law of Torts*, 9th edn (Sydney, LBC Information Services, 1998) 24; K Barker et al, *The Law of Torts in Australia*, 5th edn (Melbourne, Oxford University Press, 2012) 29–35.

thought to resemble the mens rea requirements of the criminal law, which are also concerned with fault.

This view is problematic, however. First, the analogy with the criminal law is inapposite. In the criminal context, a defendant can be liable only if she intends to perform the actus reus, which is defined as touching without consent. Accordingly, with respect to the crime of battery:

> [T]he prosecution must … prove that the defendant *intended to apply force to the person of the victim without his consent*. If [the defendant] did not intend the whole of this italicised phrase—and in particular, if she did not realise that [the victim] had not consented—[the defendant] is entitled to an acquittal.[3]

As we will see, tort law is entirely different in this regard. It requires non-consensual and intentional touching, but in general at least—the US exceptions are examined below—it does not require touching that is intended to be non-consensual. Reflection on this point reveals that the torts are in fact forms of strict liability. As this point is most easily made in respect of the law of trespass to property, it is there that we begin.

A. Trespass to Property

If I walk on your land without consent or justification, I commit a trespass. This is so even if I reasonably and sincerely believe the land to be my own, to be a public park or the like.[4] The consequence is that trespass is a form of strict liability. Importantly, this conclusion is consistent with the law's intention requirement. An example should help to clarify this point.

Imagine that I walk on your land reasonably and sincerely believing it to be mine.[5] In this case, I satisfy the intention requirement because I am intentionally on the land. It is irrelevant that I believe the land to be my own and so am not intending-to-be-on-land-that-is-not-my-own. In other words, the fact that the land is not my own does not need to feature in my intentional state. Thus, the intentional state required for liability is not the intention to be on someone else's land, it is merely the intention to be on the land in question.

This point is well made in the second *Restatement*:

> If the actor intends to be upon the particular piece of land, it is not necessary that he intend to invade the other's interest in the exclusive possession of his land. The intention which is required to make the actor liable under the rule stated in this Section is an intention to enter upon the particular piece of land in question, irrespective of whether the

[3] A Simester and W Brookbanks, *Principles of Criminal Law*, 4th edn (Wellington, Thompson Brookers, 2012) 604.

[4] *Basely v Clarkson* (1681) 3 Lev 37, 83 ER 565.

[5] Strictly, it is possession rather than ownership that counts. For convenience, this is ignored in the following.

> actor knows or should know that he is not entitled to enter. It is, therefore, immaterial whether or not he honestly and reasonably believes that the land is his own, or that he has the consent of the possessor or of a third person having power to give consent on his behalf, or that he has a mistaken belief that he has some other privilege to enter.[6]

Thus, it was said in *Isle Royal Min Co v Hertin* that:

> [W]hen one thus goes upon the land of another … though in perfect good faith and under honest mistake as to his rights, he may be held responsible as a trespasser. His good faith does not excuse him from the payment of damages, the law requiring him at his peril to ascertain what his rights are, and not to invade the possession, actual or constructive, of another.[7]

Thus, despite being an 'intentional tort', trespass to land is a tort of strict liability. A defendant may satisfy the intention requirement without being at fault as that term is used in legal or non-legal contexts. The intention requirement is not a fault requirement.

In the Commonwealth, it is widely accepted that liability for trespass to goods is identical in form with that applicable to trespass to land. Though this has been doubted in the US,[8] that doubt seems misplaced. Again, as the *Restatement* has it:

> Such an intention is present when an act is done for the purpose of using or otherwise intermeddling with a chattel or with knowledge that such an intermeddling will, to a substantial certainty, result from the act. It is not necessary that the actor should know or have reason to know that such intermeddling is a violation of the possessory rights of another. Thus, it is immaterial that the actor intermeddles with the chattel under a mistake of law or fact which has led him to believe that he is the possessor of it or that the possessor has consented to his dealing with it … So too, a mistake of law or fact which leads him to believe even upon reasonable grounds that he is privileged to meddle with the chattel without the consent of the possessor does not prevent his act from being a trespass if the privilege is one which does not depend upon his reasonable belief.[9]

This, then, advances the same view as the one we have been examining: trespass to goods is a form of strict liability. Though it contains an intention requirement, that requirement is not a fault requirement.

B. Battery

If trespass to property is strict, this surely entails that trespass to the person should also be strict. Strict liability for the former coupled with fault-based liability for

[6] *Restatement (Second) of Torts* (St Paul, MN, American Law Institute Publishers, 1965) §163, comment b. See also *Basely v Clarkson* (n 4).

[7] *Isle Royal Min Co v Hertin* 37 Mich 332 (Mich 1877) 333.

[8] WP Keeton et al, *Prosser and Keeton on the Law of Torts*, 5th edn (St Paul, MN, West Group, 1984) 86.

[9] *Restatement (Second) of Torts* (n 6) §217, comment c.

the latter would reflect an unwarranted preference for the protection of property over the body. Despite this, however, it is common to claim that the law is in precisely this position. The clearest support for this view comes from the US, where, in conjunction with what has been said concerning trespass to property above, it is also maintained that a defendant is guilty of a battery if 'he acts intending to cause a harmful or offensive contact',[10] a view that implies fault.[11] What has led to this position?

Two answers have already been given. They are the general assumption that an intention requirement must be a fault requirement and the tendency to link the law of trespass to other areas of the law where fault is determinative. The latter is particularly tempting here because of the apparently close connection between the tort of battery and the crime of the same name. But we have seen that these are mistakes.[12] Nevertheless, matters are more complex here than with respect to trespass to property. Let us begin with English law.

i. Intention in English Law

It seems undeniable that the law of battery was once fault-based. For instance, in *Cole v Turner*, Holt CJ famously said that a battery is a touching *in anger*, a position which appears to imply that a battery exists only if the defendant was at fault:

> First, that the least touching of another in anger is a battery.
>
> Secondly, if two or more meet in a narrow passage, and without any violence or design of harm, the one touches the other gently, it will be no battery.
>
> Thirdly, if any of them use violence against the other, to force his way in a rude inordinate manner, it will be a battery; or any struggle about the passage to that degree as may do hurt, will be a battery.[13]

As we will see, the issue that concerned Holt CJ has been one of the main obstacles to recognising that liability for battery is strict.

Imagine that *A* and *B* pass in a narrow passageway and brush against each other. Is that a battery? The answer must surely be no. Such commonplace and unremarkable events cannot be legal wrongs. But what precisely is the legal justification for reaching that conclusion? It cannot be that *A* and *B* did not intend to touch

[10] ibid §13. *cf Restatement (Third) of Torts: Physical and Emotional Harm* (St Paul, MN, American Law Institute Publishers, 2010) §5.

[11] In the Commonwealth, the claim that trespass to the person is fault-based is made by Deakin, Johnston and Markesinis, 6th edn (n 2) 451–52 (compare Deakin, Johnston and Markesinis, 7th edn (n 2) 401–11); Fleming (n 2) 24; and Barker et al (n 2) 29–35, and appears to be implied by WE Peel and J Goudkamp, *Winfield and Jolowicz on Tort*, 19th edn (London, Sweet & Maxwell, 2013) 56. The claim that it is strict is made by MA Jones, *Textbook on Torts*, 8th edn (Oxford, Oxford University Press, 2005) 508–09. In the US, the near-universal assumption appears to be that battery is fault-based.

[12] For another example of the disanalogy between these actions, see A Beever, 'Transferred Malice in Tort Law?' (2009) 29 *Legal Studies* 400.

[13] *Cole v Turner* (1704) Holt KB 108, 90 ER 958, 958.

each other, though that might sometimes be true. This is because, as is examined later in this chapter, intention in this context is defined broadly so that *A* and *B* will usually have intended to touch each other in the sense required by the law.

So why is there no battery? We will have to wait until Chapter 6 for the answer to this question, but Holt CJ's answer was that they did not touch each other in anger, an answer that suggests that battery is fault-based. However, further case law has revealed this to be the wrong answer. In *Scott v Shepherd*,[14] the defendant threw a firework into a stall at a market as a practical joke. The firework injured the plaintiff. This was found to be a battery, but the defendant was not angry when he threw the firework. Similarly, if I kiss you without your consent, that is a battery,[15] but I am unlikely to kiss you in anger. For like reasons, we must also reject the claim, sometimes thought to follow from Lord Denning MR's judgment in *Letang v Cooper*,[16] that a battery requires an intention to injure.

This issue was revisited by the English Court of Appeal in *Wilson v Pringle*,[17] in which Croom-Johnson LJ distinguished between friendly and unfriendly touching, claimed that only the latter was actionable, and distinguished between the two as follows:

> [I]n a battery there must be an intentional touching or contact in one form or another of the plaintiff by the defendant. That touching must be proved to be a hostile touching. That still leaves unanswered the question 'when is a touching to be called hostile?' Hostility cannot be equated with ill-will or malevolence. It cannot be governed by the obvious intention shown in acts like punching, stabbing or shooting. It cannot be solely governed by an expressed intention, although that may be strong evidence. But the element of hostility, in the sense in which it is now to be considered, must be a question of fact for the tribunal of fact. It may be imported from the circumstances. Take the example of the police officer in *Collins v. Wilcock* [1984] 1 W.L.R. 1172. She touched the woman deliberately, but without an intention to do more than restrain her temporarily. Nevertheless, she was acting unlawfully and in that way was acting with hostility. She was acting contrary to the woman's legal right not to be physically restrained.[18]

Croom-Johnson LJ insisted that hostility is not ill-will or malevolence. But if not, then what is it? According to the *Oxford English Dictionary*, 'hostile' means 'Of, pertaining to, or characteristic of an enemy; pertaining to or engaged in actual hostilities' and 'Of the nature or disposition of an enemy; unfriendly'. Can one be or act as an enemy without having or exhibiting ill-will or malevolence? Can one with no ill-will act with hostility toward someone? Here we see the unfortunate tendency of common law judges to bend the meanings of words so as to appear to be explaining. Though Croom-Johnson LJ would be prepared to say that the defendants in *Scott v Shepherd* and *Collins v Wilcock* were hostile and that I am

[14] *Scott v Shepherd* (1773) 2 Black W 892, 96 ER 525.
[15] *cf Police v Bannin* [1991] 2 NZLR 237.
[16] *Letang v Cooper* [1965] 1 QB 232 (CA).
[17] *Wilson v Pringle* [1987] QB 237 (CA).
[18] ibid 252–53.

hostile when I kiss you without your consent, this is not what the word means in ordinary English.

Croom-Johnson LJ also tells us that the defendant in *Collins v Wilcock* was liable because she acted contrary to the plaintiff's legal right. However, without identifying and examining that right, the claim that the defendant acted contrary to the plaintiff's legal right means only that the defendant committed a battery. Nor can this mere reference to the plaintiff's rights explain the meaning of the term 'hostile'. In fact, then, it seems that the defendant's action was labelled as 'hostile' because it was thought that the defendant should not have performed it. With that we can agree, but the use of this concept does not explain why the defendant should not have done what she did.

The issue of intention was revisited in *Re F (Mental Patient: Sterilisation)*, in which Lord Goff maintained:

> In the old days it used to be said that, for a touching of another's person to amount to a battery, it had to be a touching 'in anger' (see *Cole v. Turner* ...); and it has recently been said that the touching must be 'hostile' to have that effect (see *Wilson v. Pringle* ...). I respectfully doubt whether that is correct. A prank that gets out of hand; an over-friendly slap on the back; surgical treatment by a surgeon who mistakenly thinks that the patient has consented to it—all these things may transcend the bounds of lawfulness, without being characterised as hostile. Indeed the suggested qualification is difficult to reconcile with the principle that *any touching of another's body is, in the absence of lawful excuse, capable of amounting to a battery and a trespass*. Furthermore, in the case of medical treatment, we have to bear well in mind the libertarian principle of self-determination which, to adopt the words of Cardozo J. (in *Schloendorff v. Society of New York Hospital* (1914) 105 N.E. 92, 93) recognises that:
>
>> 'Every human being of adult years and sound mind has a right to determine what shall be done with his own body; and a surgeon who performs an operation without his patient's consent commits an assault.'[19]

This strongly aligns with the position presented here. Moreover, even if one rejects Lord Goff's specific claims, as his position makes clear, if liability were fault-based, then it would be impossible to explain why 'any touching of another's body is, in the absence of lawful excuse, capable of amounting to a battery and a trespass'.[20] A surgeon who sincerely and reasonably, though mistakenly, believes that a patient has consented to an operation commits a battery when that operation is performed. This cannot be because the surgeon was at fault. In general, mistake, even reasonable mistake, is no defence to a claim in battery, no matter how clearly it shows that the defendant was without fault.

It must be admitted that the support found in *Re F* for this position is not overwhelming. On the contrary, it is buried in the judgment of a single judge. Nevertheless, the submission is twofold. First, as Lord Goff intimates, the law of battery

[19] *Re F (Mental Patient: Sterilisation)* [1990] 2 AC 1 (HL), 73 (emphasis added).
[20] ibid.

must be strict if it is properly to respect individual autonomy. That argument is made in relation to US law below. Second, the fact that defendants—surgeons, for example—can be liable without being at fault reveals that in reality, this tort is strict, whatever the official position might lead one to believe. Lord Goff's judgment in *Re F*, then, should be viewed as a landmark, an example of a judge recognising and making explicit a development in the law that had already, in fact, occurred.

ii. Intention in US Law

In the US, the tort of battery seems clearly to be fault-based. As noted above, echoing the criminal law, the second *Restatement* maintains that a defendant is guilty of a battery if 'he acts intending to cause a harmful or offensive contact'.[21]

In *Mullins v Parkview Hospital Inc*,[22] the plaintiff consented to undergo a hysterectomy, but made it clear that she was concerned for her privacy and did not consent to 'the presence of healthcare learners' during the procedure. Nevertheless, an Emergency Medical Technician student attended and was permitted to practise intubation on the plaintiff. The Court held that no battery was committed in this case as the plaintiff had failed to show that the student 'act[ed] *intending* to cause a harmful or offensive contact with' the plaintiff.[23] This was because, on the evidence, the student had no idea that the plaintiff had not consented to his actions.

Through these eyes at least, the decision in *Mullins v Parkview Hospital Inc* is utterly shocking and I hopefully predict that no Commonwealth court could mirror it. Importantly, however, it can also be argued that the decision does not reflect the spirit of US law, whatever the *Restatements* might say.

Imagine that the procedure performed on the plaintiff was not a hysterectomy, but, say, an appendectomy. Here, the plaintiff did not consent to this procedure at all. Also imagine that those who performed the operation honestly believed that the plaintiff consented to that procedure. Did the medical professionals perform batteries in this case? According to the ratio of *Mullins v Parkview Hospital Inc* and the ideas expressed in the *Restatements*, they did not, as they did not have the requisite intentions. They intended to touch the plaintiff and did so in a way to which she had not consented, but they did not intend to cause harmful or offensive contact and did not intend their touching to be non-consensual. Is this really the law?[24]

If it is, how could this be said to be consistent with Cardozo CJ's maxim that: 'Every human being of adult years and sound mind has a right to determine what

[21] *Restatement (Second) of Torts* (n 6) §13. *cf Restatement (Third) of Torts* (n 10) §5.

[22] *Mullins v Parkview Hospital Inc* 865 NE 2d 608 (Ind 2007).

[23] ibid [5], quoting *Restatement (Second) of Torts* (n 6) §13.

[24] Compare *Restatement (Second) of Torts* (n 6) §49, illustration 2. This appears to indicate, as the plaintiff in our example is not willing, that there would be liability for battery in this case. See also §892A, illustration 2.

shall be done with his own body; and a surgeon who performs an operation without his patient's consent commits an assault.'[25] It could not.

Consider also a practical joker of the kind presented by *Scott v Shepherd*, an issue to which the second *Restatement* gives considerable attention:

> If an act is done with the intention described in this Section, it is immaterial that the actor is not inspired by any personal hostility to the other, or a desire to injure him. Thus the fact that the defendant who intentionally inflicts bodily harm upon another does so as a practical joke, does not render him immune from liability so long as the other has not consented. This is true although the actor erroneously believes that the other will regard it as a joke, or that the other has, in fact, consented to it. One who plays dangerous practical jokes on others takes the risk that his victims may not appreciate the humor of his conduct and may not take it in good part.[26]

This view can appear consistent with the notion that liability is fault-based only because the *Restatement* in this context concentrates on practical jokes intended to cause harm, it being arguable that a defendant who plays such a joke must be at fault. But practical jokes need not be of that form.

In *Lambertson v United States*,[27] the plaintiff was unloading a truck when the defendant's employee screamed 'boo' at him, pulled his hat over his eyes, climbed on his back and rode him piggyback. This caused the plaintiff to fall, causing injury to his mouth and teeth. All agreed that the defendant's employee intended no harm to the plaintiff. He was nevertheless found liable. The Court maintained that: 'It is hornbook law in New York, as in most other jurisdictions, that the intent which is an essential element of the action for battery is the intent to make contact, not to do injury.'[28] On the face of it, this supports the position advanced here. If the requirement is that the defendant intended to make contact that is in fact unconsented to, then the tort is one of strict liability. However, in support of its claim, the Court went on to quote from *Masters v Becker*:

> A plaintiff in an action to recover damages for an assault founded on bodily contact must prove only that there was bodily contact; that such contact was offensive; and that the defendant intended to make the contact. The plaintiff is not required to prove that defendant intended physically to injure him. Certainly he is not required to prove an intention to cause the specific injuries resulting from the contact.[29]

This is unfortunately ambiguous. What does 'the contact' mean in the final clause of the first sentence? If it means the touching per se, then it supports the notion that liability is strict. But if the clause means that the defendant must intend the contact to be offensive, then that suggests that the liability is fault-based.

But the latter cannot be right. The defendant in a case of this kind does not intend to be offensive. He may be careless, but that suggests negligence rather than

[25] *Schloendorff v Society of New York Hospital* 105 NE 92 (NY 1914) 93.
[26] *Restatement (Second) of Torts* (n 6) §13, comment c.
[27] *Lambertson v United States* 528 F 2d 441 (US 1976).
[28] ibid [7].
[29] ibid, quoting *Masters v Becker* 254 NYS 2d 633 (NY 1964) [2].

battery. The fact that he is found liable in battery indicates that liability in battery is strict. The only fault apparent in *Lambertson v United States* was of the kind applicable to negligence, but the Court in that case insisted that negligence was the wrong cause of action.

The ambiguity that we find in the law, then, is to be expected. It is the kind of ambiguity that arises when the law's official position conflicts with what the law ought to be and that conflict is felt by the judges. The unfortunate result is often, as I think is the case in the US in this regard, that both the law and the way that the law ought to be become obscured.

Nevertheless, we will not here try to determine the true state of US law. Though tempted to argue that US law in practice recognises the need for strict liability in this area, I accept that the official focus on fault is so entrenched that the likely conclusion could only be that the law in practice is contradictory. Accordingly, the argument in the following will be that if the US law of battery is fault-based, then Commonwealth law is in this regard to be preferred. There, the law is and ought to be strict.

II. Rights: Control, Not Integrity

In order to develop our understanding of the torts under examination, it is necessary to clarify the nature of the rights that underlie them. Let us start with the law of battery.

A battery is an intentional and unconsented to touching of another. A paradigm case is a punch. This example helps to reveal why the right underlying this area of the law is usually conceptualised as a right to bodily integrity. It seems correct to say that I violate the integrity of your body if I punch you and the matter is even more straightforward if I stab or shoot you. However, it is trite that batteries need not be of this kind. A mere touching can suffice. So, if you tell me that you do not want to be touched and I make contact with you nevertheless, I batter you even if I cause no injury to you whatsoever. In these cases, it is misleading at best to say that there has been any interference with the *integrity* of your body.

The contemporary focus on the right to bodily integrity seems to be a product of the loss model. Through the eyes of that model, the tort of battery is concerned to prevent and respond to a certain kind of loss, damage to the integrity of the body being the most plausible candidate. From this notion we have developed the concept that a right to bodily integrity lies behind the tort. Notably, even many of those who reject the loss model have adopted this conclusion,[30] a fact that demonstrates the pervasive and often unconscious influence of that model.

[30] Including my past self. See, eg, A Beever, 'Our Most Fundamental Rights' in A Robertson and D Nolan (eds), *Rights and Private Law* (Oxford, Hart Publishing, 2011).

If the right underlying the law of battery were a right to bodily integrity, then batteries that cause no damage to the integrity of the body would have to be viewed as exceptional, as at best limiting cases of liability. But that is not the law as we find it. In the Commonwealth at least, it is trite that the law of battery is actionable per se. That means that cases where no damage to the integrity of the plaintiff's body has occurred are not peripheral or exceptional. They are as central as cases of punchings, stabbings or shootings. Our analysis of the law must reflect this.

This argument does not imply that the law of battery leaves the integrity of the body unprotected or even that there is no right to bodily integrity. The point is rather that though the law of battery does protect the integrity of our bodies, that is not its basis. The law protects the integrity of the body because it protects something even more fundamental, something that entails the protection of integrity. What is that thing?

As we have seen, in *Schloendorff v Society of New York Hospital*, Cardozo CJ said that: 'Every human being of adult years and sound mind has a right to determine what shall be done with his own body.'[31] This passage nicely reveals what is implicit in the discussion earlier in this chapter: that the tort protects one's entitlement to control the use of one's own body.

The basic idea is simple. My body is mine. It is absolutely fundamental that only I have the power to choose the purposes to which it is put. If another puts my body to her purposes without my consent, then she infringes that fundamental right. This is a concern not with integrity, but with control. Thus, while you interfere with the integrity of my body when you punch, shoot, stab or operate on me without my consent, the essential reason these are batteries is because they violate my right to control the use of my own body. These actions put my body to your purposes without my consent. This is also why it is no less a battery to kiss me or to touch me in any way to which I do not consent, even in the absence of harm or even if the touching is of benefit to me. Though such actions leave the integrity of my body unaffected, they violate my right to control the use of my body.

In the US, it is said that a touching must be harmful or offensive to constitute a battery.[32] As has been argued, harmful contact violates the plaintiff's right to control her own body. But what is to be said of the latter requirement?

In *Fuerschbach v Southwest Airlines Co*,[33] the plaintiff was subject to a mock arrest as a result of a practical joke played on her by her co-workers. She was manhandled and handcuffed. The Court held that this touching was offensive and therefore illegal. But why was the touching deemed to be offensive? Because the Court had already decided that it violated the plaintiff's entitlement. And what was that entitlement? I submit that it is best understood as the plaintiff's right to control the use of her own body. The touching was offensive because it put the plaintiff's body to the defendants' purposes without the plaintiff's consent.

[31] *Schloendorff v Society of New York Hospital* (n 25) 93.
[32] *Restatement (Second) of Torts* (n 6) §§ 13, 18.
[33] *Fuerschbach v Southwest Airlines Co* 439 F 3d 1197 (US 2006).

In *Cohen v Smith*,[34] the plaintiff consented to undergo a caesarean section on the condition that her naked body would not be seen by a male. The defendant, a male nurse, allegedly saw and touched the naked plaintiff. The Court held that:

> Although most people in modern society have come to accept the necessity of being seen unclothed and being touched by members of the opposite sex during medical treatment, the plaintiffs had not accepted these procedures and, according to their complaint, had informed defendants of their convictions …
>
> Accepting as true the plaintiffs' allegations that they informed defendants of their religious beliefs and that defendants persisted in treating Patricia Cohen as they would have treated a patient without those beliefs, we conclude that the trial court erred in dismissing both the battery and the intentional infliction of emotional distress counts.[35]

Of course, the touching was not rightly characterised as offensive merely because the plaintiff was offended by it. That is not what the requirement of offensiveness means, nor was that understanding adopted by the Court. The Court's position was that the touching was offensive because it was performed against the expressed wishes of the plaintiff. But this assumes that the plaintiff is entitled to control the use of her own body. Here, it is the plaintiff's right that determines the meaning of offensiveness and not the other way round.

Again, this is not to deny that we have a right to bodily integrity. We do have such a right. It is an aspect of the right to control the use of our own bodies. Nor is it to deny that the law of battery is concerned with the right to bodily integrity. On the contrary, that law is necessarily concerned with the right as it is an aspect of the more fundamental right to control the use of our own bodies. The claim is only that it is this more fundamental right and not the right to bodily integrity that is the key to understanding the law of battery.

Similarly, a person who enters my land or touches my goods without my permission is a trespasser, even though she in no way damages (interferes with the integrity of) the object in question.[36] We have a right to the integrity of our property, but that is because that right is an aspect of the more general right to control the use of our property. The fundamental right here is to control, not to integrity. That is the key to understanding the nature of all of the torts of trespass.

III. The Nature of Trespassory Wrongdoing

Our task now is to take this right and use it to explain the basic features of the law as we find it. We begin by examining the nature of the wrongdoing involved in this

[34] *Cohen v Smith* 648 NE 2d 329 (Ill 1995).

[35] ibid [13]–[15].

[36] Here I dissent from the decisions in cases such as *De Marentille v Oliver* 2 NJL 379 (NJ 1808) and *Paul v Slason* 22 Vt 231 (Vt 1850). For a helpful discussion of these cases that relates to the analysis presented here, see Keeton et al (n 8) 87.

area of the law. It will help to envisage examples that confront us with the nature of the problems that must be solved. Let us begin with two cases. In the first case, A_1 touches B_1 without B_1's consent, without causing any physical injury, and in the sincere and reasonable belief that B_1 consented.[37] In the second case, C_1 negligently falls into D_1, again not causing any damage. In the first case, A_1 commits a trespass. In the second case, C_1 does not and (in usual circumstances) commits no tort whatsoever. Why is this?

It will also help to have examples that relate to the law of trespass to property. These mirror the examples given above. In the first, A_2 parks his car on B_2's land. A_2 believes that the land belongs to a public car park and he leaves the land undamaged. In the second case, C_2 loses control of his car while driving. The car spins off the road and enters D_2's property, again without damaging it. The issues are the same. Why is A_2 but not C_2 liable?

These pairs of cases reveal two relevant issues. First, why is there any legal wrong in the first cases? After all, neither B_1 nor B_2 suffers loss. In fact, as Arthur Ripstein points out, the actions of the defendants in such cases can be Pareto efficient.[38] In our example, A_2 is made better off while B_2 is materially unaffected. Why then find A_2 liable? Second, how can an answer to the first question be consistent with the absence of liability in the second cases? In all examples, the plaintiff suffers no loss, so why is anyone liable? What is more, the defendants in the second cases are at fault, while those in the first are not. So why are only those in the first cases liable?

Presenting the issues in this way reveals that a mere appeal to the rights of the parties, or to the importance of the relevant rights, is insufficient to answer our questions. It is not sufficient, for instance, to argue that the law of battery has the form it does because an act of battery involves the violation of the plaintiff's right to his body and, because the law takes the relevant right seriously, it imposes liability even if the defendant is faultless and the plaintiff is materially unaffected.[39] It is, of course, true to say that the right is to be taken seriously. But what reason is there to think that taking it seriously will result in the law of trespass? Why would it not result in something quite different? What does it mean to take the right seriously? Why does taking the right seriously result in strict liability for intentional, but fault-based liability for unintentional, behaviour? And so on. Answering these questions will take us well beyond the suggestion under consideration. Moreover, given the nature of our law, what we need to know most particularly is why it is illegal for those who are faultless and who cause no harm to touch others intentionally when it is not illegal for them to do so inadvertently. The suggestion under examination provides no answer. This is not because the suggestion is wrong; it is

[37] We should assume that the reasons for A_1's belief are not attributable to the actions of B_1, ie, B_1 has not *indicated* consent to A_1 intentionally or unintentionally. For discussion of this issue, see Ch 6.

[38] A Ripstein, *Force and Freedom: Kant's Legal and Political Philosophy* (Boston, MA, Harvard University Press, 2009) 92.

[39] *cf* WVH Rogers, *Winfield and Jolowicz on Tort*, 18th edn (London, Sweet & Maxwell, 2010) 139 (the relevant passage has been deleted from the 19th edn).

not wrong. The problem is that it is insufficiently developed to answer the questions that confront us.

Let us begin with the first question. Why does A_1 commit a trespass against B_1? The first point to note is that A_1's action constrains B_1. The form of the constraint is control. The action puts B_1's body to A_1's purposes without B_1's consent. This is so even if A_1's action was a mere touching. That conclusion leads to the question: is this a form of constraint that can be justified on the basis of equal maximum freedom? The answer is No. B_1's body is B_1's. A_1 cannot be entitled to use it unless he has B_1's consent or some other relevant justification applies.[40]

The position is the same with respect to A_2 and B_2. In parking his car on B_2's land without B_2's consent, A_2 constrains B_2.[41] A_2 exercises control over B_2 by putting B_2's property to his purposes. Is that constraint consistent with equal maximum freedom? No. B_2's land is B_2's. A_2 cannot be entitled to use it unless he has B_2's consent.

These cases involve a particularly stark form of control that we can call *use*: the defendant exercises control over the plaintiff by using his body or his property.[42] In my view, all batteries and trespasses to property involve use by the defendant of the plaintiff or the plaintiff's property. But it is important not to be tied down by terminology. Some may be inclined to use 'use' more narrowly than I and so reject this view. That is not important. What matters is the defendant's exercise of control over the plaintiff in the sense of 'control' defined in Chapter 2.

Note that the conclusions reached above are indifferent to fault. The issue is the impact of A_1's and A_2's actions on B_1 and B_2, not on A_1's and A_2's blameworthiness or the like. From A_1's perspective, his use of B_1's body is perfectly reasonable. A_1 in no way behaves unethically. Nevertheless, A_1's use of B_1's body remains a use of that body without B_1's consent. Thus, as between the parties, the action is unjust. It is a form of wrongdoing. Likewise, though from A_2's perspective his use of B_2's land is perfectly reasonable and though A_2 behaves perfectly ethically, A_2's use of B_2's land remains a use of that land without B_2's consent. Again, as between the parties, the action is unjust, a form of wrongdoing. Also note that loss is likewise irrelevant. B_1 and B_2 are coerced, though they suffer no material loss and may indeed undergo no negative influence whatsoever.

Thus, imagine that I am trying to teach students by drawing lines on a whiteboard. Exasperated by their lack of comprehension, I thrust a pen into the hand of one of them, grab her arm and force it to draw a line. 'See?', I say, 'Can you not see that connection?' Here, I have put the student to my purposes. This is

[40] These matters are examined in Ch 6. For convenience, justification is generally ignored in the remainder of this chapter.

[41] Naturally, this assumes that one is connected with one's property in a way such that one can be constrained and coerced when that property is interfered with. As noted above, this book takes acquired rights as we find them in law.

[42] *cf Restatement (Second) of Torts* (n 6) §217: 'A trespass to a chattel may be committed by intentionally ... using or intermeddling with a chattel in the possession of another.'

so even though my purpose is to benefit the student. It is so even if my purpose is self-sacrificing and entirely focused on advancing the student's interests. It is also irrelevant whether the action succeeds in benefiting the student. Influence is immaterial, whether positive or negative. For this reason, the surgeon who operates on a patient without the patient's consent puts the patient to her (the surgeon's) purposes, even though the surgeon's purpose is to benefit the patient rather than herself and even if the patient is advantaged by the operation.[43] All of these cases involve wrongdoing of the same kind: control.[44] The law, then, is right to hold that they fall under the same tort.

Why, then, do C_1 and C_2 escape liability? They were at fault, remember. Because this question is tied up with the further question—'Why does liability for negligence require proof of damage?'—it cannot fully be answered until Chapter 12. It must suffice for the moment to show that these cases are different in kind from the examples just examined. In that regard, the point is that, unlike A_1, C_1 does not exercise control over the plaintiff's body. Because A_1's touching is intentional (though entirely without fault), A_1 puts B_1's body to his purposes. But because C_1 touches D_1 inadvertently, C_1 does not put D_1's body to his purposes. Thus, no control is exercised. Likewise, unlike A_2, C_2 does not put the plaintiff's land to his purposes. Because A_2's parking on the land is intentional (though entirely without fault), A_2 uses B_2's land. But because C_2 enters D_2's land only accidentally, C_2 does not use D_2's land. D_2's land is not put to C_2's purposes; C_2 does not subject the land to his control.

Accordingly, in distinguishing between strict and fault-based liability as it does, the law tracks the moral distinction between cases in which one person puts another or another's property to his purposes without consent, which is coercive even without fault, and cases in which one person does not put another or the property of another to his purposes and hence does not thereby coerce the other, even if at fault. In other words, the law is tracking the distinction between what we have defined as control and injury.

It may also help to think of this example. Imagine that a person touches me without my consent, where the touching is intentional. In these circumstances, if I respond angrily, you might well regard that as justified. But if I am touched with the same force, in the same place etc, but unintentionally, you would not regard the same response in the same way. You might say something along the lines of: 'Calm down. It was just an accident.' What is the force of the comment? What is meant by saying that it was *just* an accident? On the view advanced here, the

[43] Though I have heard this doubted, it cannot sensibly be doubted. If the surgeon did not put the patient to her purposes, then was she acting without a purpose? Was her action purposeless? There is a difficulty here only if one insists on interpreting the notion of putting another to one's purposes as implying fault and/or loss to the plaintiff. That, of course, is directly counter to the thesis presented here.

[44] Note that this is not to say that the wrongdoing is equally *blameworthy* or that the defendants are equally *culpable* in each case. These notions turn on ethical assessments that are not relevant in this context.

point is that, while the touching in the first case was a use of my body without my consent, the touching in the second, as unintended, was not. The first involved control, but the second could involve only injury.

It is undeniable that we respond differently to touchings of the kinds just imagined. Moreover, we do not respond differently merely because we find the first kind more offensive than the second. Rather, we find the first more offensive because we think that it is more offensive. Similarly, the first is not worse because it will have a greater impact on the plaintiff—because he will be more upset for instance. It will have a greater impact on the plaintiff and he will be more upset because he thinks it worse.

IV. The Elements of Trespass

The above analysis helps us to understand the three key doctrines of the law of trespass: that the torts are actionable per se, that they are torts of strict liability and that the torts require intention. We examine these issues in turn.

A. Actionable Per Se

Why are the torts of trespass actionable per se? Because the form of wrongdoing to which the torts respond is control: the unconsented to putting of the plaintiff's person or property to the defendant's purposes. The wrong lies in the control itself, not in the negative influence that flows from it. Hence, establishing liability in trespass does not require proof of damage. Of course, if the plaintiff has been damaged, then that will be reflected in the quantum of damages payable by the defendant. That, however, does not change the nature of the wrong or affect the analysis of liability.

Here again we see that US law is wrong to place such emphasis on harm. The third *Restatement* maintains as a general principle governing liability in this area that: 'An actor who intentionally causes physical harm is subject to liability for that harm.'[45] That is correct. However, the law of trespass is not best analysed in terms of this principle. That law is not correctly viewed as an instantiation of the principle coupled with many counterexamples in which defendants without that intention or who do not cause harm are nevertheless held liable. Rather, it is important to see that the law is founded on a different principle. It is concerned with control, not harm; with constraint, not with negative influence.

[45] *Restatement (Third) of Torts* (n 10) §5.

B. Strict Liability

It is also clear why these torts are forms of strict liability. Fault is irrelevant, because the exercise of control is itself coercive. The wrongful action is the intentional putting of the plaintiff or of the plaintiff's property to the defendant's purposes where that is done without consent. This can be done entirely without fault. Again, however, fault can affect the quantum of damages. Most importantly, if the defendant is at fault, then this can lead to the availability of aggravated or punitive damages.[46] But that is another matter.

C. The Intention Requirement

If the torts in question are forms of strict liability, why do they contain an intention requirement? The answer, as we have seen, is that this requirement is the law's way of tracking the morally significant distinction between control and injury, between the putting of someone or someone's property to one's purposes without consent and the damaging of someone or someone's property so that they are unable to act according to their purposes. In order to see this fully, we must examine intention in detail.

i. Intention in Tort Law

'Intention' as used in the Commonwealth law of trespass (both to the person and to property) has a wider meaning than in ordinary discourse. The best way to approach the law of trespass in this regard is by comparison with the criminal law. As a matter of criminal law, P performed an action a with an intention to do x if x was the purpose for which P performed a or if P performed a knowing that x would follow in the ordinary course of events. If, however, P performed a knowing that a would produce a significant risk of x, then P is said not to have intended x, but to have been reckless with respect to x.[47] The importance of this distinction is revealed, for example, in the fact that the crime of murder requires intention, recklessness being insufficient.

This division between intention and recklessness is closely mirrored in US tort law. Thus, according to the third *Restatement*: 'A person acts with the intent to

[46] Here punitive damages must be included because, in the US, these include what Commonwealth lawyers refer to as aggravated damages. This should not be taken to support damage awards that actually are punitive or exemplary. For analysis, see A Beever, 'The Structure of Aggravated and Exemplary Damages' (2003) 23 *Oxford Journal of Legal Studies* 87.

[47] A Ashworth and J Horder, *Principles of Criminal Law*, 7th edn (Oxford, Oxford University Press, 2013) 171–72; Law Commission, *Criminal Law: A Criminal Code*, Law Com No 177, HC 299, cl 18. I take this to summarise and clarify the consequence of cases such as *R v Nedrick* [1986] 1 WLR 1025 (CA) and *R v Woollin* [1999] 1 AC 82 (HL), which extend intention beyond purpose in the context of

produce a consequence if … the person acts with the purpose of producing that consequence; or … the person acts knowing that the consequence is substantially certain to result.'[48] Alternatively: 'A person acts recklessly in engaging in conduct if … the person knows of the risk of harm created by the conduct or knows facts that make the risk obvious to another in the person's situation, and … the precaution that would eliminate or reduce the risk involves burdens that are so slight relative to the magnitude of the risk as to render the person's failure to adopt the precaution a demonstration of the person's indifference to the risk.'[49]

Because it raises special issues, the discussion of recklessness is left until last. Our focus begins with the two listed senses of intention.

a. Intention

It will help to have in mind examples of the two relevant categories of intention. First, I place a bomb in my house in order to kill my wife. Here, I intend to kill her in the sense that I act with the purpose of killing her. Second, I plant a bomb in my house because I want to blow it up and claim on my insurance policy. I also know that my wife will be in the house when the bomb explodes. Again, in the language of the law, I intend to kill my wife because I act in a way that I know will kill her in the ordinary course of events, where the killing of her is substantially certain to occur, even though my purpose in planting the bomb was not to kill anyone.

In the first example, it is clear that I put my wife's body to my purposes. As I do this without her consent, I coerce her. And this is just as clear in the second case. Though my purpose is not to kill her but to gain the insurance money, I put my wife to that purpose without her consent. My act, then, is coercive and is coercive in the same sense as was my act in the first example: both acts exercise control. The more difficult question is whether this can be said when the defendant was reckless.

b. Recklessness

In this area too, Commonwealth and US law differs, though again the difference is less significant than it may appear at first sight. Let us begin with US law.

According to US law, recklessness is insufficient for liability in this area. Thus, as the third *Restatement* explicitly notes, as a general matter, a reckless defendant will be liable only when and in the same way in which a negligent defendant

murder as follows: 'Where the charge is murder and in the rare cases where the simple direction is not enough, the jury should be directed that they are not entitled to find the necessary intention unless they feel sure that death or serious bodily harm was a virtual certainty (barring some unforeseen intervention) as a result of the defendant's action and that the defendant appreciated that such was the case.' Any differences between the approach in those cases and the one supported by Ashworth and the Law Commission are not important here.

[48] *Restatement (Third) of Torts* (n 10) §1.

[49] ibid §2.

would be liable.[50] There are exceptions, however. The clearest is that a defendant who acts recklessly may be liable in the tort of intentional infliction of emotional harm.[51] Also, the line between what is known as 'wilful or wanton misconduct'—understood to include negligence—and intention is a hazy one.[52]

On the other hand, though it is a point that has been little remarked upon, recklessness is sufficient for liability in Commonwealth law. This is because, as far as Commonwealth tort law is concerned, 'intention' is defined to encompass what criminal and US tort lawyers call intention and recklessness.[53] In Commonwealth law, however, recklessness is not well described. It is somewhat ironic, then (though not untypical), that US law precisely defines the concept, but does not use it in this context, while Commonwealth law uses it without properly defining it.

Because of this obscurity, Commonwealth commentators who draw their definitions from the case law have been forced to provide inadequate accounts. Thus, it has been claimed that recklessness occurs 'where the actor foresees, but does not desire, a particular result that is not regarded as inevitable'[54] and that: '"Recklessness" is usually categorized with intention, where it [is] used to signify the defendant's advertence to a risk that the consequences will result from his act.'[55] These definitions are too broad. One is often aware of relatively small risks, but one is not reckless if those risks materialise. Imagine that I injure you as the result of driving that fell just below the standard of care. In those circumstances, I can be liable in negligence, but not in battery. The inability to sue in battery is inconsistent with the definitions listed above, as I am always aware of the relevant risks when driving and can foresee injuries of the relevant kinds. What is more, one is often aware of very small risks, risks too small to constitute negligence. If a wheel falls off my car through no fault of mine and I collide with you, you can sue me in neither negligence nor battery. But this is a risk of which I am aware and the injury is one that I can foresee. I have, after all, written about them in this chapter. In consequence, then, if these definitions of recklessness were correct, a great many of the actions we perform in our adult lives would be reckless. That, however, is not the law. These definitions must be narrowed.

Criminal lawyers do so by insisting that recklessness involve a '*high degree* of carelessness'[56] or the 'conscious taking of an *unjustified* risk'.[57] In other words, in the eyes of the criminal law, a person is reckless only if she exhibits a sufficient degree of personal fault. That is appropriate because the focus of the criminal law

[50] ibid §2, comment b.
[51] ibid §46.
[52] See, eg, the examinations of recklessness in the citations of *Restatement (Second) of Torts* (n 6) §13.
[53] For discussion, see A Beever, 'Transferred Malice in Tort Law?' (2009) 29 *Legal Studies* 400, 418–19.
[54] Deakin, Johnston and Markesinis, 7th edn (n 2) 27.
[55] Jones (n 11) 9.
[56] Ashworth and Horder (n 47) 176 (emphasis added).
[57] ibid (emphasis added).

is on the defendant's culpability and hence the relevant question is whether the defendant was sufficiently culpable to warrant punishment. This is not the appropriate position for the torts of trespass, however, which do not impose fault-based liability.

Similarly, US law has effectively defined recklessness as what we might call gross negligence. There, a person is said to be reckless if the risk was quite obvious and the defendant had no good reason not to eliminate it.[58] In itself, that is fine. The problem is that there is a form of intentionality that justifies liability in battery and yet does not fit the third *Restatement*'s definition of intention. The submission is that Commonwealth law should conceive of its version of recklessness in this light. Let me explain.

Imagine that I play a version of Russian roulette with you in which I pull the trigger and you are unaware of what is happening. Here, then, there is a one in six chance that the gun will fire. As it happens, the gun does fire, but, though injured, you survive. Can you sue me for battery? On the face of it, the answer must be no. As the chance of your being struck was only one in six, this cannot be described as a case in which the contact with you would happen in the ordinary course of events or was a substantial certainty. Nevertheless, I submit that there is a battery.[59] This is because, in this case, I intentionally take a chance *with* you. The use of that preposition is instructive. It indicates that my action is an exercise of control over you. In playing this game, I am putting you to my purposes without your consent.

Note that my purpose is not to shoot you. I may actually hope that you are not shot—and I may have money riding on it. My purpose is not to shoot you, but to play the game. The point is that this game is constituted in part by exposing you to the risk of being shot. This is crucial. The game involves taking this risk with you. Thus, it is right to say that I am putting you to my purposes.

Recall the previous examples involving my wife. In the first case, I place a bomb in my house in order to kill her. Here I am liable because I act with the purpose of killing her, putting her to my purposes. In the second case, I plant a bomb in my house because I want to blow it up and claim on my insurance policy, knowing that my wife is inside. Here I do not act with the purpose of killing my wife; my purpose is to obtain the insurance money. Nevertheless, I put my wife to my purposes because I use her as a means to obtaining that end. Imagine now that I plant the bomb, not knowing that she is in the house, but knowing that there is a significant chance—say 0.8—that she is there. Here again, I submit that if she is struck by the explosion, I put her to my purposes. This is not because my purpose was to strike her. It is because my purpose was to gain the insurance money and I was prepared to place my wife at this risk in order to get it. When the bomb explodes and she is struck, I exercise of control over her body without her consent. I ought to be liable.

[58] *Restatement (Third) of Torts* (n 10) §2.

[59] *cf People v Sandoval* 35 Cal Reporter 227 (Cal 1963); *Minor v State* 583 A 2d 1102 (Mld 1991).

In tort law, recklessness ought to be defined as the conscious taking of a significant risk *with* another. In the US, it would perhaps be easiest to widen the definition of intention to reach the same position.

Compare these examples with the following case. Imagine that I suffer from a phobia that makes me reluctant to touch objects in public spaces. I get into a crowded train carriage and stand without holding on. I am aware that there is a good chance—say 0.8—that I will collide with someone when the train changes velocity. This risk materialises and I fall into one of the passengers. Is this a battery?

The issues raised by this example—by all of these examples—cannot be solved merely by applying the definitions of coercion given in Chapter 2. Those definitions are not algorithms, but principles that are intended to guide deliberation. Because of this, reasonable people can sometimes disagree as to the best way in which to realise those principles in particular cases, and different legal systems can be equally reasonable and yet draw the line between actionable and non-actionable behaviour in slightly different places. Nevertheless, the contention is that there is no battery in this case.

In the earlier case, my purpose is to get the money and I use my wife's body as a means of realising that purpose. In this case, however, my purpose is to avoid touching objects in public, and I am prepared to place the passengers at risk accordingly. This suggests—and the example gains much of its force from the hidden fact—that, the passengers being 'objects in public' too, I do not wish to touch them either. Thus, when I fall into one of the passengers, that touching is not a means to the realisation of my purposes. On the contrary, the touching is the result of my failure to realise my purposes. This tends strongly to the conclusion that I was not putting the passenger I struck to my purposes. The example would appear in a very different light were I concerned only about handles and the like and were quite happy to fall into the passengers, regarding the possibility of doing so as a means to achieving my ends. In that case, a battery would likely have occurred.

Thus, we can conclude that a defendant's wrongdoing is of the same kind whether he acted intentionally in the two relevant senses or recklessly in the sense defined here. The wrongdoing in question is control. Consequently, the law is right to treat all of this wrongdoing as falling under the same heading.

This also explains the different treatment of recklessness in tort and criminal law in the Commonwealth. As noted above, the criminal law separates intention and recklessness, holding, for instance, that recklessness is not sufficient for the crime of murder. This is appropriate, because that law is focused on the culpability of the defendant and a reckless defendant is (at least characteristically) less culpable than one who intends the actus reus. Why, then, does Commonwealth tort law not reflect this distinction? The short answer is that tort law is not interested in the defendant's culpability per se, but in the moral status of the interaction between the parties. In this particular context, this means that the question is whether the defendant exercised control over the plaintiff without justification, not whether he did so culpably or sufficiently culpably.

c. Intention and 'Intention'

Before we end the discussion of intention, it is useful to consider John Finnis' objection to the use of this terminology. Finnis argues that defining intention so that an outcome is intended if the agent knows that the outcome will occur in the ordinary course of events or is reckless with respect to that outcome stretches the meaning of 'intention' beyond breaking point. As he summarises this line of argument, 'the golfer whose only hope of winning at the last hole is to take a very long drive across the water "intends" [according to the view supported here] to miss the green and lose the ball in the pond'.[60] This is, of course, absurd.

The absurdity lies in the fact that the word 'intend' does not, in common parlance, cover the situation under examination. This provides an argument for not using 'intention' to identify the relevant concept. But it does not show that the law is wrong to utilise the concept that it does. As Finnis would certainly accept, that turns on an assessment of the relevant moral issues. In these circumstances, the central issue is coercion. Thus, a relevant example would be the following. Imagine that I lend the golfer my ball, allowing him to use it, but on the condition that he not hit the ball into the water. If he nevertheless attempts the shot knowing that it is very likely to go into the water, has he used the ball in a way (ie, put the ball to a purpose) to which I have not consented? My answer is that he has.[61]

D. The Directness Requirement

Commonwealth law insists that a defendant can be liable only if the contact between him and the plaintiff or the plaintiff's property is direct.[62] This is no longer the position in US law.[63] In this regard, US law is to be preferred. However, it is important to say that, to an extent, the Commonwealth's directness requirement can be justified because it can be used to track coercion. Nevertheless, the

[60] J Finnis, 'Intention in Tort Law' in D Owen (ed), *Philosophical Foundations of Tort Law* (Oxford, Oxford University Press, 1995) 243.

[61] Nevertheless, Finnis is right. We ought to abandon the use of 'intention' in this context if better terminology is available. The problem is that no terms suggest themselves. Accordingly, as is not uncommon in law, we have to utilise words bearing in mind that in these contexts they do not possess their ordinary meanings.

[62] The view taken in *In Re Polemis and Furness* [1921] 3 KB 560 (CA) regarding remoteness, which relies on directness, is supported in R Stevens, *Torts and Rights* (Oxford, Oxford University Press, 2007) 152–58. However, Stevens' argument concentrates on defending the outcome of that case and criticising the different approach propounded in *Overseas Tankship (UK) Ltd v Morts Dock & Engineering Co Ltd (The Wagon Mound (No 1))* [1961] AC 388 (PC) or, more accurately, the way in which that approach has been applied in subsequent cases. Stevens is right that there are significant problems with that approach (for my attempt to deal with these problems as they relate to the law of negligence, see A Beever, *Rediscovering the Law of Negligence* (Oxford, Hart Publishing, 2007) 129–66), but that does not support the position advanced in *Polemis*. In fact, as I read him, Stevens does not argue, and does not intend to argue, in support of directness itself.

[63] *Restatement (Second) of Torts* (n 6) §13(b).

requirement must ultimately be regarded as objectionable, as it only generally tracks coercion. The argument for this position begins by rejecting the idea that directness could have a justification other than the one proffered here and then moves to consider the extent to which it fits that justification.

The aim of the following is not to legislate against the use of the word 'direct'. After all, I employ the word in this book. The point is that this use is appropriate only if accompanied by the recognition that the distinction between the direct and the indirect cannot approach precision or the terms are given a meaning in a particular context that renders that distinction there sufficiently precise. So, for instance, we all know what is meant by saying during a game of Monopoly that one must go directly to jail, even if it is not clear exactly how one would justify a judgement that a particular path was direct or indirect. When playing Monopoly, precision in this regard is not required. Conversely, as used here, control is said to be direct if the defendant does something to or with the plaintiff and indirect if the defendant does something to or with a third party that results in control over the plaintiff. Here the distinction is given sufficient precision for this particular context. The problem examined below is that, as used in the law of trespass, the distinction between directness and indirectness requires precision in circumstances where that precision is unavailable.

i. Directness in Fact

The concept of directness can be understood in two different ways. First, it can be viewed as an entirely factual notion. On this view, directness must refer to one or both of two things: the length of the causal chain or the length of time between the defendant's action and the violation of the plaintiff's right. According to this view, then, shooting someone with a gun counts as a battery in part because there is a very short causal chain that runs from, and/or because very little time elapses between, the pulling of the trigger and the striking of the plaintiff.

The problem with this view is that there is, in fact, no such thing as a purely factual understanding of directness. Let us take an example. In *Scott v Shepherd*,[64] the defendant threw a firework into a market. A third party saw the firework and threw it to another part of the market, where another third party also saw the firework and threw it to yet another part of the market. The firework then exploded, injuring the plaintiff. The majority of the Court of King's Bench found that the contact with the plaintiff was sufficiently direct to conclude that the defendant had committed a battery.

How many steps in the causal chain were there in *Scott v Shepherd*? There is no incorrect or uniquely correct answer to this question. The chain is as short or as long as one cares to describe it. The question is like asking: how many numbers are there between 1 and 10?

[64] *Scott v Shepherd* (n 14).

When we focus on time, things seem clearer. Say that the whole sequence from the throwing of the firework to the plaintiff's injury took 7.46 seconds exactly. Here it is possible to be precise. But when we ask the further question 'Was there direct contact between the defendant and the plaintiff?', how could 'The sequence lasted 7.46 seconds' provide the answer? Similarly, even if we could say that there were precisely nine steps in the causal chain, how could that answer the question that we need answered?

One point here is that directness is a relative, not an absolute concept. In that regard, it is like the concepts tall, high, hot and so on. Thus, for instance, while we might ordinarily describe 200°C as hot, if we were astronomers discussing the temperatures of stars, we would not do so. Nothing is simply hot; things are hot only relative to some baseline, a baseline that changes with context. Similarly, though lawyers are inclined to regard a punch, say, as a paradigm case of direct contact,[65] a physicist comparing a punch to the fusion that creates the sun's energy would not. Because of this, when we ask 'Was the connection between the defendant and the plaintiff direct?', we do not mean what we say. There is no answer to that question. What we are really asking is whether the contact is direct relative to some assumed baseline.

The crucial point is that the baseline is selected by us in accordance with our purposes. If the air temperature is 40°C, we regard the day as hot, but if our coffee is the same temperature, we consider it to be cold because of the different ways in which the weather and coffee relate to our purposes. Thus, there is no fact of the matter as to whether something is hot or not. Likewise, there is no fact of the matter as to whether something is direct or indirect. In this regard, causation and directness are different kinds of concepts. When we ask 'Did the defendant cause the plaintiff's injury?', that question has a purely factual answer.[66] The question 'Was the defendant's action a direct cause of the plaintiff's injury?' does not. Causation is in the world entirely independently of our purposes. Directness is not. Whether or not something is direct is a judgement we make in the light of our ends.

This is well brought out by *Scott v Shepherd*. As we have seen, the majority of the Court in that case ruled that the contact between the parties was sufficiently

[65] In fact, the example that has most frequently been pressed on me is a punch *in the face*. I take this to be revealing. Surely, it makes no difference to directness where on the body the punch connects. Thus, the insistence that it is specifically a punch *in the face* that evinces directness appears to reveal that the lawyer is operating with a concept of directness that is not entirely factual. Note also that the issue under examination has nothing to do with predictability. The issue is not that one cannot predict what the courts will decide regarding directness. One usually can predict and the thesis of this chapter helps to explain why. Our focus now is on the meaningfulness and utility of the concept in question.

[66] Some have apparently denied this, suggesting that policy concerns must be consulted in this context. This is not the place to examine that issue here, but it should be stressed that the question at issue here is 'Did the defendant cause the claimant's injury?', not 'Should we say that the defendant's action passes the causation or cause-in-fact stage of the legal enquiry?' The answer to the first question cannot rely on policy unless reality is literally (and absurdly) responsive to our desires.

direct to justify liability. Blackstone J, however, disagreed. But the judges were not disagreeing about what the facts were. Blackstone J argued that the contact was not direct because the actions of third parties had been involved in the causal chain from the defendant to the plaintiff.[67] That this had occurred was, of course, a purely factual matter, but that it did (or did not) show that there was indirect contact between the parties was not. That other agents rather than natural causes were involved does not make the causal chain any longer or shorter (to the extent that the idea is even coherent). But it arguably makes a moral difference.

This is also reflected in the majority's replies. Nares J argued that the defendant was liable because he 'is the person who … gave the mischievous faculty to the squib. That mischievous faculty remained in it till the explosion. No new power of doing mischief was communicated to it by [any other party]'.[68] What matters here is not causation *simpliciter*, but 'mischievous causation'. This turns on a moral judgement. Likewise, De Grey CJ maintained that the contact with the plaintiff was direct because of the nature of the defendant's intention in throwing the firework.[69] Again, this is no appeal to the facts alone. The defendant's intentions are a matter of fact, but only a moral judgement makes that fact relevant to determining the 'directness' of the contact with the plaintiff.

Determinations of directness in law involve moral judgement. This idea is examined now.

ii. Directness as a Moral Judgement

According to the view now under examination, directness itself is or at least involves a moral judgement that indicates whether the defendant ought to be liable. What is to be made of this idea?

Take three examples. First, imagine that *A* shoots you from close range and *B* shoots you from a distance. *A*'s action seems to be more direct than *B*'s, but there is no moral significance in this. Second, *C* shoots you in person while *D* sets up a spring gun that is triggered when you enter your office. *C*'s action is more direct than *D*'s. So what? *E* is a terrorist who makes a nuclear bomb and sets it off in central London. *F* is also a terrorist, but she breaks into an intercontinental ballistic missile (ICBM) silo in Russia and manages to launch an ICBM, intending to and succeeding in striking central London. Again, *F*'s action is less direct than *E*'s, but this is quite irrelevant. Simply, the appeal to directness itself has no moral justification.[70]

That appeal is meant to establish that there is a close enough connection between the defendant's act and the plaintiff. But what does close *enough* mean?

[67] *Scott v Shepherd* (n 14) 527.

[68] ibid 526.

[69] ibid 528.

[70] The claim here is not that distance cannot be relevant. It can be, but when it is, that is not because of directness. For instance, in the law of negligence, distance between the parties can mean that the plaintiff's injury was not a reasonably foreseeable consequence of the defendant's negligent action.

Close enough for what? 'Close enough for liability' is the obvious answer. But directness is meant to be a tool that courts can use to determine whether a defendant ought to be liable. In fact, though, courts must first decide as a matter of intuition whether the defendant should be liable and then, in the light of that decision, describe the facts as displaying directness or not.

It has been claimed that throwing water on someone, riding a horse at someone so that the horse hits that person and pulling a chair from under a person sitting down so that they hit the floor are batteries, but that blowing smoke, shining a light or radiating heat at someone are not.[71] But one will look in vain for the purely factual element that makes the contact direct in the first cases yet indirect in the second. The distinction drawn between them is not purely factual, but if it is moral, then it is not made in terms of directness. It is simply the result of the feeling that some of these cases are batteries and some are not.

iii. Directness in Law

What is the content of this feeling? In line with the theory expounded above, I suggest that the law is tracking control. Throwing water on a person, riding a horse at a person so that the horse hits that person and pulling a chair from under a person sitting down are exercises of control over of that person's body. They involve putting the person to one's purposes. Blowing smoke, shining a light or radiating heat at a person are (at least usually) not. In general, a person or a person's property is put to another's purposes only in circumstances where we are inclined to describe the contact as direct. If I am putting you to my purposes, it is normally because I am there grabbing, pulling or pushing you. If I am putting your property to my purposes, it is normally because I am walking on it, cutting the grass on it, taking fruit from it, driving it, sitting on it and so on. In this context, then, 'directness' is really concerned with control.

The problem is that one can put someone or someone's property to one's purposes in ways that one would not ordinarily be inclined to describe as direct. When this happens, courts are faced with a dilemma. They can either do what seems and is right and find the defendant liable, or they can hold on to the directness requirement as traditionally understood and commit what seems to be and is an injustice. Courts are more likely to take the second option in circumstances where there is general agreement about the meaning of directness; they are more likely to take the first option in areas where that agreement does not exist. For this reason, it is still generally thought that poisoning someone—say that the defendant places poison in the plaintiff's coffee, who then drinks the coffee—cannot constitute a battery

[71] Peel and Goudkamp (n 11) 58–59. The cases mentioned in this regard are *Pursell v Horn* (1838) N & P 564, 112 ER 966; *Hopper v Reeve* (1817) Taunt 698, 129 ER 278; and *Murray v Ministry of Defence* [1985] 12 NIJB 12.

because of the insufficiently direct contact between the parties.[72] This thought is a product of the fact that the paradigm agreed on examples of direct contact in the law of battery involve actual physical contact, eg, punching someone. In the law of assault, however, things are quite different. There, it was never entirely clear what directness meant, as the bodies of the parties did not come into contact. The non-existence of any agreed-upon paradigms meant that in *R v Ireland*, the House of Lords was able to rule that an assault could be committed over the telephone by a distant defendant.[73]

Lord Steyn said:

> Take now the case of the silent caller. He intends by his silence to cause fear and he is so understood. The victim is assailed by uncertainty about his intentions. Fear may dominate her emotions, and it may be the fear that the caller's arrival at her door may be imminent. She may fear the *possibility* of immediate personal violence.[74]

Though his argument was directed at a different point, Lord Steyn was saying that the defendant's interaction with the plaintiff may be such that fear of the defendant overwhelms the plaintiff. In those circumstances, there could be liability. And those circumstances are ones in which the defendant exercises control over the plaintiff. The intention of individuals in this defendant's position is precisely to put those in the plaintiff's position to their purposes, and on the facts of *R v Ireland*, the defendant succeeded.

If courts choose to do what is right, as the House of Lords did in *R v Ireland*, then they again have two options available. First, they could realise that the directness requirement is causing their dilemma, is inappropriate and should therefore be abandoned. Alternatively, they could simply stretch the scope of 'directness' so that it fits the instant case, even if that deprives the concept of any even apparent meaning. Because of the nature of the common law, courts are much more likely to take the second option than the first, even though it is obscurantist and will generate confusion. Thus, we have now reached the stage where 'directness' remains a necessary condition for liability in the English law of assault and yet has no apparent meaning. The preferable course of action is to do as the Americans have done and eliminate this requirement altogether.

Let us return to our poisoning case. As we have seen, there is general agreement that a poisoning cannot be a battery. But that does not mean that poisoning constitutes no civil wrong. It is often thought that poisoning must fall under the tort in *Wilkinson v Downton*[75] that allows a plaintiff who suffers harm intentionally inflicted by a defendant to recover, even if that harm was caused indirectly. The

[72] See, eg, WVH Rogers, *Winfield and Jolowicz on Tort*, 18th edn (London, Sweet & Maxwell, 2010) 143. Compare Peel and Goudkamp (n 11) 70–71.

[73] *R v Ireland* [1998] AC 147 (HL). This was a criminal case, but there is no reason to believe that the findings would not also apply in tort law.

[74] ibid 162.

[75] *Wilkinson v Downton* [1897] 2 QB 57.

availability of this action helps to close the gap, but it only helps. The problem with it is that it requires the plaintiff to have been damaged and this seems quite inappropriate.[76]

Imagine the following case. I put poison in your coffee in order to kill you. I watch you until you have finished and then exclaim: 'Got you. I put XYZ poison in your coffee and you will die within 10 minutes.' At which point, someone in the room turns to you and says: 'What a stroke of luck. I happen to have the antidote to XYZ here in my pocket. Drink this.' You take the antidote and suffer no physical (or psychiatric) injury as a result. Are we really to believe that a legal system that holds (rightly) that mere unconsented to touching is a battery can find no civil wrong here at all?

The point of this example is not to reveal that such a situation might well occur and that we had better be ready for it (though the happening of an analogous event is not impossible). The example is rather a thought experiment that reveals that a poisoning can be wrongful even if it does not cause damage and hence that the suggestion that poisoning should be actionable under *Wilkinson v Downton* but not in the law of trespass is mistaken.

What would happen if a case of this kind were to come before a court? My guess is that a court would rule that there was a trespass, though it would do so by stretching the directness requirement. In other words, the court would ensure that directness tracked control, regardless of the fact that it would stretch the term beyond breaking point.

The directness requirement is understandable, but it should go. It is understandable because, in the relevant contexts, control is usually direct. But it should go because, even in those contexts, control is only usually direct. This has happened in the US[77] and it is past time that the Commonwealth followed suit.

[76] This is also why recourse to the law of negligence would be inappropriate in this context.
[77] *Restatement (Second) of Torts* (n 6) §13(b).

5

Trespass in General

The previous chapter presented a theory of trespassory liability concentrating on the torts of battery and trespass to property. This chapter extends that discussion to the torts of assault, false imprisonment, intentional infliction of emotional distress, conversion and detinue.

I. Assault

The tort of battery protects the right to control the use of one's own body. The same right is protected by the law of assault. This is why both assault and battery are species of the more general trespass to the person.

An assault is the intentional creation in another of an apprehension of an imminent battery. It is an exercise of control. Let us start with a paradigm case. The defendant pulls a gun on the plaintiff and leads the plaintiff to believe that he will be shot. Naturally, if the defendant fires and hits the plaintiff, the defendant will exercise control over the plaintiff's body. But it takes little imagination to see that, even before the trigger has been pulled or even if it is not pulled, the defendant asserts control over the plaintiff. This can be brought out by observing that the plaintiff will normally feel compelled to flee or at least flinch in response to the threat. In general, the point is that the plaintiff's realisation that he may be shot leads him to experience his body as the mechanism through which the defendant threatens his death. The threatened shooting makes the plaintiff experience his body as a means to another's ends.

Anyone who has faced the threat of physical violence understands the nature of this observation. If I threaten to punch you on the arm, your arm is experienced as a potential source of the pain I am looking to inflict on you. You are likely to flee, flinch, move to protect yourself or something of the kind. But even if you do none of these things, even if you are entirely unafraid, the fact that you apprehend that I am about to strike you on the arm means that you can no longer view your arm as under your control free of my purposes.

This is also true of non-violent cases. Imagine, for instance, that I shape to kiss you on the cheek. Here, in order to avoid the use of your body to which you have not consented, you are forced to act, for example, by moving away or blocking me. More fundamentally, while it appears that I am about to kiss you, you cannot regard your cheek as under your control free of my purposes.

This explains why there is no equivalent of assault in the law of trespass to property. We relate to our bodies differently from how we relate to our property. This is because our purposes are contained in our bodies in a way that they are not contained in our property. Property is a means to our ends. But because we are our bodies, they are ends as well as means. A threat to my body undermines my ability to regard my body purposively; a threat to a mere object does not have the equivalent effect. Thus, you do not put my car to your purposes simply by threatening to steal it.[1] The car is merely the object of my purposes—my body is the source.

This also explains why assault and battery are separate actions. A battery is the exercise of control over another by putting that person's body to one's purposes. An assault is the exercise of control over another by threatening to put that person's body to one's purposes. It further explains why the plaintiff's level of fear or concern is irrelevant. The tort is focused not on negative influence, but constraint. The issue is whether control over the plaintiff has been exercised, not the psychological or emotional impact on the plaintiff. For the same reason, it makes no difference if the defendant believes that he will be able to defend himself with ease from the threatened attack. That shows only that the negative influence was small. That the defendant planned to defend himself reveals the constraint.

It is not a requirement for assault that the defendant ever be in the position to batter the plaintiff. The defendant in *Stephens v Myers*[2] advanced on the plaintiff with a clenched fist, but was halted by others before getting close enough to throw a punch. The Court held this to be an assault.[3] This is because the plaintiff was subject to the defendant's control, a fact that can be brought out by seeing that the plaintiff would likely have been inclined to rise, flee, protect himself and so on.[4] On the other hand, if the plaintiff knows that he cannot be struck, say because he knows that the gun being held by the defendant is not loaded, or is unaware of the defendant's activity, then there can be no assault.[5] This is because this plaintiff is not subject to the defendant's control in these circumstances.

This analysis further enables us to understand what would otherwise appear to be a quite incongruous feature of the law: the demand that the plaintiff apprehend an *imminent* battery.[6] On the face of it, the rationale for this rule is opaque. Why is it an assault if I shape to kiss you, but slip and miss, when it is not an assault if I tell you that I will kill you a month from now, even if you have no reason to doubt that

[1] Conversely, it is possible to imagine cases in which you put me (not my car) to your purposes by threatening to steal my car, eg, when I need the car in order to get to a hospital in order to save my life.

[2] *Stephens v Myers* (1840) 4 C & P 349, 172 ER 735.

[3] See also *Restatement (Second) of Torts* (St Paul, MN, American Law Institute Publishers, 1965) §33.

[4] Again, it is important to stress that these inclinations reveal the wrong; they do not constitute the wrong. The claim is not, for example, that assaults are wrongful because they cause people to flee.

[5] *R v Kerr* [1988] 1 NZLR 270 (CA); *Restatement (Second) of Torts* (n 3) §§22, 24.

[6] See especially *Restatement (Second) of Torts* (n 3) §29(2).

I can and will carry out my threat? The first action seems comparatively trivial. The second is very significant and may in itself cause serious harm. In that light, the law's insistence on imminence appears irrational. It is obvious that the threat to kill you is likely to have a greater negative influence on your life than the threat to kiss you, and yet only the latter is an assault.

The answer to this difficulty is to note again that the law is unconcerned with negative influence, but is focused instead on the right to control the use of the body. Given that focus, it is natural to regard a threat of *immediate* unconsented to touching as interfering with that right. Again, this can be supported by noting that people react to imminent threats in physical ways, by flinching or fleeing etc, but not to distant threats. Because of this, my threat to touch you now interferes with your right now, while my threat to kill you in a month does not violate that right now (though it might violate a different right now). The first is a threat that violates your right to control your body, while the second is a threat to violate that right in the future.

II. False Imprisonment

The tort of false imprisonment is commonly said to protect the right to freedom of movement. This can be a helpful definition, but it is not strictly correct. It is another error produced by the loss model. Again, the idea is that the harm usually caused by an act of false imprisonment is loss of movement and so it is thought that the tort protects a right to freedom of movement. However, the tort generates no right to move wherever one wants.[7] Moreover, it would not be a false imprisonment wrongfully to refuse permission for someone to leave the country.[8] It is not flatly wrong to say that false imprisonment is about the right to freedom of movement, but it is more accurate to say that the tort protects one's right to control the use of one's body.

If I lock you in a room, I deprive you of your ability to move around. That is wrongful because it is an assertion of control over the use of your body. But, though it in some way interferes with freedom of movement, it is not an assertion of control over your body to prevent you moving in one particular direction (without committing an assault, battery or other relevant wrong)[9] when you can

[7] *Bird v Jones* (1845) 7 Ad & El (NS) 742, 115 ER 688.

[8] WE Peel and J Goudkamp, *Winfield and Jolowicz on Tort*, 19th edn (London, Sweet & Maxwell, 2013) 68.

[9] Hence, I accept that if the defendant in *Bird v Jones* (n 7) had not been a policeman, then a tort would have been committed. But that is because such a defendant could have prevented the plaintiff's continuing only by completely restraining the plaintiff or by committing a tort on the plaintiff other than false imprisonment.

easily go elsewhere.[10] Similarly, if the plaintiff is easily able to 'escape' the area of alleged imprisonment, then no control has been exercised.

Moreover, in order for there to be a false imprisonment, the defendant must intend to control and succeed in controlling the plaintiff's body through imprisonment. The issue is not whether the defendant intends to or succeeds in imprisoning the plaintiff. Again, the focus is constraint, not influence; in this context control, not loss. So, a defendant who places the plaintiff in a room with an unlocked door and convinces the plaintiff that the doorknob is electrified commits a false imprisonment even if the doorknob is not electrified and thus the plaintiff not in fact imprisoned.[11] What matters is that, by convincing the plaintiff that he cannot touch the doorknob, the defendant has gained control over the plaintiff's body where the form of control is imprisonment, ie, preventing the plaintiff from moving. That the plaintiff is not in fact imprisoned is beside the point. This is also why it can be a false imprisonment wrongfully to assert legal authority over a person, restraining his movements.[12]

Similarly, it is possible to be falsely imprisoned even in circumstances in which one is incapable of movement, for example, when one is too ill to move.[13] Again, the issue is not whether the defendant's actions had a negative influence on the plaintiff; it is whether the defendant exercised control over the plaintiff's body. If I lock you in a room, then I exercise that control even if you are unable to leave the room had I not locked it.

US law maintains that a plaintiff who is unaware of her imprisonment has no cause of action.[14] The reasoning for this appears to be that a plaintiff unaware of her imprisonment cannot have suffered negative influence. As the law of the Commonwealth recognises, however, that is the wrong approach.[15] Influence is not the issue. If I lock you in a room, I am exerting control over you even if you are unaware of it. Thus, the House of Lords has held that a school that refused to allow a child's parents to collect him for the holidays on the basis that they had failed to pay his school fees falsely imprisoned the child, even though the child was unaware of the situation.[16]

On the other hand, it has rightly been said that a hospital does not falsely imprison a patient in a coma merely by keeping the patient in hospital,[17] and that is so even if, when the patient awakes, she truthfully reports that she would not have agreed to be kept at the hospital had she been able to express herself. This

[10] ibid; *Restatement (Second) of Torts* (n 3) §36.

[11] *Restatement (Second) of Torts* (n 3) §§38–40.

[12] *Symes v Mahon* [1922] SASR 447 (SCSA); *Restatement (Second) of Torts* (n 3) §41.

[13] *Grainger v Hill* (1838) 4 Bing NC 212, 132 ER 769.

[14] *Restatement (Second) of Torts* (n 3) §§35(c), 42.

[15] *Meering v Graham-White Aviation Co Ltd* (1920) 122 LT 44 (CA); *Murray v Ministry of Defence* [1988] 1 WLR 692 (HL).

[16] *Murray v Ministry of Defence* (n 15), discussing *Herring v Boyle* (19834) 1 Cr M & R 377, 149 ER 1126.

[17] Peel and Goudkamp (n 8) 66–67.

is because the hospital is not, by keeping the patient, exercising control over the patient's body by imprisonment. Of course, the hospital does exercise control over the patient's body, for example, by feeding the patient, but that is not an exercise of control by imprisonment.[18] There is no intention to imprison the patient at the hospital. (It is also not a battery for the reasons discussed in Chapter 6.)

III. Intentional Infliction of Emotional Distress

The defendant in *Wilkinson v Downton*[19] told the plaintiff as a practical joke that her husband had been involved in an accident, had broken both his legs, was lying at The Elms at Leytonstone and that she needed to collect him in a cab. This news caused her to suffer severe shock, resulting in 'vomiting and other more serious and permanent physical consequences at one time threatening her reason, and entailing weeks of suffering and incapacity'.[20]

The law has not found it easy to deal with cases of this kind.[21] The decision in favour of the plaintiff in *Wilkinson v Downton* has been understood as turning on the defendant's intention to harm the plaintiff (hence the tort's sometimes name of '*intentionally causing* emotional distress') and has been tied up with the issue of mental injury (hence its sometimes name, 'intentionally causing *emotional distress*').[22] None of this seems to be right. It is far from clear that the defendant intended harm to the plaintiff in *Wilkinson v Downton* and it is wrong to think that the tort applies only to mental injury.[23] The problem again is the focus on negative influence.

This was a practical joke that went too far. But in what sense did it go too far? In the sense that the joke had not only a negative influence on the plaintiff—itself irrelevant to liability—but resulted in an exercise of control over the plaintiff to such an extent that she was for a while unable to direct her own life (her 'reason was threatened').

This is even clearer in *Janvier v Sweeney*,[24] where the defendant private detective, in an attempt to obtain some papers, told the plaintiff that he was a police officer and that she was in danger of being arrested for being a German spy. Here the defendant was trying to control the plaintiff, to force her to give him the papers, by playing on her fears. In another case, *Khorasandjian v Bush*,[25] the defendant

[18] See also *R v Bournewood etc NHS Trust* [1999] 1 AC 458 (HL).
[19] *Wilkinson v Downton* [1897] 2 QB 57.
[20] ibid 58.
[21] See also *Rhodes v OPO* [2015] UKSC 32.
[22] For discussion, see Peel and Goudkamp (n 83) 70–71.
[23] ibid.
[24] *Janvier v Sweeney* [1919] 2 KB 316 (CA).
[25] *Khorasandjian v Bush* [1993] QB 727 (CA).

caused the plaintiff severe stress by making harassing phone calls, though there was no evidence of physical or psychiatric injury. The English Court of Appeal upheld the trial judge's issuing of an injunction. This decision is to be supported. The defendant in this case made the phone calls in an attempt to gain control over the plaintiff's life and had to an extent succeeded. It is incumbent on the law to put a stop to such coercion.

IV. Conversion and Detinue

The previous chapter revealed that the tort of trespass to property protects the plaintiff's right to control the use of her property and that the tort focuses specifically on unauthorised uses of the plaintiff's property. There is much overlap between trespass and conversion in this regard. The explanation for this is historical. This need not concern us here. What is important now is that conversion and detinue are capable of dealing with cases of coercion that do not amount to trespasses, cases that involve control through the operation of law or through omission.

The plaintiffs in *Hiort v Bott*[26] were corn merchants. They regularly employed Grimmett as their broker. As a result of a telegram from Grimmett, they sent a shipment of barley to Birmingham and sent the defendant a letter containing an invoice for the barley, stating that the barley was to be 'sold by Mr. Grimmett as broker between buyer and seller'. The letter also contained a delivery order, making the barley deliverable 'to the order of consignor or consignee'. In fact, the defendant had not ordered the barley. When Grimmett called on the defendant, he said that the situation was the result of a mistake of the plaintiffs and asked the defendant to endorse the delivery order so that he, Grimmett, could return the barley to the plaintiffs. The defendant did so. Grimmett took the barley, disposed of it and absconded.

The defendant was found guilty of committing a conversion though he did not make physical contact with the goods. This was because he intentionally, though innocently, took control over the barley by signing the delivery order when he had no right to do so. This action was inconsistent with the plaintiffs' right to control the goods. The decision, then, is directly in line with the theory presented here. It recognises that one can assert control over the property of another without making physical contact with it and that doing so is wrongful.

In the UK, the law of detinue has been absorbed into the law of conversion.[27] This need not concern us here. Suffice it to say that a detinue is—or, in the UK,

[26] *Hiort v Bott* (1873–74) LR 9 EX 86.
[27] Torts (Interference with Goods) Act 1977 (UK) s 2.

conversion includes—the failure to deliver goods to a person who has a right to receive them. Again, it is clear why this is so. The failure to deliver is inconsistent with the plaintiff's right to control the use of the goods. That is so whether or not the defendant makes physical contact with the goods or the plaintiff suffers any negative influence.

In these cases, then, we see the law recognising that one may control the property of another without using it. Because of this, the law of trespass to property must be extended. The common law has done this through the torts of conversion and detinue.

6

Defences to Trespass

This chapter examines the following important defences to a claim in trespass: consent, licence, self-defence, the defence of others, self-help and necessity. It demonstrates that these defences are best explained in terms of the theory advanced here.

I. Consent and Licence

We begin with the defences of consent and licence. Though listed in law as separate defences, at the level of theory they are two names for the same thing, a fact that US law has effectively recognised.[1] With respect to trespass to the person, the defence is called consent, while with respect to trespass to property, it is labelled licence, but both turn on the defendant having a permission from the plaintiff to perform the action in question.[2]

A. The Nature and Scope of Consent

Let us begin with a simple example of consensual touching. Meeting you for the first time, I reach out my hand in order to shake yours. You reach across and grasp mine. Why is this not a battery? The answer, of course, is that the touching is consensual, the consent being implied by our behaviour. But what we need to know is how the consent functions in order to make our actions legal. That is a somewhat more difficult question, or at least the answer is more complicated than it may seem at first.

[1] *Restatement (Second) of Torts* (St Paul, MN, American Law Institute Publishers, 1965) §§167–75, 252–58. The discussion of irrevocable licence in §§176–84 does not constitute a counter-example. These are merely the reflections on the consequences of the withdrawal of consent.

[2] Occasionally, the permission will be from someone able to consent on behalf of the plaintiff: a parent in the case of a minor or a co-occupier of land, for instance.

It will help to describe what is involved in this seemingly uncomplicated event. When I hold out my hand, I indicate to you that I have a particular purpose: to greet you. When you return the gesture, you act with the same purpose. But it is essential to the psychology of this phenomenon that we do not merely act in order to realise identical purposes. We do that, but that is not sufficient. We also act in order to realise each other's purposes. So when you return my handshake, you not only fulfil your purpose in greeting me, you also fulfil my purpose in greeting you and, assuming that you are sincere, fulfilling my purpose is part of your purpose. Likewise, when I shake your hand, I both fulfil my purpose and willingly fulfil yours. Shaking hands is not an event in which two people realise their separate, congruent purposes; it is an event in which two people join together to realise a common purpose. That purpose may be relatively trivial, but the joining together is a crucial element of what it means to greet someone.[3]

Of course, the claim is not that all consensual activity is just like this. But the claim is that consent functions as a defence in battery because, in the presence of the plaintiff's consent, the defendant's touching of the plaintiff is in accordance with a purpose that the parties share. This feature of the defence must be stressed. In order to enjoy the defence, the defendant must be acting in accordance with a purpose that she and the plaintiff have together.[4] It is not sufficient for the defendant merely to be acting in accordance with a purpose that the plaintiff has—it is not enough if the parties' purposes are congruent.

I mean especially to distance the position advanced here from that presented in the second *Restatement*:

> Upon the recommendation of A, his doctor, B assents to an operation for the removal of a septum from his nose. Nothing whatever is said about performing a tonsillectomy. Actually B has had trouble with his tonsils and desires that A remove them too, but he forgets to mention it. A removes the septum and the tonsils while B is under a general anesthetic. Although B has not assented to the tonsillectomy, his actual willingness to submit to that operation constitutes consent to it and A is not liable to B.[5]

This position seems to rest on the notion that, as *B* wanted the surgery, *A* did not subject him to negative influence in performing it. But the position is most objectionable. *B*'s liberty is to be determined in accordance with his decisions, not in accordance with his desires—who is to say that *B* would have chosen to follow this desire?—still less the perceptions that others have of his desires, even if these perceptions are veridical. This position fails to give proper respect to the patient. Think of the consequences of applying this notion to cases of sexual battery, for instance.

Things may be different if *A* knows that *B* desires the tonsillectomy. This is not because that knowledge is decisive in itself. It is rather because *A*'s possessing that

[3] Compare it, for example, to two individuals unknowingly and simultaneously sending greeting emails to each other. The greeting is not complete without at least one reply.

[4] A Ripstein, *Force and Freedom: Kant's Legal and Political Philosophy* (Cambridge, MA, Harvard University Press, 2009) 109.

[5] *Restatement (Second) of Torts* (n 1) §49, illustration 2.

knowledge suggests—ie, presents some evidence to think that—*B* has in fact indicated his consent. But the presentation in the *Restatement* appears to rule this out.

The position in the Commonwealth is and ought to be that consent is required. Thus, it is a battery to grab my hand and shake it, even if it could be shown that I did want and intend to shake your hand. That is an action in accordance with my purposes, but it is not in accordance with a purpose that we share. Likewise, it is a battery for a surgeon to operate on me without my consent, even if it can be proven that I desperately wanted the operation, would have consented if asked and the operation was a success significantly benefiting me. In these circumstances, the surgeon's purpose is to benefit me and I have a congruent purpose, but there is no purpose that we share. If she obtains my consent, however, then the operation is in accordance with our shared purpose.

It should be evident from the foregoing that the defence requires communication from the plaintiff to the defendant, though that communication can of course be implicit. It is my holding out my hand that makes it possible for you to grasp it as the realisation of my purposes and it is my consent that makes it possible for the surgeon to operate on me in order to bring about a joint aim.

This helps to settle a related difficulty. On the face of it, consent is an entirely subjective matter: whether the plaintiff consents is determined by that person's intentions. But that is not the position taken by the law. Why not? Because, as we have seen, the issue is not merely whether the plaintiff subjectively consents, it is whether the parties have a shared purpose, something that they can possess only if the plaintiff communicates her consent to the defendant. For this reason—because the focus is on communication and shared purpose—the existence of consent is determined by taking the positions of both parties into account.

In *O'Brian v Cunard SS Co*,[6] the immigrant plaintiff was given a vaccination while aboard one of the defendant's steamships. The plaintiff testified rather oddly that:

> [A]bout 200 women passengers were assembled below, and she understood from conversation with them that they were to be vaccinated; that she stood about 15 feet from the surgeon, and saw them form in a line, and pass in turn before him; that he 'examined their arms, and, passing some of them by, proceeded to vaccinate those that had no mark [of a previous vaccination];' that she did not hear him say anything to any of them; that upon being passed by they each received a card, and went on deck; that when her turn came she showed him her arm; he looked at it, and said there was no mark, and that she should be vaccinated; that she told him she had been vaccinated before, and it left no mark; 'that he then said nothing; that he should vaccinate her again;' that she held up her arm to be vaccinated; that no one touched her; that she did not tell him she did not want to be vaccinated; and that she took the ticket which he gave her, certifying that he had vaccinated her, and used it at quarantine.[7]

[6] *O'Brian v Cunard SS Co* 28 NE 266 (Mass 1891).
[7] ibid 274.

Knowlton J ruled that: 'If the plaintiff's behavior was such as to indicate consent on her part, he [the surgeon] was justified in his act, whatever her unexpressed feelings may have been.'[8] That is entirely correct. Communication is of the essence and it is not the passage of subjective intentions through mind reading or the like.[9] The approach here, then, is the same as in the law of contract and related areas of the law.[10]

Also for these reasons, consent must be distinguished in principle from wishing, wanting, submitting, knowing and so on. The defendant in *R v Day*[11] was accused of sexually assaulting a 10-year-old child. His defence was that she did not resist. That argument rightly failed and should have done so even if the victim were an adult. The issue is whether the activity in question was in accordance with a shared purpose. Submission in the sense of the failure to resist does nothing to show that there was a shared purpose. This can be brought out by observing that in *R v Day*, one could not say that the parties engaged in sexual touching *together*.[12] On the contrary, the touching was something that the defendant did to the victim. Of course, in practice, the line between submission and consent can be a fine one, at least when speaking of adults. But in principle, the distinction is clear.

R v Day can usefully be compared to *Norberg v Wynrib*.[13] The plaintiff was a patient of the defendant general practitioner. Because she was addicted to pain-killers, she agreed to the defendant's suggestion of a 'sex-for-drugs arrangement'. In the Supreme Court of Canada, La Forest, Gonthier and Cory JJ held that the defendant was guilty of battery when engaging in sex with the defendant on this basis. Though finding the defendant liable on other grounds, McLachlin, L'Heureux-Dubé and Sopinka JJ disagreed.[14] They were right to do so. The parties in *Norberg v Wynrib* had sex together, they had a shared purpose, no matter how inappropriate the defendant's behaviour. There is all the difference in the world between the claim that parties had sex together even though it was wrong for the defendant to have so behaved and the claim that the defendant subjected

[8] ibid 273.

[9] See also *Restatement (Second) of Torts* (n 1) §49(1).

[10] For discussion, see A Beever, 'Agreements, Mistakes, and Contract Formation' (2009) 20 *King's Law Journal* 21; A Beever, *Forgotten Justice: A History of Political and Legal Theory* (Oxford, Oxford University Press, 2013) 132–37.

[11] *R v Day* (1841) 9 C & P 722, 173 ER 1026.

[12] This is a rough-and-ready guide only. If it is natural to say that the parties were doing the action in question together, then it is all but certain that the defence of consent/licence will apply. However, the reverse is more difficult. If it is unnatural to say that the parties were doing the action together, this tends to show that the defence will not apply. But it is sometimes unnatural to say this because one party is active while the other is passive, and this distinction is irrelevant here. So, for instance, it is unnatural to say that a surgeon and a consenting patient perform an operation together when the patient is unconscious. Nevertheless, there is a joint purpose here and the defence applies. Note, alternatively, that we have no difficulty saying of partners who are engaging in sexual activity where one partner is passive that *they* are having sex.

[13] *Norberg v Wynrib* [1992] 2 SCR 226.

[14] Stevenson J played no role in the judgment.

the plaintiff to sexual activity. It is clear that the latter did not occur in *Norberg v Wynrib*.[15] That must impact on the assertion of wrongdoing as between the parties. Conversely, had the plaintiff's addiction been such that she was unable to control herself, then matters would have been different. There, it would not have been possible to say that the parties had sex together and that they shared a purpose, the plaintiff in these hypothetical circumstances not acting purposively at all.

A more difficult case is *McNamara v Duncan*.[16] The parties were playing a game of Australian rules football when the defendant made a late tackle on the plaintiff, striking him with the fist or elbow in the head. The plaintiff was severely injured.

First, the Supreme Court of the Australian Capital Territory recognised that touching in accordance with the rules of the game cannot constitute a battery. When one consents to play a game, one consents to any touching allowed for by the rules of the game. The reason for this is obvious. The game is something that the players are doing together, playing the game is their common purpose and the content of that purpose is determined in part by the rules of the game as those rules constitute the game that the players are playing together.

In *McNamara v Duncan*, the defendant violated the rules of the game. It is tempting to conclude, therefore, that the plaintiff did not consent to the defendant's actions and thus the defendant was guilty of a battery. As the Court recognised, however, things cannot be quite this simple. This is because touching in violation of the rules of the game is ubiquitous in many sports. For instance, it is common for players to enter a ruck from an offside position in rugby union, to jostle in the penalty area during the taking of a corner in association football (soccer), or to engage in pass interference or holding in American football. If all touchings in violation of the rules of the game were illegal, then these sports would contain copious illegality. That, it seems clear, cannot be right. The issue is how to account for this.

It is tempting to respond that these rule violations do not constitute batteries because, as they occur frequently, players must be taken to have consented to them when they agree to play. As the defendant pointed out in *McNamara v Duncan*, 'a little bit of foul play is a common, if not invariable, concomitant of a game of football'.[17] That might seem to indicate that the plaintiff consented to this form of touching too. However, while this line of argument is not completely mistaken, it cannot be entirely right either. In *McNamara v Duncan*, for instance, it is perfectly clear that the plaintiff did not consent to be struck in the way that he was, and this

[15] In fact, the plaintiff admitted 'that she "played" on the fact that [the defendant] liked her and that she knew throughout the relationship that he was lonely': *Norberg v Wynrib* (n 13) [8].

[16] *McNamara v Duncan* (1971) 45 FLR 152 (SC ACT).

[17] ibid 155.

remains so even if he knew that he might be so struck. Similarly, though I know that some people intentionally drive dangerously (ie, intentionally or recklessly) and though I choose to drive in that knowledge, if I am struck by such a person, we will surely not say that I consented to the dangerous driving. *Sciens* is not *volens*. Knowing about something and choosing to expose oneself to the risk associated with it is not itself consent to the existence of that risk.

In *McNamara v Duncan*, the Court held that:

> A footballer consents to those tackles which the rules permits, and, it is thought, to those tackles contravening the rules where the rule infringed is framed to maintain the skill of the game; but otherwise if his opponent gouges out an eye or perhaps even tackles against the rules and dangerously.[18]

This position seems to suggest that a touching that violates the rules designed to make the game enjoyable to play and watch etc ('skill rules') will enjoy the defence of consent, whereas violating the rules designed to protect player safety ('safety rules') will not. This closely resembles the American position—the safety rule advanced in *Narbonzy v Barnhill*:

> [W]hen athletes are engaged in an athletic competition; all teams involved are trained and coached by knowledgeable personnel; a recognized set of rules governs the conduct of the competition; and a safety rule is contained therein which is primarily designed to protect players from serious injury, a player is then charged with a legal duty to every other player on the field to refrain from conduct proscribed by a safety rule.[19]

I contend that this position is by and large correct, but not entirely so. Again, let us take some examples.

The rule of rugby union that a player must enter the ruck 'through the gate' is (feebly) designed to speed up the game so that it is interesting to watch. It is a skill rule. But imagine a player who enters entirely from his opponents' side of the ruck because he sees an opponent in a compromising position and intends to injure him. Here, though the player violates only a skill rule, I submit that the player cannot enjoy the defence. Perhaps even more clearly, the requirement that only 11 players per team be on the field at any one time in American football is designed to ensure the numerical equality between the teams necessary for enjoyment of the game. That rule is a skill rule. However, imagine that an offensive player for the team currently on defence enters the field during a play in order to tackle the opposition quarterback, which he does in a way that would otherwise have been legal, blindsiding the quarterback and injuring him. Again, I submit that though this player has violated only a skill rule, he is not entitled to the defence.

Why not? Because these actions cannot be described as playing the game. The point is not that they are contrary to a particular kind of rule. It is that they are

[18] ibid 156.

[19] *Narbonzy v Barnhill* 334 NE 2d 258 (Ill 1975) 260–61. In US law, this appears to play a greater role in negligence than in battery. See, eg, *Oswald v Township High School Dist No 214* 406 NE 2d 157 (Ill 1980); *Pfister v Shusta* 657 NE 2d 1013 (Ill 1995).

so inconsistent with the rules of the game and the manner in which the game is played that they cannot be regarded as acts of playing the game. As such, they are not in accordance with the players' common purpose.

The quarterback sacked and injured by a defensive lineman guilty of holding is nevertheless injured by an action that was part of the game that the quarterback was playing. It was in accordance with the players' common purpose. But a quarterback sacked by an offensive lineman running on the field from the side-line is not. Likewise, a rugby union halfback (scrum half, if you really must) illegally pulled into the ruck is touched as part of the game he is playing, though that touching constitutes a penalty offence. But a halfback pushed into the ruck by an opponent entirely on the halfback's side of the ruck intending to injure the halfback is not.

That argument shows that touchings that violate skill rules can be batteries. It is also true that touchings that violate safety rules can enjoy the defence of consent, though that will seldom be the case as such touchings are infrequently part of the game. Consider the following examples, however.

At one stage, Australian rugby league's State of Origin matches, which pitch New South Wales' and Queensland's best players against each other, could not be said to have really begun until an all-in brawl had occurred. Now, if it were really the case that such an event was a de facto *requirement* of a State of Origin match—as one seems entitled to assume given their frequency and their former use in the promotion of State of Origin games—then it is at least arguable that this was consented to by the players. Engaging in those brawls was part of what it meant to play in the State of Origin. Similarly, prior to the 2013 season, so-called shoulder charges were permitted in rugby league. In practice, these were frequently higher than the rules allowed. The shoulder charge was thought to be such an integral part of rugby league that it is again arguable that if one were hit high but, say, below the nose, then that was just part of what it meant to play rugby league as it used to be. Another example is ice hockey, where fighting between certain players seems to be part of the offered entertainment, and indeed there is a rather absurd ritual that these players engage in—throwing off the gloves as they circle each other while being watched by the referees who will step in before anyone really gets hurt etc—before the fighting can begin. When it does begin, a safety rule is broken, but it is again at least plausible to suggest that the defence operates in at least many of these cases as this form of fighting is part of the game of ice hockey.[20]

It is important to stress that where the defence applies, it does so because, in the circumstances, the players have consented to the touching in question. A player agreeing to play in the State of Origin in the early 1990s may have consented on the basis that agreeing to play meant that in the inevitable brawl, he would fight the stuck-up New South Welshmen or Neanderthal Queenslanders. It is not enough that the player knew that the touching might or would occur and chose to play in

[20] Of course, this does not mean that all fighting is covered by this defence.

the light of that knowledge. For this reason, though I know that some people drive dangerously and, though I choose to drive in that knowledge, I do not consent to such driving. Driving in that way does not relate to any common purpose that I share with the idiot who crashes into me.

B. Vitiating Consent

We turn now to the rule that the plaintiff's consent is vitiated if obtained through force or fraud. Though the wisdom of this approach is clear, it nevertheless presents difficulties for our understanding of the law.

Imagine, for instance, that a man obtains a woman's consent to sexual intercourse by threatening to shoot her. Naturally, it is clear that a tort is committed here. But it is not immediately clear that the law is right to hold that the tort is battery. After all, though the law's position is that the plaintiff's consent is 'ineffective',[21] it maintains correctly that the consent is nevertheless given. On that basis, it seems that legal principle demands that the tort is constituted by the duress rather than the consented to touching.

Consider also the following case taken from the *Restatement*: 'A consents to a [seemingly] friendly boxing match with B. B knows that A is unaware of the fact that A has a defective heart. B punches A in the chest and A suffers a heart attack. B is subject to liability to A for battery.'[22] Strictly, it seems that the legal position rather ought to be that the illegal action performed by B is obtaining A's consent given the circumstances, as B's striking of A is consensual.

Compare that case to *R v Linekar*.[23] The defendant had sex with a prostitute after promising to pay her £25. The jury found that the defendant did not and never intended to pay. The trial judge directed the jury that, in these circumstances, if the prostitute consented in the belief she would be paid, then the defendant's fraud vitiated the complainant's consent. The defendant was convicted of rape. The English Court of Appeal reversed this decision, saying 'the prostitute here consented to sexual intercourse with the appellant. The reality of that consent is not destroyed by being induced by the appellant's false pretence that his intention was to pay the agreed price of £25 for her services. Therefore, he was not guilty of rape'.[24]

In case the reader is inclined to doubt the correctness of that decision or its applicability to the tort of battery, consider also the following example. A knows that B is attracted to successful females. Because of this, A tells B that she is a full professor when she is, in fact, a *mere* associate. B agrees to have sex with A in the light of this representation. Is this a battery? The answer must be no.

21 *Restatement (Second) of Torts* (n 1) §892B(3).
22 ibid §892B.
23 *R v Linekar* [1995] QB 250 (CA).
24 ibid 260 (Morland J).

Let us return to the beginning. In the first two cases, the duress and the misrepresentation function as part of the mechanism by which the defendant puts the plaintiff's body to his purposes. In the first case, getting the plaintiff to consent by holding a gun to her head is one aspect of the way in which this rapist gains control over the plaintiff's body. In fact, in these circumstances, far from indicating that she is exercising her freedom and independence of the defendant, her consent is an element of the defendant's subjection of the plaintiff's body to his will. It is right, then, that the defendant be found liable for battery. Here, the plaintiff's consent does precisely nothing to show that the sexual contact was in accordance with a purpose shared by the parties. On the contrary, in this context, the consent is a manifestation of the defendant's success in putting the plaintiff to his purposes.

Note the structure of this position. The argument is not that there was no consent or that the consent was unreal. It is rather the following: the defence of consent has its basis in the fact that if the parties are pursuing a common purpose, then the defendant's action cannot have involved putting the plaintiff to his purposes. Consent generally indicates that the parties were pursuing a common purpose. But in this case, the consent does not show this. On the contrary, because of the way in which the consent was procured, the consent is itself a manifestation of the putting of the plaintiff to the defendant's purposes. Because of this, though the consent was genuine, it cannot constitute a defence.

The conclusion is the same in the second case, though here the reasoning is different. The parties consent to a boxing match. As far as that goes, there is a shared purpose and the defence applies. But B engages in the fight—at least so the example appears to assume—in order to cause injury to A via the mechanism of his weak heart. That does not correspond to any shared purpose. Again, then, the law is right to hold that the wrongdoing is a battery. Here, B's control over A achieved through boxing was not something to which A consented.

In *R v Linekar* and our fourth case, however, things are different. In *R v Linekar*, the sexual intercourse cannot constitute a battery, as that was something that the parties did together. It was their common purpose. Note the locution here. No one would say of the parties in the first case that *they* had sex. But it is right to say this in *R v Linekar*.[25] The difficulty is that the complainant would not have agreed had she been aware of the defendant's intention not to pay. But that is another matter. That is to say that, had she known of the defendant's intention, she would have had a different purpose from the one that she actually had.[26] Note also that, in the second case, B gains control over A's body in a way to which A did not consent. In *R v Linekar*, however, this did not occur. In this case, the alleged control was the sex.

[25] Recall that this is only a rough guide. See n 12 above.

[26] One might claim that the complainant intended to have sex *for payment* and that this did not relate to a shared purpose with the accused. But the point is that both intended to have sex—that was a shared purpose—and that is sufficient to show that the defence applied.

That was consented to. Having sex with someone under false pretences of this kind is not a way of exercising control separate from having sex *simpliciter*.[27]

This discussion is also usefully compared with the 1878 decision of the Irish Court of Appeal in *Hegarty v Shine*.[28] The plaintiff sued for battery after having contracted venereal disease from the defendant. There was no suggestion that the sexual activity as such was non-consensual. However, the trial judge instructed the jury that the plaintiff's consent to sexual intercourse would be vitiated if the defendant had concealed his condition. This was held to be a misdirection on appeal. Strictly, that is right. The sex was something that the parties engaged in together. It cannot have been a battery. However, had the plaintiff sued on the basis that the defendant infected her with venereal disease, then she should have succeeded, and she should have succeeded in battery. Intentionally (remembering how this term is used in the law of trespass) infecting someone with a disease is an exercise of control over that person's body. In the absence of consent relating to the infection, that is a battery.[29]

C. Implied and Presumed Consent

As we have seen, consent can be implied from behaviour. I implicitly consent to your grasping my hand when I hold it out to you. Less recognised is the fact that consent is also often presumed.

As I write, I occupy a house that has a front door roughly 10 metres from the front of my property. On the face of it, this means that any attempt to reach the door, for example, to knock on it, constitutes a trespass to my land. We all know, however, that this is not the law. People are permitted to enter my land to knock on the door as long as they do so with a legitimate purpose.

The ability to do so is said to rest on the existence of an implied licence. In some circumstances, this label is accurate. If, for instance, I place a doorbell on the outside of my front door, this could reasonably be taken to imply that I consent to people entering my land in order to use it. Similarly, it is arguable that having a post slot in one's door, as is typical in the UK, implicitly invites the postal officer onto the land in order to deliver the mail. But often the facts are otherwise. In my own case, there is nothing to indicate that people are entitled to enter my land for any reason whatsoever.[30]

In these cases, in fact the standard cases, the consent or licence is presumed rather than implied. Think of the matter this way. In the absence of the licence, anyone who wanted to contact me would be forced to yell from the footpath to

[27] I do not suggest that there are no circumstances in which it could be, however.

[28] *Hegarty v Shine* (1878) 14 Cox CC 145, 4 LR Ir 288 (CA).

[29] *cf R v Konzani* 2005 EWCA Crim 706, [2005] 2 Cr App R 14 (CA); *Crowell v Crowell* 105 SE 206 (NC 1920).

[30] I take it that the existence of a path etc is not such evidence. After all, it might well be there only for myself and for those I authorise to enter my land to use.

try to get my attention so that I could consent for them to come to my front door. Naturally, this would be very inconvenient.[31] Generally, we want people to be able to come to our front door and knock.[32] The law acknowledges this by recognising the licence. It is not that I have done anything that implies that I consent to people coming to my front door—certainly not to, say, someone who has never been in the area before and is lost, seeking directions from me. Rather, the law recognises a general presumption that people consent to others entering their land to knock on their front doors.

This presumption also exists with respect to bodily touching, though the law has been very slow to see this. Its clearest statement is found in *Collins v Wilcock*, where Robert Goff LJ said that: 'Generally speaking, consent is a defence to battery; and most of the physical contacts of ordinary life are not actionable because they are impliedly consented to by all who move in society and so expose themselves to the risk of bodily contact.'[33]

Imagine the alternative—that the members of an audience at a rock concert were prohibited from touching each other. If that were so, attending a concert would be impossible. Similarly, we generally do not want people to have to interrupt our conversations at cocktail parties in order to get past; we are happy for them gently to push on our backs, for instance. And so on. These are not batteries, not because the touching is not in anger, non-hostile or the like, but because it is in accordance with a presumed consent. Conversely, if the touching is genuinely in anger, hostile etc, then it constitutes a battery, because consent to such touching cannot be presumed.

One way to test this is to imagine that you press on someone's back at a cocktail party in order to pass only to have the person accost you for doing so. You may well feel affronted by this. Why, exactly? Surely it is because this is a form of touching that you expect people to accept. (It is not because you think the person ignorant for not realising that such activities, though prima facie wrongful, cannot for practical reasons count as illegal.)

This is all in line with the theory presented here. The reason that the consent is presumed is that the plaintiff is engaged in an activity that has a shared purpose as part of the nature of that activity. There is no direct communication between the parties, then, but undertaking the activity is itself a form of communication. Attending a cocktail party is not an activity one can do alone. It involves engaging oneself in a shared purpose with others. Part of the general understanding of that

[31] Importantly, it does not follow that it is the inconvenience itself that justifies the implied licence.

[32] In the UK, because of subdivision and the like, this must often in practice be extended to include the back door, which is often the only external door in general use. Naturally, cultural differences of this kind affect the application of the relevant principles in practice.

[33] *Collins v Wilcock* [1984] 1 WLR 1172, 1177. His Lordship went on to say that: 'Although such cases are regarded as examples of implied consent, it is more common nowadays to treat them as falling within a general exception embracing all physical contact which is generally acceptable in the ordinary conduct of daily life' (ibid). That is, unfortunately, correct.

purpose is that, at least in ordinary circumstances, people at the party try not to interrupt others' conversations, but instead gently indicate their wish to pass. This touching is therefore in accordance with a shared purpose.

This is less obvious, but no less true, with respect to occupying land. Occupying land is an activity with many purposes. Two of these are to give security and privacy. But that is not understood to mean security and privacy to the exclusion of all contact with the outside world. On the contrary, one of the many purposes of having front doors is so that people are able to use them in order to contact us. Thus, when you walk down my path in order to knock on my door, you rightly take yourself to be acting in accordance with a common purpose. As we see immediately, if you cannot take yourself to be doing this, then you are not entitled to enjoy the defence.[34]

This presumption can be defeated. If, for instance, I put a sign on my property stating 'No admittance to anyone without authorisation', then anyone who enters without my consent (express or implied but not presumed) commits a trespass. Likewise, if I wear a hat to a cocktail party proclaiming 'Do not touch', it is then a battery to press on me without my permission, no matter how annoying I am being.[35]

The rule that the otherwise trespasser must enter the land with a so-called legitimate purpose is a reflection of this principle. In the relevant sense, a purpose is legitimate if it is reasonable to assume that the defendant would have consented to it. This too is determined by the parties' purposes. Imagine that a person walks down my front path and knocks on my front door and then, receiving no answer, turns and leaves. That is no trespass if the person did so in order to talk to me, to ask for directions or the like. Why? Because, without evidence to the contrary, it can be presumed that I consent to such. But she cannot do exactly the same thing if her intention is to 'case the joint' in preparation for a burglary. Why not? Because I cannot be presumed to consent to entry for that reason. Similarly, if she decides to wait for three hours at the door until I return, even without malicious intention, that is a trespass, because my consent to her remaining that long cannot be presumed. Likewise, at least outside of the UK,[36] if she sees through the door that I am playing in the back of the house with my children, that does not entitle her to come around the side of the house. Again, my consent cannot be presumed.[37]

The same reasons apply when the defendant is a police officer, subject, as always, to statute. So, it is presumed that I consent to police officers entering my land in

[34] This reveals that the line between a presumption and an implication can be a fine one. Nevertheless, it is there in principle. Here, the claim is not that having a path and a door implies that I consent; rather, the consent is presumed, because occupying a house is generally done for certain purposes.

[35] Of course, this is true only if the message on the hat appears serious. It is also important to remember that I can always be asked to leave and if I do not, for reasons that we are about to see, I can be ejected.

[36] See n 32.

[37] See, eg, *Robson v Hallett* [1967] 2 QB 939 (CA).

order to give me information, question me about events in the neighbourhood and so on. But the police cannot enter in order to search for evidence without a warrant, because it cannot be presumed that I consent to this.[38]

Unfortunately, in jurisdictions with a less than ideal concern for the rule of law, this position has been undermined. Consider, for instance, the High Court of Australia's judgment in *Halliday v Nevill*.[39] Two police officers entered private land without a search warrant or the occupier's consent. They did so in order to arrest a man strongly suspected of criminal activity. The majority of the High Court held that this action was not a trespass as the police officers enjoyed an implied licence. This was because the officers were trying to arrest a suspected criminal and, of course, that was held to be a legitimate purpose.

In dissent, Brennan J revealed the unacceptable consequences of this position:

> Once it is admitted that the police officers have an implied licence to enter to arrest, might a licence for other police purposes be implied? To install a traffic radar device on the driveway? Or carry out surveillance of neighbouring premises from there? The presence of the police officers on the [land] was not for any purpose with which the person in possession was concerned. I am unable to see in the facts of the case any ground for inferring that the police had a licence from that person to come on to his driveway without his permission for the purpose of arresting a suspected offender.[40]

The problem is that the majority interpreted 'legitimate purpose' to refer to the public interest. They held that if the officer's actions were in the public interest, then they were in accordance with a legitimate purpose and the officers enjoyed an implied licence. But, as Brennan J pointed out, that cannot be right. First, it would lead to the conclusion that a great many activities would be legitimated by an implied licence when that is not the law. Second, it would mean that an implied licence could come into conflict with an express licence or lack thereof. Imagine that the occupier of the land in question had expressly refused the police officers entry. It remains the case that the entry is a 'legitimate purpose' as defined by the majority. So can the officers enter or not? The fundamental problem is that the majority misidentify the meaning of 'legitimate purpose' in this context. It is not concerned with the public interest. It is concerned with the scope of the presumed consent. The purpose is said to be legitimate if and only if it is reasonable to presume that the occupier would have consented to it. That was not reasonable in *Halliday v Nevill*. Again, as Brennan J pointed out, if that were not so, then the law relating to search warrants would look quite different than it does.

[38] See, eg, ibid 953–54; *Shattock v Devlin* [1990] 2 NZLR 88.

[39] *Halliday v Nevill* (1984) 155 CLR 1 (HCA). See also *AG v Hewitt* [2000] 2 NZLR 110. Compare *Restatement (Second) of Torts* (n 1) §§204–11. It is also significant to note that the objection is not necessarily to the outcomes of these cases, but to the ways in which those outcomes were reached. There may have been other ways to have reached those outcomes.

[40] *Halliday v Nevill* (n 39) 20.

II. Self-Defence, the Defence of Others and Self-Help

There is a tradition of treating self-defence as an excuse or justification for what is in itself wrongful behaviour.[41] On this view, the fundamental theoretical question is thought to be: 'How does one provide a theoretically illuminating explanation of why considerations such as self-defence are moral justifications for conduct that would otherwise be immoral?'[42] Compare this to the position taken by Kant, here speaking of coercion in general:

> Resistance that counteracts the hindering of an effect promotes this effect and is consistent with it. Now whatever is wrong is a hindrance to freedom in accordance with universal laws. But coercion is a hindrance or resistance to freedom. Therefore, if a certain use of freedom is itself a hindrance to freedom in accordance with universal laws (i.e., wrong), coercion that is opposed to this (as a *hindering of a hindrance to freedom*) is consistent with freedom in accordance with universal laws, that is, it is right. Hence there is connected with right by the principle of contradiction an authorization to coerce someone who infringes upon it.[43]

Some may find this obscure. Certainly, a modern philosopher would not choose to express herself this way. Nevertheless, the point that Kant is making is highly intuitive and his position is far more so than the one taken by many modern theorists.

It will be instructive to compare the structure of these analyses with reference to an example. In the example, *A* attempts to strike *B*, but is prevented because *B* strikes *A* in self-defence. The orthodox view begins with the notion that unconsented-to touching is prohibited. It therefore holds that *A* attempts to perform a prohibited action. But *B*'s touching of *A* is also non-consensual. That means that it too is prohibited prima facie. Hence, we must look for some consideration that justifies or excuses *B*'s action.

This analysis is the result of not pursuing one's enquiry sufficiently deeply. With the orthodox view, we begin with the notion that unconsented-to touching is prohibited. But we should want to know why. Our answer has been because an unconsented-to touching is an exercise of control over another's body. But that is not true of all unconsented-to touchings. Touchings that are aimed only to prevent an agent gaining control over the bodies of others are not themselves attempts to gain control over the agent's body. An attempt to prevent you controlling me need not be an attempt to control you. The same is true of an attempt to prevent you controlling a third party. Of course, the act has an unwanted effect on the other, but that is a different point entirely.

[41] eg, HLA Hart, *The Concept of Law*, 2nd edn (Oxford, Oxford University Press, 1994) 179.

[42] R Ladenson, 'In Defense of a Hobbesian Conception of Law' in J Raz (ed), *Authority* (Oxford, Blackwell, 1990) 36.

[43] I Kant, *The Metaphysics of Morals*, M Gregor (trans) (Cambridge, Cambridge University Press, 1996) 6:231.

On this analysis, *A* attempts to exercise control of *B*'s body. *B*, however, neither attempts to exercise nor exercises control over *A*'s body (though he effects that body). *B* merely prevents *A*'s control of his body, preserving *B*'s control of his own body. This analysis reflects the intuition held by non-theorists that an act of self-defence is not of the same order as the act that provoked it. It is therefore not an act that needs to be excused or justified.

This also explains why *D* is permitted to slap away the hand of *C* who is about to touch him unintentionally and without causing harm. This case is significant because *C*'s action is not a candidate for liability, it is not illegal, and yet *D* is entitled to take self-defence. Why? Because *D*'s intentionality is such that his action does not exert control over *C*. *D* is not putting *C* to his purposes, he is merely protecting his ability to preserve his control over his body.

However, it is possible for *B* to act so as to exercise control over *A*'s body in such cases. Imagine in our original case that *B* could have prevented *A*'s action by stepping back, but instead shot *A* dead. Here, *B*'s action is not rightly interpreted as an attempt merely to preserve control of his own body. It is that, but it is also an exercise of control over *A*'s. Thus, the defence does not apply.[44]

It is helpful to examine the rules in the second *Restatement* in this light. The *Restatement* imagines four scenarios:

(1) *A* threatens to strike *B*. *B* can defend herself without killing or seriously injuring *A*. *B* is entitled so to defend herself, even if she could avoid being struck in other ways, by, eg, retreating or complying with *A*'s demands (assuming that they are not too onerous etc).[45]
(2) *A* threatens to strike *B*. *B* cannot defend herself without killing or seriously injuring *A*. *B* is entitled so to defend herself if and only if she is threatened with similarly serious injury and cannot avoid injury by retreating, complying with *A*'s demands etc.[46]
(3) *B* becomes aware that she will be negligently injured by *A* and can prevent this happening by striking *A* without killing or seriously injuring *A*. *B* is entitled so to defend herself if and only if she cannot avoid injury by retreating, complying with *A*'s demands etc.[47]
(4) *B* becomes aware that she will be negligently killed or seriously injured by *A* and can prevent this happening by striking *A*. *B* is entitled so to defend herself even if it means that *A* will be killed or suffer serious injury.[48]

[44] *Lane v Holloway* [1968] 1 QB 379 (CA).
[45] *Restatement (Second) of Torts* (n 1) §63.
[46] ibid §65.
[47] ibid §64.
[48] ibid §66.

I do not claim that this is the only scheme consistent with the theory advanced here, but it is consistent.

In (1), *A* is attempting to exercise control over *B*. *B* is entitled to resist. In these circumstances, requiring *B* to retreat, comply or the like would be to permit *A* to succeed in exercising control, though perhaps not the control intended. So, for instance, if we asked *B* why she retreated, she might say: 'He made me.'

In (2), however, things are different. First, imagine that *B* is not threatened with death or serious injury and strikes *A*, killing or seriously injuring him. Here, it is arguable that, though *B* acts to prevent *A* gaining control over her, she does so in a way that exerts control over *A*.[49] This must not be permitted. Second, imagine that *B* is threatened with death or serious injury, but can avoid that injury and strikes *B*, killing or seriously injuring him. Here again, it is arguable that in acting as she does, though *B* prevents *A* gaining control over her, she does so in a way that exerts control over *A*.[50] However, if the only way *B* can avoid death or serious injury is to inflict the like on *A*, then if she does so, in those circumstances, all she is doing is preventing *A*'s control of her.

In (3) and (4), matters are different, because *A* is not attempting to exert control over *B*. We cannot at this stage analyse these cases in any depth, as the law of negligence is not examined until Chapter 12, but I submit that it is already apparent that (3) and (4) can readily be interpreted as attempts to achieve justice as between the parties along the lines of the theory presented here.

So far, we have examined self-defence. A feature of this theory is that it holds that the same analysis applies to the defence of others and the various self-help remedies.

For instance, just as *B* can strike *A* in self-defence because in doing so she prevents *A* exercising control over her without asserting control over *A*, *C* can strike *A* in order to prevent *A* exercising control over *B* without asserting control over *A*. Likewise, if you are trespassing on my land and I can remove you only by forcibly ejecting you, then I am entitled to do so. This is because, in these circumstances, my action is rightly understood as preserving my control over my land rather than exercising control over your body. And this principle has precisely the same limits. If I could remove you by pushing you, but instead shoot you, then my action cannot rightly be viewed merely as preserving my control of my land.

Note the significance of the party's intention. If you are on my land and I push you off because it is the only way that I can get you off my property, then I am not attempting to control your body. But if you are on my land and I push you

[49] I say that this is arguable, because I think it often wrong, though I accept that reasonable people may differ in this regard. I would argue that, here again, the *Restatement* is a little too influenced by the idea that tort law revolves around negative influence, the idea being that the law must act so as to minimise negative influence. Why, though, should I be forced to suffer negative influence just because you threaten me in a way that means that I am, as it were, the lowest negative influence avoider?

[50] However, see ibid.

off because I see this as an opportunity to assert my physical dominance over you, then I am attempting to control you. The intention makes all the difference.

III. Necessity

We start with a simple, now almost cliché, case that we owe to Joel Feinberg. Imagine that *A* is starving in the woods and comes across *B*'s cabin. *A* breaks in and consumes *B*'s food. Ordinarily, this would constitute a trespass. However, because *A* is acting under necessity—ie, because she needs the food in order to survive—she is at liberty so to act. What makes the case more difficult to understand is that, despite this liberty and despite the fact that she is not guilty of trespass, she must compensate *B* for the loss of his food etc.[51]

In legal circles, this is a notorious problem.[52] The case seems to fall between legal stools. The duty to compensate could easily be explained if *A* committed a trespass, but the defence of necessity indicates that she committed no such tort. Alternatively, as no tort was committed, some maintain that *A* is unjustly enriched at *B*'s expense or that there is some other restitutionary claim.[53] But that is also problematic, at least philosophically. Surely, if *B* is entitled to claim, it is because of his loss, not because of *A*'s gain, not even because of *A*'s gain at his expense. Put most simply, *B*'s claim is: 'That was my food that you ate.' It is not: 'You wrongly gained from eating my food.'[54]

This is one area in which the philosophical analysis is easier than the legal. The account proceeds in two steps: the first shows why there is no trespass and the second why compensation must be paid.

First, prima facie, *A* is not entitled to exercise control over *B*'s cabin or chattels. In our example, however, *A* must do so in order to preserve her control over her own body. She must break in and eat *B*'s food or die. *A*'s right is innate, *B*'s is acquired. This means that the breaking in and the eating of the food cannot be wrongful, as it is done in order to preserve a right in *A* more fundamental than the right in *B*. Thus, there is no way of describing *A*'s actions as wrongful consistent with the rights of both parties.

[51] *Vincent v Lake Erie Transportation Co* 124 NW 221 (MN SC 1910).

[52] R Stevens, *Torts and Rights* (Oxford, Oxford University Press, 2007) 104, maintains that the case is best understood in the following terms: 'the defendant had a privilege to [break in and eat the food], but … this privilege was qualified and did not excuse it from having to pay for damage suffered as a result of its exercise. The duty of the [defendant] became, in the emergency, a duty not to cause loss in [breaking in], and not a duty not to [break in] at all'. The problem with this *from the perspective of theory* is that, while it accurately describes the legal position, it does not explain anything. Why does the defendant have precisely these privileges?

[53] eg, EJ Weinrib, *The Idea of Private Law* (Cambridge, MA, Harvard University Press, 1995) 196–203.

[54] The issue is not, therefore, the quantum of damages or the method by which they are calculated, but the nature of the wrong in question.

Second, *A*'s actions nevertheless assert control over *B*'s property. To the extent that this control can be separated from *A*'s entitlement to control her own body, it is wrongful. And that control is exercised not only by breaking in and eating the food, but also by leaving the property in that condition.[55] It is this for which *A* must compensate *B*, as (eventually) the property does not have to be left in that condition in order to preserve *A*'s control over her own body. This position reflects what seems to be the intuitive response to the example. From *A*'s perspective, the position is: 'I was entitled to do what I did, but I can't leave you like this.' This theory explains why.

Is the duty to compensate tortious or restitutionary? Why expect a definitive answer to this question? The duty could be conceptualised either way. The important point is that the duty is justified.

Other cases have an entirely different structure. Imagine, for instance, that I am about to be struck by a bus when you pull me back from danger. I did not consent to this touching. Can I sue for battery? The answer is no. Similarly, if I arrive at hospital unconscious and require urgent surgery to save my life, the hospital is entitled to perform the surgery despite the absence of consent. There is no battery even if I can later prove that I would not have consented to the operation.

In the Commonwealth, these cases are standardly understood to involve the defence of necessity. The idea is that you and the hospital are entitled to a defence because you are acting in circumstances of necessity. That is not correct. The defence of necessity is not involved here. US law correctly characterises these cases as involving consent.[56] They are yet more situations where consent is presumed.

This is evident from the nature of the situations envisaged. It is also revealed by the moral force of the defence. Pulling me out of the path of a speeding bus is permissible not because you have to do it—you do not have to do it—but because it is reasonable to assume that I would have consented had it been possible to ask me. This is also why the defence will fail in circumstances where it is apparent that the consent would not have been given.

In *Malette v Shulman*,[57] the plaintiff was taken to hospital in a semi-conscious state after a traffic accident. She required a blood transfusion in order to save her life. Her state of mind made her unable to consent, or refuse consent, to the procedure. However, a card was found in the plaintiff's purse that read (in translation):

> No Blood Transfusion!
>
> As one of Jehovah's Witnesses with firm religious convictions, I request that no blood or blood products be administered to me under any circumstances. I fully realize the

[55] For analysis, see Beever, *Forgotten Justice* (n 10) 262–66.

[56] See, eg, *Restatement (Second) of Torts* (n 1) ch 45; WP Keeton et al, *Prosser and Keeton on the Law of Torts*, 5th edn (St Paul, MN, West Group, 1984) 117–18; DB Dobbs, *Torts and Compensation Personal Accountability and Social Responsibility for Injury*, 2nd edn (Los Angeles, West Group, 1993) 70.

[57] *Malette v Shulman* (1989) 67 DLR (4th) 321 (Ont CA). See also *Wons v Public Health Trust of Dade County* 541 So 2d 96 (Fla 1989).

> implications of this position, but I have resolutely decided to obey the Bible command: 'Keep abstaining … from blood' (Acts 15:28, 29).

Despite this, she was given a blood transfusion.

The Ontario Court of Appeal upheld the finding that this was a battery. Rightly so.[58] The finding of the card was decisive; it meant that the transfusion could not be performed. But that had nothing to do with necessity. The finding of the card did not make the transfusion any less necessary than it would otherwise have been. What it did do was undermine the presumption that the plaintiff would have consented to the operation had she been able to do so.

[58] See also *Chambers v Nottebaum* 96 So 2d 716 (Fla 1957); *Schloendorff v Society of New York Hospital* 105 NE 92 (NY 1914); *Restatement (Second) of Torts* (n 1) §892D(b).

7

Deceit

The second part of our investigation ends by considering a tort that fits the model of explanation so far advanced, but where the defendant's control of the plaintiff is less immediate than it is in cases of trespass: the tort of deceit. In order to establish liability in this tort, the plaintiff must show that the defendant made a representation of fact that the defendant knew to be false or was reckless in that regard, that the defendant intended the plaintiff to rely on the statement to her detriment and that the plaintiff so relied.

At first, it seems natural to argue that this tort is based on the existence of a right not to be lied to.[1] This is attractive because it is clear that the tort is committed when a defendant lies to the plaintiff.[2] Nevertheless, this suggestion faces three difficulties.

The first is that the suggestion is ad hoc at the level of theory. As discussed in Chapter 1, one cannot provide a theoretically satisfactory explanation of tort law merely by positing rights said to underlie the various torts. This strategy may be illuminating for legal analysis in important respects, but it cannot provide the theoretical grounding for the law that we are seeking. Second, the alleged right fits poorly with the structure of the action for deceit. Most significantly, deceit requires that the plaintiff detrimentally rely on the defendant's statement and that the defendant intend this. In this regard, the tort of deceit does much less than protect a right not to be lied to.[3]

The third difficulty is the most fundamental. There can be no such right. As Kant remarked, in principle a person is at liberty to say what he wants to others, including 'communicating his thoughts to them, telling or promising them something, whether what he says is true and sincere or untrue and insincere (*veriloquium aut falsiloquium*); for it is entirely up to them whether they want to believe him or not'.[4] This passage demonstrates a crucial difference between trespass and deceit. The act of touching you without your consent is itself an exercise of control

[1] eg, R Stevens, *Torts and Rights* (Oxford, Oxford University Press, 2007) 8.

[2] For convenience, I will speak of lies even when the defendant is 'merely' reckless.

[3] Nor would it be appropriate to regard this rule as some kind of control mechanism on the operation of the right. This position implicitly admits that there is no such right in fact.

[4] I Kant, *The Metaphysics of Morals*, M Gregor (trans) (Cambridge, Cambridge University Press, 1996) 6:238.

over you. But when I lie to you, my action has no impact on you whatsoever unless you believe me or decide to act on my representation regardless. The easiest way to demonstrate this point is to imagine a person telling you something you know to be false. It is hard to see how that could be regarded as a violation of your rights and it is clear that you cannot sue.[5]

Of course, this does not mean that lies are morally neutral. As Kant further explains:

> Telling an untruth intentionally, even though merely frivolously, is usually called a lie (*mendacium*) because it can also harm someone, at least to the extent that if he ingenuously repeats it others ridicule him as gullible. The only kind of untruth we want to call a lie, in the sense *bearing upon rights*, is one that directly infringes upon another's right, e.g., the false allegation that a contract has been concluded with someone, made in order to deprive him of what is his (*falsiloquium dolosum*). And this distinction between closely related concepts is not without basis; for when someone merely says what he thinks, another always remains free to take it as he pleases.[6]

This is to say that a lie is (legally) wrongful only if it results in the violation of the plaintiff's rights, either acquired or innate. On this view, the tort of deceit is not about any right not to be lied to. Rather, it recognises that lying to another can be a mechanism by which a different right is violated. In order to unpack this idea, it will be useful to examine Kant's contrasting analyses of lying and false promising.

In the *Metaphysics of Morals*, Kant defines lying as a violation of one's duty to oneself as a moral being.[7] We must notice the self-regarding nature of this wrong. As Kant explains:

> [C]ommunication of one's thoughts to someone through words that yet (intentionally) contain the contrary of what the speaker thinks on the subject is an end that is directly opposed to the natural purposiveness of the speaker's capacity to communicate his thoughts, and is thus a renunciation by the speaker of his personality, and such a speaker is a mere deceptive appearance of a human being, not a human being himself.[8]

We need not fully come to terms with these difficult ideas here. Suffice it to say that Kant understands lying to be wrongful because it is a violation of the liar's own dignity.

Compare this to Kant's analysis of false (ie insincere) promising:

> [H]e who has it in mind to make a false promise to others sees at once that he wants to make use of another human being *merely as a means*, without the other at the same time containing in himself the end. For, he whom I want to use for my purposes by such a promise cannot possibly agree to my way of behaving toward him, and so himself

[5] If there is an assumption of the responsibility by the utterer, then it might be possible to sue, but in that case the action would be for breach of the assumption of responsibility, not for the falsehood.

[6] Kant (n 4) 6:238.

[7] ibid 6:428–31. Kant also defines lying in a special legal sense at 6:429. That use is not the ordinary use of the term, however.

[8] ibid.

> contain the end of this action. This conflict with the principle of other human beings is seen more distinctly if examples of assaults on the freedom and property of others are brought forward. For then it is obvious that he who transgresses the rights of human beings intends to make use of the person of others merely as means, without taking into consideration that, as rational beings, they are always to be valued at the same time as ends, that is, only as beings who must also be able to contain in themselves the end of the very same action.[9]

This is an examination of the ethics and not the legality of false promising, but it is nevertheless instructive. The specific case Kant has in mind is one in which the promisor obtains money from the promisee by promising to pay the money back, where the promisor has no intention of doing so.[10] Here, the problem is not merely that the promisee has been told an untruth, it is also that the promisor gets the promisee to do something by telling the promisee the untruth. As Kant notes, the wrongdoing is particularly clear in this case because the action in question is the surrender of the promisee's property.

In our language, false promising that has this effect is coercive because it is an exercise of control over the promisee. That control is achieved by telling a lie. Here, the wrongdoing is not the telling of the lie per se, it is rather the exercise of control over the promisee accomplished through the mechanism of the lie. It is no coincidence that false promises of this kind would be actionable in deceit.[11]

The suggestion, then, is that the tort of deceit is concerned with situations in which the defendant exercises control over the plaintiff. It has this in common with all of the other torts examined in this part. With respect to deceit, that control is exercised by telling the plaintiff a lie. This is why the defendant must intend the plaintiff to rely.[12] Without that intention, there is no attempt to use the lie to exercise control. It is also why the reliance must occur. Without reliance, the attempt to exercise control cannot have succeeded.

The more difficult question is why deceit requires the making of a *false* statement. That is, why is it not illegal to tell someone something true if one intends thereby to exercise control and that indeed occurs?

The answer is somewhat complex. In part, this is because, though it cannot be a deceit, it can be illegal to tell someone the truth in such circumstances. A defendant guilty of a so-called two-party intimidation may say nothing but the truth and yet be liable for that utterance—the issuing of a sincere threat, for example. Likewise, had the defendant in *Khorasandjian v Bush*[13] said nothing but the truth—ie, were his threats sincere—there is no suggestion that this would undermine his

[9] I Kant, *Groundwork of the Metaphysics of Morals*, M Gregor (trans) (Cambridge, Cambridge University Press, 1996) 6:429–30.

[10] ibid 6:422.

[11] *Edington v Fitzmaurice* (1885) 29 Ch D 459 (CA).

[12] Recklessness is to be explained in the same way as it was in Ch 5.

[13] *Khorasandjian v Bush* [1993] QB 727 (CA).

liability for intentionally causing emotional distress. Thus, there is no rule according to which truth telling is necessarily permissible. The position is only that, in the circumstances relevant to the tort of deceit, a defendant will not be liable if he told the truth. But why is that?

In the cases just examined, the effect on the plaintiff of learning the truth is that she loses control over her actions in some way. Thus, the mechanism for gaining control over the plaintiff is the utterance, which in these examples happens to be truthful. When this occurs, the defendant's behaviour is actionable regardless of truth or falsity. The wrongdoing lies in exercising control over the plaintiff, and that control is achieved by the utterance regardless of its truth.[14] But the tort of deceit deals with different circumstances. It is concerned with cases in which the plaintiff *chooses* a course of action in the light of the defendant's utterance. If the utterance is truthful, then though it can be right to say that the plaintiff acted because of the representation made to her by the defendant, the plaintiff is still in control of her own actions. This is because she is responding to the world as it is. But if the representation were false and were intended to induce a certain course of action then, when the plaintiff chooses that course, it is right to say that the defendant exercises control over her. The plaintiff responds to the defendant's (inaccurate) representation of the world. As it were, it is the defendant's world, not the real world, to which the plaintiff is responding.

Like all of these torts, then, deceit deals with the form of coercion we are calling control. The lie is not (legally) wrongful in itself. Rather, the wrongdoing lies in the role that the lie plays in allowing the defendant to obtain power over the plaintiff.

[14] In fact, there may be cases where the truth of the utterance aids the defendant in gaining control over the plaintiff.

Part III

Indirect Control

Part II examined torts in which the defendant coerces the plaintiff directly, in the sense that the defendant acts on the plaintiff or on the plaintiff's property. This is not the only way of exerting control over another, however. It is also possible to exert control over a person by acting on a third party. This is what is meant by 'indirect control'. When I commit a tort of this kind, I gain control over another by doing something to someone else.

The area of the law with which we must deal now—the so-called economic torts—is particularly fraught with difficulty. The case law exists in a state of considerable confusion and academic disagreement on even the basic issues is deep and routine—even more so than usual. This lack of clarity makes it impossible immediately to theorise about this area of the law. Instead, we must first pick through the case law and commentary so that our subject matter can be identified with sufficient precision. Only then will we be able to diagnose the causes of the current malaise and prescribe a cure.

The picking through of Commonwealth law is done in Chapter 8. The cure is found in Chapter 9. Chapter 10 explores the corresponding area of US law. Finally, Chapter 11 applies the developed analysis to the torts of injurious falsehood and malicious prosecution.

8

The Economic Torts in the Commonwealth: The Conventional View

I. Introduction

The area of the law with which we must now deal is covered by the torts of causing loss by unlawful means, inducing breach of contract and conspiracy. Unfortunately, we have no general name for these torts. They belong to a set called the economic torts, a set that also includes the torts of deceit, malicious falsehood and passing off. I will say nothing of those last three torts now,[1] but we require a marker for the first three now under discussion. I propose to call them simply 'the economic torts' on the understanding that this label is used more narrowly than usual. Furthermore, I call the action for causing loss by unlawful means the tort of causing loss by unlawful means, even though that label did not become established until 2007. Finally, this and the following chapter concentrate for the most part on English law, as it is there that we witness the most important modern developments and analysis. It will help to begin with a brief description of these actions.

A defendant is guilty of inducing breach of contract if he persuades a third party to breach her contract with the plaintiff. The classic case is *Lumley v Gye*.[2] The diva Johanna Wagner contracted to perform exclusively for the plaintiff. Knowing this, but desiring to obtain her services, the defendant owner of a rival theatre persuaded Wagner to breach her contract.

A defendant causes loss by unlawful means if she acts illegally with respect to a third party in order to cause loss to the plaintiff. An example is that I stand outside your shop with a gun threatening to kill anyone who enters in an attempt to drive

[1] As others have argued, the tort of intimidation, at least in its three-party guise, has been incorporated into that of causing loss by unlawful means. See H Carty, *An Analysis of the Economic Torts*, 2nd edn (Oxford, Oxford University Press, 2010) 114–16, 120; JW Neyers, 'The Economic Torts as Corrective Justice' (2009) 17 *Torts Law Journal* 1, 7; R Stevens, *Torts and Rights* (Oxford, Oxford University Press, 2007) 190; J Thompson, 'Redrawing the Landscape of the Economic Torts' (2008) 12 *Edinburgh Law Review* 267, 270. The Australian High Court, however, may prove to be as attached to archaism as ever in this area. See *Construction, Forestry, Mining & Energy Union v Boral Resources (Vic) Pty Ltd* 2015 HCA Trans 122.

[2] *Lumley v Gye* (1853) 2 El & Bl 216, 118 ER 749.

you out of business. Here, I am committing an illegal action vis-a-vis the third parties in order to cause loss to you.

Conspiracy comes in two guises. Unlawful means conspiracy has the same form as causing loss by unlawful means, with the exception that two or more people must enter into some kind of agreement with the common design of injuring the plaintiff. A good example is that a friend and I take turns to stand outside your shop threatening to kill anyone who enters in an attempt to drive you out of business. Lawful means conspiracy has the same form as unlawful means conspiracy, with the exception that there is no requirement that the means employed vis-a-vis the third party be illegal. An example would be that I 'gang up' with your other competitors in some (not entirely clear sense) illegitimate though not illegal (to the third parties) fashion to influence the behaviour of third parties in an attempt to drive you out of business.

Despite these relatively simple definitions, it is generally accepted that this area of the law is beset with uncertainty. Some describe it as chaotic.[3] Because of this, contemporary debate concerns the causes of this deleterious state of affairs and the appropriate remedy for it. Though analysts disagree widely on matters of detail in this regard,[4] it is nevertheless possible to detect, at a more general level, conventional answers to these questions. There is a conventional view of the nature of these torts, of what the torts are all about, a view that provides a set of diagnoses for past and present ills and prescriptions for courses of action for the future. The ultimate aim of this analysis is to convince the courts to take their medicine and move the law in the appropriate directions.

The problem is that the conventional view is wrong. Far from providing the cure for our current difficulties, that view is the fundamental cause of the mess we are in. If we cling to it, continuing chaos is guaranteed. Demonstrating this is the primary aim of this chapter.

II. The Conventional View of the Economic Torts

Of course, the claim that there is a conventional view does not imply that the view is accepted universally. It is not. Nevertheless, the view structures the way that the majority of lawyers—academics, judges and practitioners—conceptualise this area of the law. The view forms the starting point for analysis. It has the following features.

[3] See especially H Carty, 'The Economic Torts in the 21st Century' (2008) 124 *Law Quarterly Review* 641, 660.

[4] For analysis, see Carty (n 1) 169–73.

A. Function

The view holds that the primary function of the economic torts is to regulate economic activity, specifically to prevent or deter destructive forms of competition.[5] Naturally, the target is not competition itself, which is generally to be encouraged. The focus is only undesirable competition. Moreover, this narrowed focus is coupled with the recognition that comprehensive regulation of competition for the public interest is too complicated and controversial for the courts and must be left to the legislature.[6] The following provides a useful summary: 'The common law having no general tort of unfair competition, the economic torts represent its chosen method to attack excessive (rather than simply aggressive) competition or economic endeavour, whether through diversion of custom or attacks on commercial links.'[7]

B. Historical Development

How is this attack best carried out? According to the conventional view, courts have divided on the answer to this question. To use Hazel Carty's helpful language,[8] first come the abstentionists, epitomised by the majority in *Allen v Flood*,[9] who maintain that the courts should play a relatively minor role, interfering in the operation of the market only when clear wrongs are being committed. Then come the 'interventionists', most notably the judges in *Quinn v Leathem*,[10] who propose taking a more active role in economic management.

According to Carty, the war between these factions is the primary explanation for the mess in which we find ourselves today. A coherent platform for liability was set out by the abstentionist majority in *Allen v Flood*, but that was undermined by the interventionists in *Quinn v Leathem*, a turn of events which led to disorder for much of the twentieth century.[11] Similarly, though the abstentionists on the House of Lords in *OBG Ltd v Allan* set the law back on track, it was soon again derailed by the interventionists in *Revenue and Customs Commissioners v Total Network SL*.[12]

[5] See, eg, *Mogul Steamship Co Ltd v McGregor Gow & Co* (1889) 23 QBD 598 (CA), 614 (Bowen LJ); *AI Enterprises Ltd v Bram Enterprises* 2014 SCC 12, (2014) 366 DLR (4th) 573 [29]; Carty (n 1) v, 1–2, 9, 173; WE Peel and J Goudkamp, *Winfield and Jolowicz on Tort*, 19th edn (London, Sweet & Maxwell, 2013) 570.

[6] eg, *Mogul Steamship Co Ltd v McGregor Gow & Co* (1889) 23 QBD 598 (CA), 620 (Bowen LJ); *Crofter Hand Woven Harris Tweed Co Ltd v Veitch* [1942] AC 435 (HL), 473 (Lord Wright); *AI Enterprises Ltd v Bram Enterprises* (n 5) [31].

[7] Carty (n 1) 2.

[8] ibid 1–16.

[9] *Allen v Flood* [1898] AC 1 (HL).

[10] *Quinn v Leathem* [1901] AC 495 (HL).

[11] Carty (n 1) 11, 73.

[12] *Revenue and Customs Commissioners v Total Network SL* [2008] UKHL 19, [2008] 1 AC 1174 (HL).

One particular consequence of this war is that, for much of the twentieth century, the relationship between the torts of inducing breach of contract and causing loss by unlawful means was misunderstood. According to this story, it was initially clear that the two actions were separate and based on different principles.[13] However, the interventionist ambitions of the *Quinn v Leathem* court saw the development of a 'unified theory' of liability for the economic torts that led to the view that the torts were one.[14] That theory produced 'chaos',[15] exemplified by the decisions of the English Court of Appeal in *Torquay Hotel Co Ltd v Cousins*[16] and the House of Lords in *Merkur Island Shipping Corp v Laughton*,[17] in which it was held that mere interference with contract could be actionable.[18]

Thankfully, much of this was put right in *OBG Ltd v Allan*. First, the House of Lords adopted the abstentionist approach of the majority in *Allen v Flood*. Second, the Court clearly distinguished the torts of inducing breach of contract and causing loss by unlawful means. An important consequence of this development is that it was determined that there can be no liability for interfering with contract as such. Thus, *Torquay Hotel Co Ltd v Cousins* and *Merkur Island Shipping Corp v Laughton* were deemed to be wrongly decided.[19]

Though important matters remained to be settled, not only did *OBG Ltd v Allan* clarify the actions for causing loss by unlawful means and inducing breach of contract, but without saying anything about conspiracy as such, it also set an agenda for that tort. That agenda was, of course, abstentionist and its consequences were well captured by the views of academics who suggested that the tort is either redundant or unjustified. More specifically, the tort of unlawful means conspiracy was held to be no more than a species of the tort of causing loss by unlawful means. It is simply the causing of loss by unlawful means by more than one person. That meant that there were no circumstances in which a defendant could be found liable for unlawful means conspiracy when she would not also be liable for causing loss by unlawful means. On this view, then, the tort is redundant.[20] Conversely, it was held that liability in the tort of lawful means conspiracy cannot be justified—there being no wrong committed to the plaintiff or to the third party—and thus that the tort should be abolished.[21] The hope, then, was that the economic torts would be given a rational foundation and a coherent account of liability would emerge.

[13] Carty (n 1) 17.
[14] ibid 18–21, 30–32.
[15] ibid 22–23.
[16] *Torquay Hotel Co Ltd v Cousins* [1969] 2 Ch 106 (CA).
[17] *Merkur Island Shipping Corp v Laughton* [1983] 2 AC 570 (HL).
[18] Carty (n 1) 34; Stevens (n 1) 277.
[19] See especially *OBG Ltd v Allan* [2007] UKHL 21, [2008] 1 AC 1 (HL), 61–62. According to WE Peel and J Goudkamp, *Winfield and Jolowicz on Tort*, 19th edn (London, Sweet & Maxwell, 2013) 573, the view propounded in *Torquay Hotel Co Ltd v Cousins* was 'exploded' in *OBG Ltd v Allan*.
[20] Stevens (n 1) 248–50; Carty (n 1) 125.
[21] JW Neyers, 'The Economic Torts as Corrective Justice' (2009) 17 *Torts Law Journal* 1, 5; Stevens (n 1) 251. I take it that this is also implied by the cautious language in Carty (n 1) 149.

Those hopes were not to be realised. In *Total Network*, the House of Lords breathed new life into the tort of conspiracy. Their Lordships held that conspiracy was no mere subset of causing loss by unlawful means, but a robust action in its own right. This was cemented by the fact that the Court defined unlawful means for the purposes of this tort in wider terms than the majority in *OBG Ltd v Allan* appeared to have done for the tort of causing loss by unlawful means. On this view, the tort is not redundant. More fundamentally, *Total Network* is understood to involve an implicit rejection of the abstentionist approach of *OBG Ltd v Allan* in favour of the interventionism found in cases such as *Quinn v Leathem*.[22]

The conclusion is damning. According to Carty, surely the leading analyst of this area of the law, 'the *Total* decision has arguably undermined the prospect for clarity that *OBG* represented, and thrown the economic torts back into the mess in which they were before *OBG*'.[23] The remedy, then, seems obvious. The courts must choose between the abstentionist and interventionist approaches. Only in that way can coherence be achieved. Moreover, given the difficulties of interventionism in this area, abstentionism is to be preferred.[24] Our present ills will be cured when the courts make that choice.

III. Criticism of the Conventional View

A. The Lesson of History

As we have seen, according to the conventional view, the canonical statement of the abstentionist approach was uttered in 1897. It is the decision of the House of Lords in *Allen v Flood*. Unfortunately, only four years later, the same Court in *Quinn v Leathem* opted for interventionism. And in 2007, the House of Lords once again set out along the abstentionist path in *OBG Ltd v Allan*. But the very next year, this was undermined by the interventionists in *Total Network*. What is going on?

As it were, the conventional view responds by asking: 'Why can't these judges make up their minds? Every time we reach a fork in the road, the courts turn in a different direction. One of these roads is the right one. The courts should go down it and stop looking back.' But there is another possibility. It is that both turnings lead to dead ends and the reason the law continually finds itself in reverse is that, having chosen to go down one road, it soon discovers that it cannot continue and must return. On this understanding, it is not correct to describe *Allen v Flood* and *Quinn v Leathem* as presenting the two possibilities available in this area and it is

[22] Carty (n 1) 27–29, 166.
[23] Carty (n 3) 642.
[24] This is the general theme of Carty (n 1).

not appropriate to deride the courts as intransigent for failing to commit to one of them. It is rather that, at least read according to the conventional view, these cases present two impossibilities, neither of which can be accepted. If they appear as the only alternatives, then the only available choice is between unhappy courses of action: charging boldly down one or other route to be dragged back in the near future or hanging around somewhere near the intersection indecisively fudging. The law reports reveal a few bold charges and a great deal of indecisive fudging. But there may be a third way, a straight way, available to us, blocked only by our invalid assumptions.

B. General Function

What reason might be given to support that suggestion? We can begin to answer this question by returning to the conventional view's understanding of the function of the economic torts. Take, for instance, the claim that the economic torts 'should provide a failsafe device for the common law to prevent extreme competitive or economic behaviour, but the major role in the regulation of economic behaviour should be left to the State'.[25] What is *extreme* competitive or economic behaviour?

'Extreme' has two general and related meanings. It can mean distant from a central point, as in 'the Antarctic is at the extreme end of the earth'. Alternatively, it can mean immoderate, as in 'the cake is extremely rich' where that is intended as criticism, meaning that the cake is too rich. But there is also another more colloquial sense instantiated in the phrase 'she is an extremist' said of someone who is, say, an unrepentant Stalinist. This is not intended to mean that the subject is too much of a Stalinist, that she is immoderately Stalinistic. It means that she adopts a position that is distant from the central point of contemporary political thought *and* the utterance *takes for granted* that this position is inappropriate. Hence, the claim that someone is an extremist does not argue against that person's position; rather, it *assumes* that the position is unjustified. My claim is that the definition of the law's function now under examination appears to be informative because its form suggests that it utilises the second of these meanings when it in fact exploits the third. As a consequence of this, the definition is empty.

A defendant who commits an economic tort is not guilty of competing too much. The problem is that she competes in an illegitimate fashion.[26] In *Lumley v Gye*, for instance, the plaintiff's complaint was not that he was facing an inordinate level of competition from the defendant—it was that the defendant competed with him in a way that must not be allowed. The focus on illegitimate rather

[25] ibid v.

[26] In fact, as will become obvious, I do not regard competition as of the essence of these torts in any case.

than excessive competition is apparent from the structure of the relevant actions. Liability for inducing breach of contract requires the defendant to have procured a breach of the plaintiff's contract. Liability for causing loss by unlawful means requires the defendant to have acted illegally with respect to a third party.[27] The law is not looking to assess the overall amount of competition, it is not interested in immoderate competition; rather, it targets illegitimate kinds of behaviour.

That means that the definition is unhelpful. It maintains that the torts are aimed at 'extreme' competition. In this context, however, 'extreme' means illegitimate and the definition does not tell us why certain forms of competition are illegitimate and why some are not. Without an answer to this question, we cannot even begin to understand what these torts are all about.

The problem is made worse by the insistence that 'the major role in the regulation of economic behaviour should be left to the State'. In itself, this insistence is entirely legitimate, but it has the consequence that not all forms of illegitimate competition are or ought to be tortious. The difficulty is that we are not told which forms ought and which ought not. It should not be surprising, then, that the law is in the state that it is. We are told that the law's function is to prevent something vague, and we are then told that the law must not prevent too much of that vague thing as a considerable amount of that prevention must be left to the legislature. Is it any wonder that courts have disagreed fundamentally about the direction that the law should take and that we lack anything approaching certainty?

C. The Basis of Liability in Inducing Breach of Contract

Against the argument above, it is possible to maintain that it is wrong to look for a general theory of the economic torts. Instead, clarity should be sought through the attempt to understand each tort individually. That is a position to be taken seriously. The problem is that, as we will see, the conventional view fares no better when approached in this way. We begin with the tort of inducing breach of contract.

i. The Importance of Contract

It is sometimes argued that the tort of inducing breach of contract is justified because of the importance of contract in modern life.[28] As Carty points out, however, this explanation is inadequate.[29] There is no doubt that contracts are important. The problem is that the law offers no general protection for contract. It protects contracts only from certain kinds of invasions. Appeal to the importance

[27] In different ways, I will reject both of these requirements. The point, however, is that they belong to the conventional view and yet are inconsistent with that view.
[28] For discussion, see Carty (n 1) 56–58.
[29] ibid 60.

of contract cannot account for this. It could not seriously be argued that the tort of inducing breach of contract interferes as it does in order to protect contracts when and only when they are important.

In a similar vein, it has been argued that the law contains a tort of inducing breach of contract because contracts are an essential element of our economic system.[30] But as Carty again points out, this argument is insufficient as, for the reasons just examined, it cannot explain the form of protection found in the law. As Carty also notes, appeal to the economic system cuts both ways. Competition is also an essential part of that system, an argument that alone would suggest that there be no tort of inducing breach of contract.[31]

ii. Secondary Liability

According to the analysis presented in *OBG Ltd v Allan*, inducing breach of contract is a form of 'accessory liability, dependent upon the primary wrongful act of the contracting party'.[32] The idea is that, in procuring the third party's breach of contract with the plaintiff, the defendant becomes liable as an accessory to that breach.[33] But that cannot be right.

First, accessory or secondary liability is a notion most frequently discussed in the context of the criminal law. If a mafia boss procures a hit-man to kill a victim, then along with the hit-man the boss is guilty of the murder. As criminal lawyers stress, this form of liability does not involve the creation of new offences. Rather, it extends the scope of the existing offences, so that those who procure but do not perform the actus reus with the appropriate mens rea are guilty of the relevant crime. The mafia boss in the case above is not guilty of committing the offence of being an accessory to murder. He is guilty of murder, which he commits by being an accessory.[34] We need to see that this is analytic to the concept of secondary liability. If an accessory were liable for committing the offence of being an accessory,

[30] eg, J Danforth, 'Tortious Interference with Contract: A Reassertion of Society's Interest in Commercial Stability and Contractual Integrity' (1981) 81 *Columbia Law Review* 1491.

[31] An alternative is to maintain that these arguments show that the law is a compromise between protecting contract and permitting competition. But that argument gets us nowhere. Certainly, in some sense, the law must be a 'compromise' of this kind, but what we need to know is why it is the specific compromise that it is. We need to know why liability takes the form that it does and why it does not take other forms. Being told that it is a compromise is clearly inadequate in this regard.

[32] *OBG Ltd v Allan* (n 19) 20.

[33] This analysis is accepted by Carty (n 1) 24, 60–62. See also the wealth of material discussed by Carty here.

[34] So, for instance, A Ashworth and J Horder, *Principles of Criminal Law*, 7th edn (Oxford, Oxford University Press, 2013) 418 examine an example in which *D* provides a copy of a stolen key to *P*, knowing that *P* will use the key intending to commit rape (and theft). They remark: 'In this example, D may be convicted of rape, along with P. In the eye of the law … D [is] rightly labelled a sex offender. From the moment that D realizes that a rape is one of the offences that P will commit in the house, yet nonetheless assists P, D's conduct in providing the copy of the key is regarded as so tainted by the sexual nature of the offending that it assisted that D is regarded as justifiably convicted of rape itself, and not just of an inchoate offence such as assisting rape.'

then that form of liability would be primary, not secondary. The liability in question is secondary because it arises not for performing, but for procuring, the actus reus. The problem is that when we turn to inducing breach of contract, it is clear that this is not what happens.

If a defendant in an action for inducing breach of contract were liable as an accessory, then he would be liable as an accessory to the third party's breach of contract. The action would thus be the contractual action of breach of contract, not the tort of inducing breach of contract.[35] Accordingly, if this form of liability were secondary, this would show that we do not need this form of liability. It is a peculiar fact that this explanation for the tort of inducing breach of contract—perhaps now the dominant explanation—justifies only a different form of liability that is not recognised in law, and one that would make the tort it attempts to justify redundant.

What is more, if the liability in question were secondary, then it would have the same features as the corresponding primary liability, that liability being of course breach of contract. But that is not the law. For instance, breach of contract is actionable per se, but inducing breach of contract appears to require proof of damage.[36] Moreover, the damages payable by the defendant in an action for inducing breach of contract can differ from, and sometimes exceed, those payable by the third party in an action for breach of contract.[37] Again, this shows that the liability cannot be secondary.

It is important to see that no mere legal technicality prevents secondary liability from arising in this context. Contracts generate obligations only in the parties to the contract. Hence, the contract between the plaintiff and the third party does not bind the defendant. How, then, can the defendant be liable for inducing a breach of a contract that did not bind him? And even if we can find some wrongdoing here, how can that wrongdoing be to the plaintiff? Certainly, the defendant causes the third party to commit a wrong against the plaintiff, but it is a mystery how that wrong could be a wrong as between the defendant and the plaintiff. And if there is no such wrong, then why is the defendant being held liable to the plaintiff?

This feature of contract is frequently referred to as the privity rule. I will also use this label. However, it is important to state that, as used here, the rule maintains only that contracts do not generate obligations in third parties. I take no stand on the generation of rights in third parties.

Reflection on the consequences of the privity rule reveals that liability for inducing breach of contract is entirely unlike general secondary liability. Say that I hire a thug to beat you up and to vandalise your house. There should be no difficulty

[35] See also Stevens (n 1) 276.

[36] *Jones Brothers (Hunstanton) Ltd v Stevens* [1955] 1 QB 275 (CA); *Rookes v Barnard* [1964] AC 1129 (HL), 1212; *Greig v Insole* [1978] 1 WLR 302, 332; *Time Plan Education Group v NUT* [1997] IRLR 457 (CA); Carty (n 1) 44–45.

[37] Carty (n 1) 61.

saying that I am liable for battery and trespass.[38] You hold rights to your body and to your property against both the thug and me—they are multital. Just as the thug is bound, I too am bound not to damage your body or your house, an obligation that I violate when I get the thug to perform our agreement. In *Lumley v Gye*, however, while Wagner was under an obligation to perform for the plaintiff, that obligation was generated by their contract—it was paucital and *in personam*. It was not an obligation owed by the defendant. What obligation could the defendant have violated, then, when he induced Wagner not to perform for the plaintiff?

There is an unfortunate tendency to treat the privity rule as if it were itself a mere legal technicality. It is not. It is a deep moral principle. It is most important to be clear about this issue.

First, the issue is not about the outcomes of cases—real or hypothetical.[39] Commitment to the privity rule should not be taken to imply criticism of cases now thought to turn on an exception to that rule. In fact, Chapter 9 will support the outcomes of most of these cases. The issue is the nature and basis of the rule itself. The point is this. Any exception to the privity rule is a serious violation of the liberty of the effected party. This is because the exception can be understood only in one of two ways, each entirely immoral.

The first understanding holds that a contract imposes certain kinds of obligations on third parties to the contract, including of course the defendants in these cases. But this is unacceptable, as it allows the contracting parties unilaterally to impose obligations on others.[40] It means that I can place you under obligations that you do not currently have by forming an agreement with another person, binding you without obtaining your consent. This is a fundamental violation of your liberty.[41] It is no mere technical rule that holds this is to be impossible. The second understanding maintains that, though contracts impose no obligations

[38] In principle, it seems that this should be so, though positive law appears to be unclear on the matter. If it is not possible, that makes the view under examination even weaker.

[39] It seems to me that an argument of the following kind is often employed: 'Yes, (1) the privity rule seems right. However, (2) in this [real or hypothetical] case, it seems to me that the plaintiff ought to recover. (3) The only explanation for recovery I can think of requires a violation of the privity rule. Thus, (4) it can be justified to violate that rule.' One ought to be very suspicious of arguments of this kind. The more natural conclusion from (1) and (2) is that one has to think harder about (3): one must seek to justify liability without abandoning the privity rule. In general, lawyers seem altogether too willing to surrender principles in the face of difficult cases.

[40] Unilateral, that is, as between the holder of the obligation and the holder of the right. Contracts, of course, are never unilateral (in the relevant sense) as between the contracting parties. That too would be inconsistent with the basis of the privity rule.

[41] In Kantian terms, it is a violation of the principle of 'being one's own master', a direct consequence of the innate right. I Kant, *The Metaphysics of Morals*, M Gregor (trans) (Cambridge, Cambridge University Press, 1996) 6:237. This must be distinguished from a related issue. There are circumstances in which one may want to say that an obligation is generated between *A* and *B* where that obligation cannot be contractual *due to the doctrine of consideration*. In those circumstances, the best strategy may appear to be to hold that the obligation is a consequence of a contract between *B* and *C*. But those will be circumstances in which, but for the doctrine of consideration, there would be a contract between *A* and *B*. Unfortunately, the doctrine of consideration creates considerable conceptual confusion.

on third parties, those persons can nevertheless be found liable if they procure breaches of contract. This is perhaps even worse. Here we have the suggestion that defendants are found liable for performing actions that they were under no obligation not to perform, in fundamental violation of the rule of law and the principle of innocence.

Once we recognise the moral importance of the privity rule, it becomes apparent that liability for inducing breach of contract could never be justified as a form of secondary liability. The party who breaches the contract violates an obligation to ensure that the contract is performed. But it cannot follow that the defendant violates any obligation, because that obligation must be founded in the contract and the contract binds only the parties to it. The defendant cannot justly be liable as an accessory for procuring the breach of an obligation he did not have.

iii. A Right to Contractual Integrity

Alternatively, committed to taking the privity rule seriously, some have argued that an analogy exists between contract and property that explains the defendant's obligation to the plaintiff.[42] This position too received support in *OBG Ltd v Allan*, in which Lord Hoffmann maintained that the tort of inducing breach of contract 'treats contractual rights as a species of property which deserve special protection, not only by giving a right of action against the party who breaks his contract but by imposing … liability on a person who procures him to do so'.[43] Contradicting Lord Hoffmann's other view just examined, this implies that liability for inducing breach of contract is primary rather than secondary.

This theory can take one of two forms. The first holds that contracts automatically generate obligations in others not intentionally to interfere with their performance. The second maintains that individuals have a general right not to have their contractual rights interfered with. We examine these views in turn.

According to the first view, contract formation generates two sets of rights and duties. The first is familiar: rights and duties as between the parties to performance. We can call these first-order rights and duties. The view also maintains that contract formation creates rights in the parties to the contract itself and duties in third parties that the third parties not intentionally interfere with the performance of the contract. We will call these second-order rights and duties.

The fundamental problem with this account is that it asserts without explaining the existence of the second-order rights and duties. In that sense, it is not really a theory at all. In particular, while it is sometimes suggested that there is an analogy

[42] R Epstein, 'Inducement of Breach of Contract as a Problem of Ostensible Ownership' (1982) 16 *Journal of Legal Studies* 1; Stevens (n 1) 281. For criticism, see JW Neyers, 'The Economic Torts as Corrective Justice' (2009) 17 *Torts Law Journal* 1. For a view similar to the property theory, see R Bagshaw, 'Inducing Breach of Contract' in J Horder (ed), *Oxford Essays in Jurisprudence* (Oxford, Oxford University Press, 2000).

[43] *OBG Ltd v Allan* (n 19) 27.

between contract and property, there is no analogy that is relevant. It is true that, because contractual rights can be bought and sold (assigned), contracts are sometimes regarded as proprietary. In that sense, there is an analogy between contract and property. But the fact that contracts are sometimes treated as proprietary in this way does not show what we need to have shown: how it is that contracts generate the purported obligations in third parties. There are analogies between contract and property, but not useful ones.

To express this point more concretely, the reason you are not permitted to induce another to take my property proper is the same as the reason you cannot take it yourself: the property is mine. But precisely what is mine that is being taken from me by the defendant when she induces another to breach her contract with me? It cannot be the subject matter of the contract, because that is not mine.[44] Is it the contract itself? But that contract is not mine in the necessary sense, ie, it does not generate rights in me held against the defendant—or, at least, if it does generate those rights, we have not been shown how this occurs. This argument is examined further in the following section of this chapter.

Moreover, this first version of the theory does not respect the privity rule. This rule determines that contracts cannot impose obligations on third parties. The view under examination does not answer that challenge, it merely delineates the alleged obligation, labelling it in our jargon a second-order obligation. One cannot respond to an argument showing that *x* cannot exist merely by providing a name for *x*.

A third problem is that this version of the theory does not fit the law. The tort of inducing breach of contract does not respond to all intentionally caused breaches of contract. Imagine that you have contracted to purchase a piece of equipment from a third party. Knowing this, knowing how important the equipment is to you and wanting to run you out of business, I destroy the equipment. This prevents the third party performing the contract. Here, I have intentionally caused the breach and have done so in order to harm you, and I can be liable, but not for inducing breach of contract. If the alleged analogy between contract and property existed, however, the law would be different. This indicates that the posited second-order rights and obligations do not, in fact, exist.

We turn now to the second version of the theory. This account holds that contract formation generates only first-order rights and duties, the familiar rights and duties to performance. It additionally holds that, as a matter of the general law, individuals possess a right that others not intentionally interfere with the performance of their contracts. The difference between this view and the first is that this general right is understood not to be created by contracting, but to be possessed the moment one is born. Like the so-called right to bodily integrity, it is innate.

[44] Unless, of course, due to the operation of the Sale of Goods Act 1979 (UK) or the like, it was mine. In that case, however, the claim as against the defendant would be as an accessory to trespass, assuming that this is possible. If not, then there could be no liability here at all.

Thus, if *A* and *B* contract for *x*, then *C* gains an obligation not intentionally to interfere with *x*. That is not because the contract itself generates that obligation. It is because the contract gets 'tied up with' *A*'s and *B*'s general right not to have their contracts intentionally interfered with.

It is perhaps immediately apparent that this position is no better than the one just examined. Again, the fundamental problem is that the account is based on mere assertion. We are told that a general right exists without being given an explanation as to its existence.

Second, this version of the account also violates the privity rule. The first view does so because it holds that contract formation generates obligations in third parties. That generation violates the rule. Because it points to a general right, the second view does not have that difficulty. Its problem is rather that the alleged general right is itself inconsistent with the privity rule. Take this example. I contract with another to purchase a chattel. The first and second theories hold that the formation of the contract causes you to have an obligation that you did not before have: not to behave in a way that amounts to intentionally preventing this contract being performed. The first view runs afoul of the privity rule by insisting that this obligation is a product of the contract itself. The second view tries to avoid this by insisting that the obligation is generated by the fact of the contract in combination with a general right. But that only shifts the violation of the privity rule from the contract to the general right. Both views agree that contract formation imposes obligations on third parties. They disagree as to the mechanism of that imposition. That disagreement is irrelevant. The two theories under examination give different accounts of the purported mechanism by which the privity rule is violated.

The third problem is that the theory does not fit the law. That is revealed by the example above in which I destroy the equipment that you need. In that example, my action violates the alleged general right, but there is no liability for inducing breach of contract. Again, this indicates that there is no such general right.

Some may wish to respond to this difficulty by defining the general right more narrowly, by saying perhaps that the right in question is specifically that others do not induce a contract partner to breach. But this strategy is not only ad hoc, it is also unexplanatory. One cannot account for the tort of inducing breach of contract merely by positing a right delineated so that it fits the contours of the action. That is merely to translate the remedy into a right. In order to explain the action, it is necessary to reveal why precisely that right is recognised in law and show how it relates to other rights found in the law.[45]

[45] Thus, if we can account for the tort of inducing breach of contract by inventing a right to be free of inducement etc, then why can we not invent a right to be free of negligently caused economic loss? This point is well made in NJ McBride, 'Rights and the Basis of Tort Law' in A Robertson and D Nolan (eds), *Rights and Private Law* (Oxford, Hart Publishing, 2011). However, the argument is not well directed against the position taken in A Beever, *Rediscovering the Law of Negligence* (Oxford, Hart Publishing, 2007), which purports not to provide any justification of rights, but simply to take them as they are found in the law. To put this another way, *Rediscovering the Law of Negligence* was not intended to be theoretical in the manner of this book.

In fact, in general, both versions of the theory are unacceptably ad hoc. Given the problems generated by the privity rule and the general position that contractual rights and obligations are paucital only, it is difficult to avoid the impression that the posited rights in question are being devised merely because the existence of the action for inducing breach of contract would otherwise constitute an uncomfortable counter-example to the analyst's general theory.

iv. Targeting the Contract

A final suggestion takes seriously the notion that the defendant's actions must not only intentionally cause loss but must also intentionally induce the third party to breach. According to this view, liability is justified by the fact that the defendant treats the contract as property.[46] It may help to think of the matter in the following way.

A contract between me and another is mine and his. If you induce the other to breach the contract, then you are trying to take what is mine: the contract itself. You target my contract and try to take it for yourself. The reason liability follows on this picture is that, when the court treats the contract as if it were property, it does no more than treat the contract as the defendant treated it.[47] This is the only theory that generates an account of liability that fits the form of the tort of inducing breach of contract, but it faces three important difficulties.

First, in actual cases, it is very unlikely that the defendant will treat the contract as property or target the contract in the strong sense required. In *Lumley v Gye*, for instance, the defendant did not want *the contract* between Wagner and the plaintiff—he wanted Wagner to perform in his theatre. He may have wanted a contract with Wagner, but that is not the same as wanting Wagner's contract with the plaintiff. We may loosely say that he wanted that contract, but of course what we mean is that he wanted a different contract on the same terms. Thus, the defendant did not treat the contract between Wagner and the plaintiff as property. He treated it only as a nuisance, an obstacle to his getting what he wanted. Second, even when the defendant treats the contract as property, he is unlikely to treat it as property in the relevant sense—ie, as the kind of thing that generates multital rights. In fact, his intention to induce the breach would tend to indicate that he treated the contract as a thing generating only paucital rights. Third, it would not follow from the fact that the defendant treated the contract as property that the court ought to do the same.

I conclude simply that we do not know why we have a tort of inducing breach of contract.

[46] P Benson, 'Economic Loss' in D Owen (ed), *Philosophical Foundations of Tort Law* (Oxford, Oxford University Press, 1995) 455–57.

[47] There are clear affinities here with Kant's theory of punishment: Kant (n 41) 6:331–37.

D. The Basis of Liability in Causing Loss by Unlawful Means

We turn now to causing loss by unlawful means. As we will see, the conventional view fares no better in this context.

i. *Intentionally Causing Loss*

A remarkable feature of the conventional view is that its theorists rarely attempt to justify liability for causing loss by unlawful means. Carty's analysis is particularly noteworthy in this context. Under the heading 'Rationale', she argues that there should be no general liability for intentionally causing loss and examines the alternative understandings of unlawful means presented in *OBG Ltd v Allan*.[48] All that is valuable, but it is an argument about the rationale for restricting recovery and not for the tort itself.

Like many conventional theorists, Carty seems to be of the view that, all other things being equal, it is obvious that intentionally caused loss should be actionable. Intentionally caused loss should be actionable because it is loss intentionally caused. Of course, Carty does not believe that there should be liability for all intentionally caused loss, but that is because she thinks that all other things are not always equal. Of particular importance is the notion that competition is generally to be encouraged. Consequently, Carty supports the rule that only those who act illegally should be liable.

It is worth pausing to examine the structure of this view. First, it holds that a defendant is liable for causing loss by unlawful means because he caused loss intentionally. On the face of it, that would suggest that all intentionally caused loss should be actionable. But that would be inconsistent with the policy of encouraging competition. Hence, a control mechanism must be introduced in order to prevent liability undermining that policy.[49] The suggested control mechanism is that the defendant should be liable only if he acted illegally vis-a-vis the third party. This view was explicitly endorsed in *OBG Ltd v Allan*.[50]

The position is unsatisfying, however. It posits a rule and an exception to that rule, where the exception applies far more often than the rule itself. That is, at least, very odd. We do not say of a dedicated and generally healthy employee that he always stays home from work (rule) except when he is well (exception). We say that he always comes to work (rule) except when he is sick (exception). Likewise, we do not say of a loving father of well-behaved children that he always yells at his kids (rule) except when they have not been incredibly naughty (exception). We say that he only yells at his kids (rule) when they have been very naughty (exception). This is not arbitrary. We identify the characteristic behaviour by the rule and the

[48] Carty (n 1) 101–04.
[49] ibid 94.
[50] *OBG Ltd v Allan* (n 19) 74–75.

exceptional by the exception. In our examples, it is the rule that tells you about the character of the man—that he is a committed employee or a good father—the exception is just that: exceptional. What is so strange about the first of each pair of examples is that they present the exceptional behaviour as the norm and the characteristic behaviour as the exception.

It is remarkable, then, that the analysis of tort law frequently does just this. Consider, for instance, that the law of negligence is generally understood to consist of the general principle that one is responsible for the consequences of one's negligent behaviour coupled with a list of exceptions to that principle longer than both of your arms.[51] We are in a similar position here. In practice, the unlawful means exception does much more work than the intentionally caused loss rule. This surely indicates, at the very least, that our general conception of this law is on the wrong track. We have things backwards.

ii. Transferred Malice

An alternative account maintains that causing loss by unlawful means rests on the principle of transferred malice. According to this view, in a case of causing loss by unlawful means, the defendant is liable to the plaintiff because his wrongdoing with respect to the third party is transferred to the plaintiff.[52] Again, this doctrine is borrowed from the criminal law. It holds that, taking the crime of murder as our example, if *A* shoots a gun intending to kill *B*, but misses and instead strikes and kills *C*, *A* is guilty of murder. This is because, it is sometimes said, *A*'s malice with respect to *B* is transferred to *C*. This seems analogous to the law of tort in this respect.

That is not in fact the case. Transferred malice operates in the criminal law because that law is indifferent as to the identity of the victim. This is sometimes known as the impersonality doctrine.[53] For example, the actus reus of murder is killing someone and the mens rea requirement includes intending to kill someone. There is no requirement that the person killed be the person that the offender intends to kill. Thus, in our example, *A* performs the actus reus of murder by killing *someone* (*C*, it turns out) and has the necessary mens rea because he intended to kill *someone* (*B*, as it happens). Thus, 'impersonality' is a fundamental feature of these offences. In the criminal law, malice appears to be transferred because this impersonality is built into the structure of the offences. But actions in tort cannot be like this. They cannot be indifferent as to the identity of the victim

[51] I have examined this matter in detail in A Beever, 'Justice and Punishment in Tort: A Comparative Theoretical Analysis' in C Rickett (ed), *Justifying Private Law Remedies* (Oxford, Hart Publishing, 2008); and A Beever, 'Policy in Private Law: An Admission of Failure' (2006) 25 *University of Queensland Law Journal* 287.

[52] See J Eekelaar, 'The Conspiracy Tangle' (1990) 106 *Law Quarterly Review* 225, 226.

[53] J Horder, 'Transferred Malice and the Remoteness of Unexpected Outcomes from Intentions' [2006] *Criminal Law Review* 383, 383.

because here the victim is the plaintiff. I have dealt with this argument in more detail elsewhere.[54]

Moreover, even on the incorrect understanding of the criminal doctrine, it is the offender's intention that is transferred from the intended to the actual victim, from *B* to *C* in our example. Thus, this is sometimes known as the doctrine of transferred intent. But that cannot help here. If *D* commits a battery against *T* in order to cause loss to *P*, transferring *D*'s intention with respect to *T* to *P* makes no difference. The conclusion would be only that, for legal purposes, we can say that *D* intended to batter *P*. But as *D* did not perform the 'actus reus' of battery with respect to *P*, this cannot ground liability. What is more, if we transfer the entire wrongdoing—the 'mens rea' and the 'actus reus'—*D* would be liable to *P* for battery, not for causing loss by unlawful means.

Alternatively, one might say that it is the liability that is transferred. But that will not do. For one thing, why is it not the liability for battery that is transferred? How could talk of transference justify a separate tort of causing loss by unlawful means? For another, and most importantly, this is no longer a justification. Even if something were transferred, given the inability to rely on an informative analogy with the criminal law, we are missing the justification for why that should occur. In many ways, this theory is the mirror of the secondary liability theory of the tort of inducing breach of contract and it fails for many of the same reasons.

iii. A Justified Exception to the Privity Rule

Robert Stevens has argued that this form of liability constitutes an exception to the privity rule 'justified on the basis that it prevents [the defendant] from deliberately using others as means to his own ends'.[55] The view that the basis of liability in this area lies in preventing one person from using another as the means to his ends is to be endorsed. However, this notion cannot be utilised in quite the way that Stevens employs it. Specifically, there can be no justified exception to the privity rule.

It is first necessary to say that this privity rule is not the one examined above. It is the more general rule that a defendant can be liable to a plaintiff only if the defendant violated the plaintiff's rights. On Stevens' view, then, liability for causing loss by unlawful means involves an exception to this rule, because the defendant is found liable to the plaintiff without violating the plaintiff's rights. The notion is that the defendant is liable to the plaintiff because she used a third party as a means to injure the plaintiff.

However, while it is true that the defendant puts the third party to his ends in these cases, it is not clear why the appropriate response is not the normal one: providing the third party with an action against the defendant. After all, on this theory, it is the third party who has been used. This is all the more pertinent when

[54] A Beever, 'Transferred Malice in Tort Law?' (2009) 29 *Legal Studies* 400.

[55] Stevens (n 1) 188.

we remember that, on the conventional view that to this extent Stevens endorses, the defendant can be liable for causing loss by unlawful means only if he used unlawful means with respect to the third party. This means that the third party will often already have an action against the defendant. Why, then, is that insufficient? In the language of this privity rule, it is the third party's rights that have been violated, not the plaintiff's, so why is liability to the third party not enough?

Moreover, if we assume that there is an answer to that question, that must cause us to ask why allowing third parties (in this sense) an action against defendants is sufficient outside the law of causing loss by unlawful means. If we assume that the explanation for the tort of causing loss by unlawful means is that the plaintiff must be able to sue the defendant because the defendant used the third party as a means to the defendant's ends, then why cannot any plaintiff sue when these circumstances apply? For instance, if a defendant sexually abuses a person, why cannot affected others sue? Prevention of using others as a means to an end is too broad an explanation for this tort.

Another way of revealing this is to point out that, on this view, the requirement that the plaintiff suffer loss can be only an arbitrary, policy-based control mechanism. If the aim of the tort is to prevent the defendant putting the third party to his ends, then it cannot matter whether or not the plaintiff was caused loss.

A theory of this kind was advanced in the judgment of the Supreme Court of Canada in *AI Enterprises Ltd v Bram Enterprises*.[56] It is instructive to examine it in some detail.

Cromwell J, presenting the judgment of the Court, supported an approach which involves:

> [E]xtending an existing right to sue from the immediate victim of the unlawful act to another party whom the defendant intended to target with the unlawful conduct. I will call this the 'liability stretching' rationale. The focus of the tort on this understanding is not on enlarging the basis of civil liability, but on allowing those intentionally targeted by already actionable wrongs to sue for the resulting harm.[57]

A fundamental problem with this approach is that 'liability stretching' is a metaphor, the basis of which is never explained. *Contra* Cromwell J, it is a metaphorical description of what the Court is doing, not a rationale. Why should liability be 'stretched'?

Cromwell J maintained that this position leads to certainty and clarity.[58] This argues in favour of the approach vis-a-vis other possibilities, but it does not answer our question. His Honour contended that the position 'provides a rational explanation for the expansion of tort liability which rests on pre-existing causes of action',[59] but that is not correct. The question is why the defendant is liable

[56] *AI Enterprises Ltd v Bram Enterprises* (n 5).
[57] ibid [37].
[58] ibid [44]–[45].
[59] ibid [44].

to the plaintiff. That the defendant is potentially liable to the third party cannot answer that question. To put this another way, that there could be liability to the third party does not itself explain why the liability should be 'stretched' to cover the plaintiff.

His Honour also maintained that, according to this rationale, 'the tort does not seek to create new actionable wrongs but simply to expand the range of persons who may sue for harm intentionally caused by existing actionable wrongs to a third party'.[60] That cannot be correct. Without the tort, there would be an actionable wrong as between the defendant and the third party, but not one as between the defendant and the plaintiff. The need to recognise such a wrong is, of course, what this debate is all about. The tort recognises actionable wrongs that would otherwise not exist. If it did not, there would be no point in discussing it.[61]

What is more, all accept that the defendant's liability to the plaintiff does not, in fact, turn on the defendant's potential liability to the third party. As Cromwell J explains, in order to be liable, the defendant's 'conduct must be an actionable civil wrong or conduct that would be actionable if it had caused loss to the' third party.[62] Importantly, the torts that properly require loss do so because, in the absence of loss to the plaintiff, no wrongdoing has been done to that person. This means that the defendant can be liable to the plaintiff in circumstances in which there is no actionable wrong committed against the third party. Causing loss by unlawful means is not a form of stretched liability.

iv. Unlawful Means

One further difficulty with the conventional view must be noted. There is no shortage of disagreement as to what ought to constitute unlawful means for the purposes of this tort. One view holds that unlawful means should include only torts and breaches of contract. A wider view is prepared to extend this to equitable wrongs. An even more generous view would additionally include crimes and breaches of at least some statutory duties, or even any actions that the defendant was not at liberty to perform.[63] All of these positions are represented in the case law. Divergent views are found within *OBG Ltd v Allan* and between that case and

[60] ibid [45].

[61] An alternative reading of Cromwell J's claim here is that the actionable wrong is the behaviour of the defendant per se. On this view, the wrong is not interpersonal. It is not, for instance, a wrong to the third party or to the plaintiff. It is a wrong, full stop. The question then is this: given that the defendant committed a wrong, who should be able to sue for the consequences? This is the approach to wrongdoing adopted by Andrews J and rejected by Cardozo CJ and the majority in *Palsgraf v Long Island Railroad Co* 162 NE 99 (NY CA 1928). For my objections to this view, see Beever (n 45) 123–28; A Beever, *Forgotten Justice* (Oxford, Oxford University Press, 2013) 244–59. In this specific context, one pertinent point to make is that, *contra* Cromwell J, as this position aligns wrongdoing in tort with that in the criminal law, there seems no good reason to insist that criminal wrongdoing cannot count as unlawful means.

[62] *AI Enterprises Ltd v Bram Enterprises* (n 5) [26].

[63] For discussion, see Carty (n 1) 85–92.

Total Network. If the views examined above were genuinely informative, if they really did reveal the basis and character of liability, then they would help to resolve this debate. But they do not.[64]

It is probably accurate to say that most commentators on this issue would prefer unlawful means to be restricted to torts and breaches of contract, or perhaps to draw the net only a little wider. But stepping back from the cases for a moment will reveal how odd this position is. If the use of unlawful means against a third party can ground an action in the plaintiff as against the defendant, then why on earth should that unlawful means have to be a tort or a breach of contract? The most prevalent answer seems to be that if we do not impose this restriction, then we can imagine cases where liability will flow where that seems inapposite. But that again reveals just how far we are from a proper understanding of these torts. We know, or we think we know, what must be done, but we cannot properly explain why.

A more promising explanation holds that unlawful means must be restricted to at least civil liability because, as Cromwell J put it in *AI Enterprises Ltd v Bram Enterprises*, this tort stretches liability from the third party to the plaintiff:

> Thus, criminal offences and breaches of statute would not be *per se* actionable under the unlawful means tort, but the tort would be available if, under common law principles, those acts also give rise to a civil action by the third party and interfered with the plaintiff's economic activity.[65]

The first two objections to this view have already been canvassed. They are that we lack an explanation as to why liability ought to be stretched and that liability to the plaintiff does not depend on liability to the third party, as is revealed by cases in which the third party has no action because she suffered no loss (an additional example is examined below). A third difficulty is that this view cannot explain why liability is not stretched further than it is. Recall the case in which I stand outside your shop with a gun threatening to kill anyone who enters in an attempt to drive you out of business. Imagine that this causes loss to your customers, to you and to your suppliers, and that I was aware that this would happen. Most would agree that you and your customers have a cause of action, but that your suppliers do not. But why is this? In relation to the first two losses, Cromwell J maintained that: 'Allowing recovery for only one type of loss would leave the other loss uncompensated for no obvious reason. The liability stretching rationale, as I see it, justifies imposing liability in these circumstances.'[66] That is easy to accept. But what is the

[64] Stevens (n 1) 189–90, for example, supports the narrow view, but this cannot be said to follow from his general account of the tort.

[65] *AI Enterprises Ltd v Bram Enterprises* (n 5) [45].

[66] ibid [47].

reason for refusing to extend liability to the third type of loss: the loss suffered by the suppliers?[67]

Cromwell J's answer would be that I did not intentionally cause that loss in the sense of intention relevant to this area of the law: ie, I did not target the suppliers.[68] But why should the stretching be limited in that way? If we are prepared to stretch the defendant's liability from the customers to you, then why not to the suppliers? Why should stretching be limited by the defendant's intention?

The fundamental problem here—and with many of the theories we have examined—is that it is not sufficient to find an account of the law that merely *fits* the contours of liability. In even well-settled areas of law, there are an infinite number of theories that fit the law.[69] Similarly, there are an infinite number of possible theories for the orbits of the planets, an infinite number of theories that fit those orbits (eg, gravity, the planets are living beings who choose to orbit in the way they do, God likes ellipses and so places the planets on them, there is a harmony of the spheres etc). Theory must not merely fit the phenomenon to which it applies, it must also explain that phenomenon (and, in the legal context, it must also justify it). Cromwell J's position fits, but it does not explain. Moreover, in an area as messy as this, perfect fit is impossible and, given the level of disagreement that exists in this area, the extent to which fit is even desirable is unclear.

What is more, despite the ubiquitous insistence to the contrary, it is wrong to state that liability in causing loss by unlawful means requires unlawful means. Standardly, the defendants in these cases do nothing unlawful. They merely *threaten* to do something unlawful and the threat to do something unlawful is very frequently not itself unlawful.

The parties in *Rookes v Barnard*[70] were employees of the same employer. The defendants were officials in a union who wanted to preserve universal union membership at their place of work. The plaintiff refused to join the union. Consequently, the defendants successfully pressured their employer to terminate the plaintiff's employment. Crucial to the case are the following two facts. First, the employer's dismissal of the plaintiff was entirely legal. Thus, the plaintiff had no action for wrongful dismissal or the like against the employer. Second, the defendants exerted pressure by threatening to strike, though striking would have been a breach of the terms of their employment contract. The House of Lords ruled that the plaintiff was entitled to recover his resulting loss from the defendants.

[67] In fact, in speaking of types of losses, Cromwell J appears to intend to refer to categories of loss. Thus, in the actual example he examines, the third party suffers personal injury and the plaintiff economic loss, the position being that economic loss should also be recoverable in this area. But if that is so, then why not the economic losses of the suppliers?

[68] *AI Enterprises Ltd v Bram Enterprises* (n 5) [78].

[69] This will include, of course, an account that just listed all the operative cases. Incidentally, this helps to reveal the absurdity of the view that fit is the central criteria for the assessment of a theory, legal or otherwise.

[70] *Rookes v Barnard* (n 36).

The conventional view would have us understand that the defendants employed unlawful means vis-a-vis the company and that this explains, in part, why the defendants were liable to the plaintiff. But no such means were employed. The defendants threatened to strike; they did not strike. Likewise, in the case where I destroy your business, I commit the tort of causing loss by unlawful means against you when I turn up at your shop brandishing an AK-47, making your customers flee in fear for their lives. But the wrong does not stop when they have all left and I am no longer threatening anyone with an imminent battery—ie, no longer committing an assault or other civil wrong.

I conclude that the situation is no better than with respect to inducing breach of contract. We do not know why we have this tort either.

E. The Basis of Liability in Conspiracy

There is no need to examine the tort of conspiracy in this context. This is because, as we have seen, commentators generally hold that conspiracy is either to be explained identically as causing loss by unlawful means or cannot be explained. This again entails that we do not know why we have this tort. The orthodox position seems to be that we should not have it.

IV. Conclusion

I conclude that serious problems exist with the conventional view. No version of that theory presents a solid basis for understanding these torts. Thus, if we are to achieve clarity, certainty and understanding in this area, we will have to abandon the conventional approach and begin again. That is our task now.

9

Reconceptualising the Economic Torts

I. Reconceptualising the Wrongdoing

The previous chapter suggested that the fundamental problem with this area of the law is that we misunderstand the very nature of these torts and the wrongdoing to which they respond. If that is so, then it will help to put aside the case law and legal commentary for the moment and try to think about the issue anew. In that spirit, imagine the following case.

Imagine that 10 years ago you started a small business, say a store of some kind. With lots of hard work, you grew the business, establishing a valuable rapport with your local clientele. As a result, you achieved financial stability for yourself and your family. However, envious of your success and desiring to destroy your business, I threaten to kill anyone who enters your store. Somehow getting away with this, I succeed in driving you out of business. Your store is no more. A decade's work is down the drain. And you are destitute, forced to sell your family home so that you now live in cramped, substandard rental accommodation. You are currently unemployed and looking for work. This is exactly what I set out to achieve.

Some of the theories examined in the previous chapter hold that, in this and in similar cases, I wronged only your potential customers and that you are able to sue me only as the vicarious beneficiary of my wrong to them.[1] That cannot be right. It is surely clear that I wrong you. Other theories hold that the wrong I committed against you is causing you loss. That is not completely incorrect, but it is an entirely anaemic analysis of my misconduct. If this happened to you, you would feel that you had been utterly persecuted by me. Why, exactly? I submit that it is because I succeeded in gaining control over your life, directing it to disastrous ends.

The negative things that happened to you could have occurred by chance or through the operation of the market. Had that happened, you would no doubt feel despondent. You would not, however, feel persecuted. The difference between that case and our example, then, is not simply that in the example, you can locate me as

[1] This, of course, is an allusion to Cardozo CJ's claim that this cannot be possible in *Palsgraf v Long Island Railroad Co* 162 NE 99 (NY 1928) 100.

the constant cause of the unwanted events that happened to you, as the constant cause of your loss. The difference is that I brought those unwanted events about. I gained power over you. The wrong is not the causing of loss, it is coercion.

I submit that this is the key to understanding the economic torts. The wrongdoing with which they are concerned is coercion of the plaintiff by the defendant through another: indirect control. This coercion is not a violation of the plaintiff's property or contractual rights. It is a violation of the plaintiff's innate right.

The view advanced here is found in the case law. I will not pretend that it is dominant. The arguments in the case law are too confused to describe any view as dominant. But it is nevertheless significant that the position receives noteworthy judicial support. Consider, for instance, this passage from the judgment of Lord Lindley in *Quinn v Leathem*:

> The defendants were doing a great deal more than exercising their own rights: they were dictating to the plaintiff and his customers and servants what they were to do. The defendants were violating their duty to the plaintiff and his customers and servants, which was to leave them in the undisturbed enjoyment of their liberty of action.[2]

The defendants were exercising control over the plaintiff. Similarly, Lord Brampton said that the defendants engaged in 'an unlawful conspiracy *to molest the plaintiff*'.[3] Along the same lines, Lord Evershed spoke of threats that 'are sufficiently substantial and coercive to cause real damage to the person against whom they are aimed and directed' in *Rookes v Barnard*[4] and Lord Devlin remarked that: 'The essence of the offence is coercion.'[5]

The idea also lies behind the otherwise unhelpful suggestion that the defendants in these cases violate the plaintiffs' 'right to trade'. The suggestion seems unhelpful because it is clear that there can be no such right.[6] Moreover, in *Crofter Hand Woven Harris Tweed Co Ltd v Veitch*, Lord Wright said that the explanation for liability:

> [C]annot be merely that the appellants' right to freedom in conducting their trade has been interfered with. That right is not an absolute or unconditional right. It is only a particular aspect of the citizen's right to personal freedom, and like other aspects of that right is qualified by various legal limitations, either by statute or by common law.[7]

Interestingly, though, this rejection of the right to trade theory helps to explain why that theory has proven to be so attractive.[8]

[2] *Quinn v Leathem* [1901] AC 495 (HL), 536–37.

[3] ibid 525 (emphasis added).

[4] *Rookes v Barnard* [1964] AC 1129 (HL), 1182–83.

[5] ibid 1207.

[6] R Stevens, *Torts and Rights* (Oxford, Oxford University Press, 2007) 189.

[7] *Crofter Hand Woven Harris Tweed Co Ltd v Veitch* [1942] AC 435 (HL), 463.

[8] eg, *Mogul Steamship Co Ltd v McGregor Gow & Co* (1889) 23 QBD 598 (CA), 606–07; *Allen v Flood* [1898] AC 1 (HL), 14, 112–13, 155; *OBG Ltd v Allan* [2007] UKHL 21, [2008] 1 AC 1 (HL), 31, 74.

In the English Court of Appeal in *Mogul Steamship Co Ltd v McGregor Gow & Co*, quoting Sir William Erle, Lord Esher MR said that 'a person has a right to do as he chooses with his own, whether labour or capital, within the limits set by law; that a right involves a prohibition against the infringement thereof; and that a prohibition involves a remedy for the violation thereof'.[9] Though we must accept that there can be no such right, it is possible to think of things the other way around. What happens when this 'right' is 'violated'? The answer is that the defendant prevents the plaintiff doing 'as he chooses with his own, whether labour or capital, within the limits set by law'. Once more quoting Erle, Lord Esher went on to say that: 'Every person has a right under the law, as between him and his fellow-subjects to full freedom in disposing of his own labour or his own capital according to his own will.'[10] Again, though strictly there can be no such right, the idea is that a defendant who 'violates' this 'right' coerces the plaintiff. The defendant deprives the plaintiff of the ability to direct his life 'according to his own will'. Thus, though there can be no genuine right to trade strictly speaking, the notion can be understood in the light of the theory presented here. The 'right to trade' is an aspect of the innate right.

II. Revisiting *Allen v Flood* and *Quinn v Leathem*

One may be inclined to reply to this line of argument by maintaining that while the theory under examination is supported by the judgments of some leading interventionists such as Lord Lindley in *Quinn v Leathem*,[11] it receives little support from the abstentionists. Therefore, the theory is wedded to one side of the traditional debate and, one might say, the wrong side.

However, in reality, there is no evidence of a split between abstentionists and interventionists in *Allen v Flood*[12] and *Quinn v Leathem*. In fact, it is plausible to attribute this division only to the Courts in *OBG Ltd v Allan*[13] and *Revenue and Customs Commissioners v Total Network SL*,[14] and it is arguable that it is inappropriate even there. The abstentionist/interventionist divide is a creature of modern legal analysis.

Let us return to *Allen v Flood* and *Quinn v Leathem*. Three judges sat on both Courts: Lords Halsbury, Macnaghten and Shand. Dissenting, Lord Halsbury found

[9] *Mogul Steamship Co Ltd v McGregor Gow & Co* (n 8) 607, quoting W Erle, *The Law Relating to Trade Unions* (London, Macmillan & Co, 1869) 13.

[10] *Mogul Steamship Co Ltd v McGregor Gow & Co* (n 8) 607, quoting Erle (n 9) 12.

[11] *Quinn v Leathem* (n 2).

[12] *Allen v Flood* (n 8).

[13] *OBG Ltd v Allan* (n 8).

[14] *Revenue and Customs Commissioners v Total Network SL* [2008] UKHL 19, [2008] 1 AC 1174 (HL).

for the plaintiffs in *Allen v Flood*. Unsurprisingly, he also found for the plaintiff in *Quinn v Leathem*. (However, he found for the defendants in *Mogul Steamship*.) More significantly, Lords Macnaghten and Shand were with the majority in *Allen v Flood* and did not dissent in *Quinn v Leathem*. They found for the defendants in the first case and the plaintiff in the second. This undercuts the notion that *Quinn v Leathem* represented a rejection of the decision in *Allen v Flood*. That is not how the judges who decided these cases saw things or how things were understood for a considerable time afterwards.[15] In order to fully understand why this is, it is necessary to examine *Allen v Flood* in some detail.

The plaintiffs were shipwrights who worked for the Glengall Iron Company. They were employed on a day-to-day basis and were therefore able to be discharged at any time. Other employees of the Company, ironworkers, who worked under similar arrangements, objected to the plaintiffs' employment on industrial grounds. These employees told the defendant, a delegate of the ironworkers' union, that they would cease to work for the Company unless the plaintiffs were discharged. The defendant passed this information to the Company's manager, who, dependent on the ironworkers, discharged the plaintiffs at the end of the day.

Following Lord Watson's judgment in the case, analysis focuses on the notion that the plaintiffs failed for the following reasons. First, there could be no action for inducing breach of contract because, as the plaintiffs were employed on a day-to-day basis, no contract was breached. Second, there was no action for causing loss by unlawful means because, as the ironworkers were also employed on a day-to-day basis, no breach of contract was threatened and thus no unlawful means were employed.

I will not now dispute the soundness of these rules. We will return to this matter later in this chapter. The difficulty here is that this interpretation of the decision is too narrow. It focuses on only a small, though important, element of the case and it gives undue prominence to the judgment of Lord Watson. Again, the contention is not that this judgment is unimportant. It is that it is not the only important judgment.

Lord Watson's judgment is the most influential because it is the most precise. It comes the closest to laying down clear rules. That is why those sympathetic to the abstentionist view are so impressed with it. But this precision is matched by the judgment's failure to provide any justification for the rules it prescribes.[16] And that is why those sympathetic to the interventionist view are so unconvinced by it. Let us spread our net more widely.

[15] eg, *Quinn v Leathem* (n 2) 506–07 (Earl of Halsbury LC), 508 (Lord Macnaghten), 514 (Lord Shand), 523–25 (Lord Brampton), 533–34 (Lord Lindley); *Crofter Hand Woven Harris Tweed Co Ltd v Veitch* (n 7) 474 (Lord Wright).

[16] I intend this claim literally. My eyes, at any rate, can detect no justification for his approach whatsoever in Lord Watson's judgment.

The House of Lords in *Allen v Flood* decided 6:3 in favour of the defendant. Eight judges were also asked to assist the House. Remarkably, they came out 6:2 in favour of the plaintiffs. Is this evidence of the clash between the abstentionist and interventionist views? It is not. As Lord Brampton said in *Quinn v Leathem*,[17] the split in *Allen v Flood* was mostly down to differing interpretations of the facts. Take, for instance, the description of Lord Shand, arguing in favour of the defendant:

> The fact is that the defendant was not actuated by malice towards the plaintiffs, in anything he said or did, in his communications with the employers, taking that word in its popular and ordinary sense, as meaning personal ill-will. He did not even know the plaintiffs. He came on the scene only because he was sent for by the boiler-makers, and he acted only officially as their delegate and representative.
>
> If anything is clear on the evidence, it seems to me to be this—that the defendant was bent, and bent exclusively, on the object of furthering the interests of those he represented in all he did—that this was his motive of action, and not a desire, to use the words of the learned judge, 'to do mischief to the plaintiffs in their lawful calling'.[18]

On this reading of the facts, the defendant was not trying to injure the plaintiffs. He was merely reporting the intentions of others to the Company. All he was doing was telling the truth, passing on important information that the Company needed to know. His actions were therefore to be commended.[19]

The majority came to this conclusion in part because they viewed the defendant more as an individual than as a representative of the union. Thus, Lord James maintained that the plaintiffs would have been better off pursuing the ironworkers.[20] This is an important point, because it indicates that those judges who adopted this view cannot have accepted Lord Watson's position. As we have seen, according to Lord Watson, the plaintiffs failed because of the absence of illegality (breach of contract or unlawful means vis-a-vis third parties). In this respect, the ironworkers were in precisely the same position as the defendant. On Lord Watson's view, then, if the defendant could not be liable, then nor could the ironworkers. But that was not the view taken by the others in the majority. This reveals that their reason for denying liability was not the absence of illegality—it was because, in their view, the defendant had behaved responsibly. That may not have been true of the ironworkers and that is why the plaintiffs may have succeeded had they pursued those persons. This is a quite different position from Lord Watson's.

If the majority found that the defendant's action should be described as responsibly informing the Company about the intentions of third parties, the dissenters took a completely different view. They found that the defendant threatened the Company in order to damage the position of the plaintiffs. The dissenters came

[17] *Quinn v Leathem* (n 2) 523.
[18] *Allen v Flood* (n 8) 162–64.
[19] For other clear statements of this view, see ibid 148 (Lord Macnaghten), 177–78 (Lord James).
[20] ibid 178.

to this conclusion in part because they were prepared to view the defendant as the spokesperson for and representative of the ironworkers.[21] This is also why the majority of the assisting judges favoured the plaintiffs' position. They were asked to proceed on the basis that the plaintiffs' version of the facts was correct.[22]

Thus, the dissenters and the majority of the assisting judges found for the plaintiffs because they felt that the defendant had acted coercively. But the majority of the House of Lords felt that the defendant did no such thing. This is what the division on the Court was about. It was not about abstentionist versus interventionist policy preferences—it was about different interpretations of the facts.

We now turn to *Quinn v Leathem*. The plaintiff prepared meat for a butcher with the help of men who were not members of a union. The defendants, opposed to the plaintiff's use of non-union labour, informed the butcher that union members upon whom the butcher relied would cease work if he continued to deal with the plaintiff. In an attempt to defuse the stand-off, the plaintiff offered to pay the men's fees so that they could join the union. This was rejected, however, and the defendants' threat was sufficient to cause the butcher (legally) to break off his relationship with the plaintiff.

The judges were convinced that this case was entirely different from *Allen v Flood*.[23] Why? Because here the defendants were trying to strike at the plaintiff. They were trying to control the way in which he ran his business. This explains the significance of the fact that the defendants had rejected the plaintiff's offer. That rejection showed that the defendants were not merely seeking to protect their position—allowing the workers to join the union at the plaintiff's expense would have been sufficient for that. Rather, the defendants were looking to punish the plaintiff for employing non-union labour. Their act was coercive.

This is what *Allen v Flood* and *Quinn v Leathem* really stand for. They are not rightly understood as competitors. On the contrary, as Lord Wright said in *Crofter*, *Quinn v Leathem* 'was in fact the complement of *Allen v Flood*'.[24] The theory that underlies both cases is the one presented here.

III. The Elements of Causing Loss by Unlawful Means

We turn now to examine the individual tort of causing loss by unlawful means in detail. The aim is to show that the theory advanced here provides a powerful explanation of the structure of this tort.

[21] See especially ibid 74–75, 80–81, 84–85 (Lord Halsbury LC), 112–14 (Lord Ashborne), 155–57 (Lord Morris).

[22] *Quinn v Leathem* (n 2) 523.

[23] ibid 506–07 (Earl of Halsbury LC), 508 (Lord Macnaghten), 514 (Lord Shand), 523–25 (Lord Brampton), 533–34 (Lord Lindley).

[24] *Crofter Hand Woven Harris Tweed Co Ltd v Veitch* (n 7) 474.

A. Causation

In order to be liable, a defendant must cause harm to the plaintiff. This is readily explicable. The tort deals with coercion of the plaintiff through another. As the coercion is via the medium of other persons, a plaintiff who suffers no loss cannot have been coerced.

Take the example in which I set out to destroy your business by threatening to kill those who enter your shop. If, at the moment I decided to do this, you independently decided instead to sell online so that my actions have no effect on you, then you are not coerced. My attempt to coerce you has failed.

B. Intention

Only a defendant who intends harm to the plaintiff will be liable. This has frequently been interpreted as a requirement that the defendant must target or aim at harm to the plaintiff, a view that Hazel Carty in particular has supported.[25] In *OBG Ltd v Allan*, however, Lord Hoffmann adopted a different approach that focused on means and ends.[26] It has been argued that this view is both unmotivated and unfortunate.[27]

The view that targeted harm is required is supported in some case law,[28] but it is not the dominant view. As Carty herself notes:

> Lord Watson in *Allen v Flood* noted that liability would ensue where the defendant had used illegal means 'directed against' the claimant. This was applied by the majority of the Court of Appeal in *National Phonographic Ltd v Edison Bell*[29] … In *Lonrho v Fayed*,[30] Dillon LJ asserted that liability could arise where fraud on a third party was 'aimed specifically at the plaintiff', it having been conceded by the claimant that he must prove that the unlawful act 'was in some sense directed against' him or intended to harm him. Ralph Gibson LJ in the same case supported the narrower view of intention, alluding to the requirement that the conduct be 'directed against' the claimants …
>
> Overall, paraphrasing Ralph Gibson LJ in *Lonrho v Fayed*, the intention provides the sufficient 'nexus' between the means employed and the harm caused to the claimant. The fact that the claimant is the defendant's target (for whatever reason) was seen as important: as Lord Lindley noted in *Quinn v Leathem* 'the intention to injure the plaintiff … disposes of any question of remoteness of damage'.

[25] eg, H Carty, *An Analysis of the Economic Torts*, 2nd edn (Oxford, Oxford University Press, 2010) 80–82.

[26] *OBG Ltd v Allan* (n 8) [62].

[27] eg, Carty (n 25) 79–84.

[28] eg, *Mainstream Properties v Young* [2006] QB 125 (CA).

[29] *National Phonographic Ltd v Edison-Bell* [1908] 1 Ch 335 (CA).

[30] *Lonrho v Fayed* [1990] 2 QB 479 (CA).

> And indeed, some Commonwealth decisions mirror this narrow view of intention: Cooke J in the New Zealand Court of Appeal decision in *Van Camp Chocolates Ltd v Aulsebrooks Ltd*[31] asserted that this tort required deliberate interference … In *Cheticamp Fisheries Co-operative v Canada*[32] the Court of Appeal of Nova Scotia asserted that the harm must be 'directed at the plaintiff'.[33]

In the light of what has gone before, we can see that these comments do not support the view that the defendant must target *the harm* to the plaintiff. Rather, they support the notion that the defendant must target the plaintiff, which he does by attempting to cause the plaintiff harm. The difference here is small and usually insignificant, but it is crucial for our purposes. Causing loss is not the key to understanding this tort. Nor is the tort about responding to caused loss per se. It is about responding to wrongdoing achieved by causing loss. The required intention is to target the plaintiff, to attempt to exercise control over that person. This is achieved by causing loss, but it is the control that matters and not the loss itself. The loss is either the mechanism by which the coercion is achieved or at least partly constitutes that coercion.

In *OBG Ltd v Allan*, Lord Hoffmann said:

> A defendant may intend to harm the claimant's business either as an end in itself or as a means to an end. A defendant may intend to harm the claimant as an end in itself where, for instance, he has a grudge against the claimant. More usually a defendant intentionally inflicts harm on a claimant's business as a means to an end. He inflicts damage as the means whereby to protect or promote his own economic interests.[34]

In these cases, the defendant has the requisite intention. However:

> Lesser states of mind do not suffice … In particular, a defendant's foresight that his unlawful conduct may or will probably damage the claimant cannot be equated with intention for this purpose. The defendant must intend to injure the claimant. This intent must be a cause of the defendant's conduct.[35]

This is at once an improvement on the targeted harm approach and misses the mark in the same way as that approach.

The issue is surely not whether the defendant intended *the harm* as an end or as a means to an end. What could the significance of that be? The defendant does not wrong the harm. The issue is whether the defendant used the plaintiff as a means to his ends. So, while Lord Hoffmann was wrong to focus on the harm, his appeal to means and ends is enlightening. It helps to reveal that the issue is whether the defendant's intentions were such that the plaintiff was used as a means to the defendant's ends. The harm must be either the mechanism by which the coercion

[31] *Van Camp Chocolates Ltd v Aulsebrooks Ltd* [1984] 1 NZLR 354 (CA).
[32] *Cheticamp Fisheries Co-operative v Canada* (1995) 123 DLR 121 (Nova Scotia CA).
[33] Carty (n 25) 80–82 (citations omitted).
[34] *OBG Ltd v Allan* (n 8) 57.
[35] ibid.

is achieved (a 'means to an end' in Lord Hoffmann's language) or must at least partly constitute that coercion (an 'end in itself').

That the loss could be foreseen is insufficient because in cases where the loss is merely foreseeable, the defendant will not have used the plaintiff as a means to his ends. He will merely have caused the plaintiff loss. Recall again our initial example, but imagine now that I have no desire to injure you—I merely hate having shoppers in my neighbourhood. In this case, you may well feel resentful of my actions and believe that I should be stopped (as I will be), but you will not feel that I am persecuting you. This is because my actions are directed at the shoppers and not at you. Though the material effect on you is identical, I do not take control of your life. I do not coerce you.

This is also the appropriate way to deal with the pizza delivery example examined in *OBG Ltd v Allan*[36] and *Total Network*.[37] The case imagines a company that swallows the market share of its rivals by delivering faster as a result of instructing its drivers to run red lights. Though this behaviour is illegal, all agree that the company cannot be liable to its competitors. According to Lord Walker in *OBG Ltd v Allan*, the example reveals the importance of ensuring that the correct control mechanisms are in place to prevent liability getting out of hand.[38] According to Lord Mance in *Total Network*, the example shows that unlawful means must be appropriately delimited.[39] Neither view can be right. This pizza delivery business does not wrong its competitors. It does not coerce them. It does not attempt to control the way that they do business. It is not using its competitors as means to its ends. That is why there is no liability.

As is often pointed out, competitors intend to cause their rivals loss. And, indeed, they often target certain kinds of loss. They intend harm to another as a means to the realisation of their self-interest. For instance, television programmers routinely attempt to entice sought-after demographics away from their competitors and draw up detailed plans to do so. We will never understand this area of the law if we adopt theories according to which this is prima facie wrongful, though immune from liability because of control mechanisms. These actions are not even prima facie wrongful.

In general, we must recognise that competition is an inescapable aspect of the human condition. No non-utopian theory can hold it to be even prima facie wrongful. Intentionally causing loss to others is the unpreventable consequence of living a life with one's eyes open to the results of one's actions.[40]

[36] ibid 74.

[37] *Revenue and Customs Commissioners v Total Network SL* (n 14) 1259.

[38] *OBG Ltd v Allan* (n 8) 74.

[39] *Revenue and Customs Commissioners v Total Network SL* (n 14) 1259.

[40] I am not advancing the view that modern capitalism is natural. Of course it is not. It is the creature of modern modes of production and regulatory systems of various kinds. But the point is that competition itself is not introduced into the world by this. On the contrary, modes of production and regulation merely channel competition into certain forms.

Imagine that during the school holidays, a boy decides that he wants to operate a lemonade stand on the street outside his house in order to save for a new bicycle. The girl who lives in the neighbouring house sees this and decides to emulate him. Her lemonade tastes better and she causes him loss. Why can she do this? Because she is living her own life. But things are different if she sets up shop in order to gain control over her neighbour's life, in order to harm him, for instance, as revenge for teasing her about her freckles. Then her actions are coercive and she can be stopped.

This discussion provides us with the necessary materials to answer a potential difficulty. The difficulty is this. Chapter 4 noted that intention in the law of trespass encompasses what criminal lawyers refer to as intention and recklessness (and that US tort law ought to do so). It is apparent, however, that intention is defined differently in this area of the law.[41] The question, of course, is why? The answer is that, while intention plays the same role in the two areas of the law, the different factual circumstances relevant to these torts means that, in order to fulfil that function, the intention requirement must change.

The function of the intention requirement is to determine whether the defendant had the state of mind necessary to have exerted control over the plaintiff. In trespass, because the control is direct in the sense of being unmediated by third parties, even recklessness is sufficient. But here, because the control is achieved through another, recklessness is not enough. Rather, as we have seen, the defendant must have the control as his goal. In fact, then, this shows that intention in this context is defined more narrowly than it is in the criminal law. Here, intention is identified only with purpose.

C. Motive and Intention

This understanding of intention is sure to attract criticism. It seems flatly inconsistent with that most sacred aspect of the abstentionist view: the insistence that liability cannot turn on the motive of the defendant. I argue now that, to the extent that this inconsistency is real, the insistence must be abandoned.

The plaintiff in *Bradford v Pickles*[42] owned land containing water springs that for more than 40 years had supplied the town of Bradford with water. The defendant owned land on a higher level than the plaintiff. Under the defendant's land was a natural reservoir and water flowed from this reservoir to the plaintiff's springs. The defendant sank a shaft into his land in order to alter the flow of the water, seriously reducing the amount of water that flowed into the springs. He did so not in order to provide any direct benefit to himself, but so as to deprive the plaintiff of water in order to come to a beneficial financial arrangement with the town.

[41] eg, *OBG Ltd v Allan* (n 8) [62].
[42] *Bradford v Pickles* [1895] AC 587 (HL).

The plaintiff insisted that this was malicious and hence that it was entitled to an injunction.

The House of Lords disagreed. Lord Watson said that: 'No use of property, which would be legal if due to a proper motive, can become illegal because it is prompted by a motive which is improper or even malicious.'[43] This view was also echoed in *Allen v Flood*, where his Lordship said that 'the law of England does not, according to my apprehension, take into account motive as constituting an element of civil wrong'.[44]

But it is also significant that Lord Halsbury, who dissented in *Allen v Flood* and wrote the leading judgment in *Quinn v Leathem*, also found for the defendant in *Bradford v Pickles*. After deciding that the plaintiff had no case absent the allegation of malice, Lord Halsbury LC said:

> The only remaining point is the question of fact alleged by the plaintiffs, that the acts done by the defendant are done, not with any view which deals with the use of his own land or the percolating water through it, but is done, in the language of the pleader, 'maliciously'. I am not certain that I can understand or give any intelligible construction to the word so used. Upon the supposition on which I am now arguing, it comes to an allegation that the defendant did maliciously something that he had a right to do. If this question were to have been tried in old times as an injury to the right in an action on the case, the plaintiffs would have had to allege, and to prove, if traversed, that they were entitled to the flow of the water, which, as I have already said, was an allegation they would have failed to establish.
>
> This is not a case in which the state of mind of the person doing the act can affect the right to do it. If it was a lawful act, however ill the motive might be, he had a right to do it. If it was an unlawful act, however good his motive might be, he would have no right to do it. Motives and intentions in such a question as is now before your Lordships seem to me to be absolutely irrelevant.[45]

Notice that, though *Bradford v Pickles* was not such a case,[46] Lord Halsbury recognised that in appropriate cases, the intention or motivation of a defendant can determine whether the plaintiff's rights were violated. Compare this with Lord Watson's view in *Allen v Flood*:

> Any invasion of the civil rights of another person is in itself a legal wrong, carrying with it liability to repair its necessary or natural consequences, in so far as these are injurious to the person whose right is infringed, whether the motive which prompted it be good,

[43] ibid 598.

[44] *Allen v Flood* (n 8) 92.

[45] *Bradford v Pickles* (n 42) 594.

[46] In *Bradford v Pickles* (ibid), the defendant's motive was irrelevant because he was using only his own land. As long as one does not interfere with the more fundamental rights of another, one is entitled to use one's land as one chooses (A Beever, *The Law of Private Nuisance* (Oxford, Hart Publishing, 2013)). But in the cases under examination, the defendant is alleged to have used the plaintiff—to have put the plaintiff to his own purposes. And in that context, motive in the relevant sense is crucial. One puts another to one's purposes only if one has the relevant kinds of motivation/intention.

> bad, or indifferent. But the existence of a bad motive, in the case of an act which is not in itself illegal, will not convert that act into a civil wrong for which reparation is due.[47]

Despite possible appearances, Lord Watson and Halsbury did not disagree; rather, they spoke of different things.

Lord Halsbury discussed the defendant's intentions. In *Bradford v Pickles*, because the defendant was using his own land, his intentions were irrelevant. But intentions are clearly relevant in other cases, most obviously in the 'intentional torts'. Lord Watson, on the other hand, was asking whether the fact that the defendant's intentions or motivations were considered improper could ground liability. He quite rightly said that it could not. When an intention grounds liability, it does so because it shows that the defendant performed an action that violated the plaintiff's rights. It does not ground liability because it is regarded independently as bad—ie, independent of the plaintiff's rights—as unethical, socially undesirable and the like. A defendant who intentionally touches a plaintiff who has not consented is guilty of battery because the intention reveals that he put the plaintiff to his purposes without that person's consent. It is not because the touching was innocent per se, but was performed with an intention separately judged to be bad. Likewise, a defendant who intentionally causes loss to another in the way examined in this chapter is liable because his intention reveals that he put that person to his purposes, not because his intention is independently appraised negatively. In Lord Watson's sense, motive is irrelevant. In Lord Halsbury's sense, motive is routinely relevant. It is that sense of motive employed here.

IV. Unlawful Means

We have now uncovered the most fundamental difference between the conventional view and the one presented here. The latter maintains that liability is premised on the defendant's exercise of control over the plaintiff through another, a control that is achieved by intentionally causing the plaintiff loss. On this view, intentionally caused loss is necessary but not sufficient for liability. Most importantly, liability is meaningfully delineated in accordance with the understanding of wrongdoing just discussed. There is no need for any policy-based control mechanisms.

On the other hand, because the conventional view focuses on loss for its own sake, it cannot reach the same conclusions. Because it holds both that those who intentionally cause loss ought to be liable in principle and that unrestricted liability for intentionally caused loss is intolerable, the conventional view cannot provide a coherent understanding of the law. Instead, it posits a principle that is far

[47] *Bradford v Pickles* (n 42) 598.

too broad and then introduces policy based control mechanisms inconsistent with that principle. The practical consequence of the fact that the conventional view's principle is too broad is that that law has been forced to place a great deal of emphasis on these control mechanisms. Because of this, they seem to constitute the essence of the law.

Thus, it was once thought that the action we now know as causing loss by unlawful means was concerned only with injury to trade. That rule is now recognised as an unnecessary control mechanism. Today, the crucial mechanism is, of course, the requirement that the defendant has engaged in unlawful means. It is interesting to note that Carty refers to this requirement as the 'magic' of the tort.[48] I cannot claim certainty as to what this was intended to mean, but I do agree that it is unreal. In fact, there are five serious problems with the requirement.

The first is the point noted in Chapter 8: there is both widespread disagreement as to what constitutes unlawful means and no principled way of settling that dispute. The reason for this is that there is no principled basis for the requirement.

The second problem has also already been noted in Chapter 8. It is that, despite official doctrine, unlawful means are not necessary for liability. In short, the tort of causing loss by unlawful means does not require unlawful means. It is uncontroversial that the threat of unlawful means can be sufficient, even if it is not itself unlawful. The reason for this is that when unlawful means are threatened, it is usually the case that the defendant is trying to exert control over the plaintiff. The threat is part of the attempt to achieve this control. But what is important is the control, not the unlawful means. Thus, as discussed in Chapter 8, the defendants did not employ unlawful means in *Rookes v Barnard*,[49] but were nevertheless liable because they exercised control over the plaintiff.

A similar case is *AI Enterprises Ltd v Bram Enterprises*, recently heard by the New Brunswick Court of Appeal[50] and the Supreme Court of Canada.[51] The parties possessed interests in a building controlled by a syndication agreement. This agreement included a clause stating that, in circumstances that in fact obtained, the property would be marketed to the public and sold. The defendants, however, sought to block any sale. They filed a notice of right of first refusal on the title, initiated arbitration proceedings, registered liens against title and refused entry to the plaintiffs for inspection by prospective purchasers. In consequence of this activity, two lucrative sales failed to close, causing loss to the plaintiffs.

For our purposes, the fundamental difficulty for the plaintiffs was that 'No one has been able to identify a sustainable cause of action upon which' a third party would have been able to sue the defendants.[52] In other words, there was no

48 Carty (n 25) 84, 86, 104.
49 *Rookes v Barnard* (n 4).
50 *AI Enterprises Ltd v Bram Enterprises* 2012 NBCA 33, (2012) 350 DLR (4th) 601.
51 ibid.
52 ibid [8].

unlawful means. However, the Court of Appeal held that 'principled exceptions'[53] to the unlawful means rule ought to be recognised and:

> [T]he facts of the present case warrant exceptional treatment … the intentional erection of legal barriers, some of which are enforceable through statutory processes not subject to prior judicial authorization, in circumstances where those barriers rest on rights fabricated with arguments of sand, warrants redress under the tort of unlawful means … Alan Schelew's manipulation of, and reliance on, the syndication agreement provided him with a convenient pretext for opposing any sale, and with access to self-help mechanisms that were effective in interfering with the respondents' exercise of their contractual right to negotiate and sell to a third party.[54]

In other words, despite there being no unlawful means used in this case, the defendants nevertheless must be liable because Schelew's actions amounted to an illegitimate exercise of power over the plaintiff.

The Court of Appeal attempted to downplay its departure from the conventional view by describing its position as committed to the unlawful means rule per se, though prepared to acknowledge 'principled exceptions'. As the passage advancing this view is somewhat humorous—in the way that, say, the sinners' self-justifications in *The Divine Comedy* can be humorous—it is worth repeating here:

> It seems to me that the Supreme Court of Canada typically eschews the formulation of rules or frameworks which do not admit exceptions. The question is whether one is prepared to trade off some certainty for some flexibility in the law. In my view, judges need 'wiggle room' if they are going to adequately respond to unanticipated factual scenarios or changing circumstances. A legal requirement that unequivocally states that no action for unlawful interference is sustainable unless the impugned action is independently actionable does not provide the necessary flexibility.[55]

This exercise in camouflage cannot disguise the fact that the called for 'wiggle room' and 'flexibility' are required precisely because unlawful means is not, in fact, properly a necessary condition for liability. To put this another way, the 'exception' can only genuinely be 'principled' if it is not really an exception.

The problem with creating exceptions was recognised by Cromwell J in the Supreme Court.[56] However, that Court chose to reassert the conventional view, holding that, as the defendants committed no tort against any third party, the defendants could not be liable in this tort to the plaintiffs.

The Court nevertheless found the defendants liable to the plaintiffs. They held that Schelew was a fiduciary of the plaintiffs and breached the duties he owed to them.[57] This was very 'convenient' and, from the legal theorist's perspective, rather

[53] ibid [82].

[54] ibid.

[55] ibid [81].

[56] 'My difficulty with the 'principled exception' approach is that I cannot, with respect, find any principle on which it is based.' ibid [85].

[57] And that the second defendant was liable for knowing assistance in the breach of fiduciary duty.

unfortunately provided an 'escape' for the Court. Standing back from legal doctrine to examine the facts of this case, it is surely clear that the defendant ought to have been liable. He manipulated the situation in order to exercise control over the plaintiffs. This ought to generate liability even in the absence of fiduciary obligations.[58]

The third problem is that unlawful means, even in conjunction with the other elements of the action, are not sufficient for liability. This is brought out by the pizza case mentioned above. In that case, the company intentionally causes loss to its competitors by committing illegal actions, but all agree that there can be no liability.

It might be suggested that the appropriate way to solve the difficulties raised by this example is to define unlawful means narrowly to include only, say, torts and breaches of contracts, so that the pizza business is not guilty of unlawful means. But that is the wrong kind of answer. We feel that there should be no liability in this case, but the source of that feeling is not the belief that the defendant's action was illegal under the wrong legal category. Just change the example. Say that the pizza delivery company attempts to gain market share by breaching its supply agreements with or committing torts against uninvolved third parties. This is the 'right' kind of illegality—breach of contract and tort—but it does not change our attitude as to the correct outcome.

It is rightly said that this example reveals that the defendant's illegal action must connect with the plaintiff's injury.[59] But why is that? It is because the defendant will be using the illegal means as a way of exercising control over the plaintiff only if that connection exists. Again, the illegal means are, in themselves, irrelevant.

The fourth problem is the most important. It is that the unlawful means requirement is entirely without rational warrant. Liability of one person to another cannot be justified on the ground that a third party was wronged. Nor can the absence of liability of one person to another be justified on the ground that no third party was wronged. Again, this is no mere technical rule of law or fetish of legal formalism. The point is logical. If the question is 'Why is *A* liable to *B*?', how could 'Because *A* wronged *C*' be the answer? There is a logical chasm here. Without a wrong to the plaintiff, what is the motivation for finding the defendant liable to that person? Without a wrong, what is one meant to be remedying?

In fact, despite the number of arguments holding that it is the defendant's wrong to the third party that justifies liability to the plaintiff, I submit that unless one felt that the defendant wronged the plaintiff, one would not feel the urge to posit liability in the first place. Thus, the conventional view is in the curious position of

[58] Moreover, why does the breach of the fiduciary obligation to one plaintiff not justify stretching liability to the other?

[59] eg, R Bagshaw, 'Can the Economic Torts be Justified?' (1998) 18 *Oxford Journal of Legal Studies* 729.

being motivated to support liability by the feeling that the defendant wronged the plaintiff, but insisting that the liability be rationalised on the basis that this wrong did not occur. The potential liability to the third party is a red herring, a control mechanism that we have had to lean on because of an inadequate understanding of the historical cases and the basis of the liability found in them.

The fifth problem is that, notoriously, when two or more defendants are involved, the unlawful means requirement goes out the window. We know this as the tort of lawful means conspiracy. We will turn to this in a moment.

It is very important to note that this discussion does not imply that illegality is never relevant. It can be relevant, as we see in section VI below. The point is that it is not appropriately viewed as a necessary condition for the relevant kind of wrongdoing and so should not be an element of the action.

V. Conspiracy

A defendant who joins with another with the purpose of striking at the plaintiff can be liable even if no unlawful means are used. The question is why. Why does there need to be a combination? Modern commentators tend to be scathing of this requirement, but it is worth pointing out that it has considerable pedigree.[60] The intuitive justification of the idea seems clear: in general, one person ought to be unable to gain control over the life of another—it being merely one on one—but two or more people have greater power. And in general, that is correct. Ganging up on someone is much more serious than going it alone. However, this assumes that the parties are of roughly equal power and, of course, that is often not the case. The point is that, on this theory, the rule is understandable even if ultimately unjustified. It is no mere piece of idiocy.

Contempt for the rule is unjustified. Though the rule must be abandoned, it is trying to get at something important. This is that the defendant or defendants must not be allowed to gain control over the plaintiff. Defendants who gang up on plaintiffs must be especially carefully watched in this regard. It is quite understandable, then, that conspiracy has turned out to be more 'plaintiff-friendly' than causing loss by unlawful means. As is the unlawful means rule, the combination rule is a defective proxy for what really matters.

This also explains two further features of the law of conspiracy. First, liability requires that the defendants' purpose was to strike at the plaintiff. This is because

[60] See, for instance, the foundations of Roman law's *Actio Iniuriarum*. For discussion, see R Zimmermann, *The Law of Obligations: Roman Foundations of the Civilian Tradition* (Oxford, Oxford University Press, 1996) 1053–54. Conspiracy is also, of course, of major concern to the criminal law. For a discussion that relates to the position advanced here, see A Ashworth and J Horder, *Principles of Criminal Law*, 7th edn (Oxford, Oxford University Press, 2013) 416–19.

defendants who have a different purpose are not attempting to exercise control over the plaintiff. So, for example, if the defendants are primarily trying to advance their own interests, then they are living their own life rather than trying to control the plaintiff's.

This leads to the second point. In lawful means conspiracy, a defendant can rely on the defence of justification. Most interestingly, it has been argued that this defence means that a defendant escapes liability if she shows that she was motivated by self-interest.[61] On the face of it, this is extremely odd. It is surely unintuitive to say that a person is exculpated *because* she was being selfish. No, the reason for this defence is not that self-interest is exculpatory. It is because a defendant who acted out of self-interest in this way was living her own life, pursuing her own interests and was not trying to gain control over the plaintiff.[62] Again, we see the law attempting to work itself towards the theory here presented. With this in mind, it is time to revisit the case law.

VI. Revisiting the Case Law

A. The Standard Cases

Causing loss by unlawful means and conspiracy are the same action, separated only by their unnecessary and invalid control mechanisms. On a correct understanding, liability in these 'torts' is to be explained identically. Let us turn to the case law.

In *Mogul Steamship Co Ltd v McGregor Gow & Co*, the defendant ship owners entered into an association in order to raise their profits. They agreed to restrict the number of ships that they sent to various ports, to give a five per cent rebate on freight to all shippers of stock who dealt exclusively with the association, and that agents of members would be dismissed if they refused to deal exclusively with the association. The plaintiff was not a member of the association. It sent a ship to a port to load cargo. In response, the association sent more ships and underbid the plaintiff. It also threatened to dismiss agents or withdraw rebates from anyone who dealt with the plaintiff. The plaintiff suffered loss as a result and sued. Both the Court of Appeal and the House of Lords held that, as the defendants were

[61] Stevens (n 6) 252–53.

[62] Consider also *Brimelow v Casson* [1924] 1 Ch 302, in which the defendant persuaded chorus girls to breach their contracts with the plaintiff theatre. The defence was held to apply in this case, as the defendant was motivated by the fact that the women's wage was so low that they were forced to supplement it by resorting to prostitution. Though targeting another's contract is usually an exercise of control, in this case it was not.

legally pursuing their own interests, they could not be liable. That, of course, is exactly in line with the argument advanced here.

It is also worth pausing to note that the sole dissenter in the case, Lord Esher in the Court of Appeal, said the following:

> Each has a right to carry on his trade in a free course of trade, according to his own free will and judgment. So long as the one so carries on his trade, the other cannot, without infringing on the right of his rival, effectively complain. So long as each so carries on his trade, though such carrying on produces the utmost extent of competition, and consequent lowering of gain, neither can validly complain. Each is exercising the free course of trade. But if one goes beyond the exercise of the course of trade, and does an act beyond what is the course of trade, in order—that is to say, with intent—to molest the other's free course of trade, and which does molest the other's free course of trade, he is not exercising his own freedom of a course of trade; he is not acting in, but beyond, the course of trade; and then it follows that his act is an unlawful obstruction of the other's right to a free course of trade; and if such obstruction causes damage to the other, he is entitled to maintain an action for the wrong … 'Every person has a right under the law, as between him and his fellow-subjects to full freedom in disposing of his own labour or his own capital according to his own will. It follows that every other person is subject to the correlative duty arising therefrom, and is prohibited from any obstruction to the fullest exercise of this right which can be made compatible with the exercise of similar rights by others. Every act causing an obstruction to another in the exercise of the right comprised within this description—done, not in the exercise of the actor's own right, but for the purpose of obstruction—would, if damage should be caused thereby to the party obstructed, be a violation of this prohibition.'[63]

Here again we see that it is the interpretation of the facts that makes the difference, not a dispute between abstentionist and interventionist policies. According to the majority of the judges, the defendants were looking out for their own interests. According to Lord Esher, they were exercising control over the plaintiff.

Allen v Flood has been dealt with above. According to the majority of the House of Lords, the defendant was merely informing the company of the intentions of third parties. According to the other judges, the defendant was the representative of a group trying to assert control over the plaintiffs. On the majority's view, the defendant was not acting coercively and so was not found liable. On the alternative view, the defendant was acting coercively and liability should have followed.

Quinn v Leathem has also already been examined. The House of Lords found for the plaintiff because it held that the defendants were trying to punish the plaintiff for hiring non-union labour and/or force the plaintiff to inflict their (the defendants') retribution on the plaintiff's employees for not belonging to the union.

The next case is *Crofter*. This concerned a dispute between two groups producing Harris Tweed. The first group manufactured the tweed in accordance with tradition, utilising spinning mills on Harris Island to produce yarn that was then

[63] *Mogul Steamship Co Ltd v McGregor Gow & Co* (n 8) 607–08, quoting Erle (n 9) 12.

woven into tweed by crofters in their homes on Harris. The second group obtained yarn from the mainland at cheaper prices, which was then also woven by crofters in their homes on Harris. Most of the first group were members of a union that included dockworkers at Stornoway, the port on Harris through which the yarn was handled. They colluded with the other members of this union, instructing the dockworkers to refuse to handle yarn imported from the mainland destined for the second group. The dockworkers, without acting illegally, obeyed these instructions and the second group, including the plaintiff company, suffered loss. The defendants were representatives of the relevant union.

The House of Lords held that there could be no liability as the purpose of the action was to promote the interests of the first group. In other words, these people were trying to protect their traditional way of life against the threat posed by the second group's more innovative methods. They were not trying to gain control over the plaintiffs.

We have also dealt with *Rookes v Barnard*. Recall that the defendants were officials in a union who wanted to preserve universal union membership at their place of work. The plaintiff refused to join. The defendants successfully pressured their employer to terminate the plaintiff's employment. The pressure was a threat to strike illegally. Had the threatened strike not been illegal, the plaintiff would have failed. At first glance, this case appears on all fours with *Crofter*. In fact, there is one crucial difference. This difference is a product of the fact that in *Rookes v Barnard*, the defendants threatened to act illegally.

Noticing this difference and holding that it is decisive in this case does not imply that illegality is a proper element in the action. The claim is not that the illegality makes any legal difference in its own right. It is instead that the illegality affects the nature of the facts. In *Crofter*, the defendants were able to claim that they were attempting to preserve their way of life. But in *Rookes v Barnard*, the fact that the defendants' threat was to do something illegal meant that no such claim was possible.

In *Rookes v Barnard*, the defendants were trying to advance their own interests in terms of universal union membership. That is why they targeted the plaintiff. In that respect, their actions were irreproachable. But that was not all that they did. They also decided to act illegally by striking in violation of their contractual obligations. Note that the focus here is on this decision and not on the threat per se. Note also that the decision was itself an action. Because the defendants performed that action, they could not claim merely to be living their own lives. This is because they were not entitled to live their lives in the way that they decided to act.[64] That is decisively different from the position of the defendants in *Crofter*.

On the other hand, had the defendants threatened only legal behaviour, they could have legitimately claimed to be living their own lives. That explains the

[64] Strictly, the position is not that the decision to strike was illegal and thus the defendants were not entitled to act in this way. The position is that the decision to strike was, while in itself legal, a decision to do something illegal and the defendants were not entitled to act in that way.

decision in *Morgan v Fry*.[65] The plaintiff was an employee of a third party and a member of a certain union. The defendants were members of a rival union and believed that the first union was a threat to industrial peace. Because of this, they pressured the third party to terminate the plaintiff's employment. Ultimately, the defendants threatened the third party that unless the plaintiff was dismissed, members of the second union would strike. The planned strike, however, would have been entirely legal. Because of that, the English Court of Appeal held that no tort was committed. The only significant difference between this case and *Rookes v Barnard* is that the defendants' threat in the latter case was a threat to do something illegal. Why is this difference significant? Because in *Morgan v Fry*, but not in *Rookes v Barnard*, the defendants could claim to be merely trying to live their own lives.

In these cases, it is the decision to perform an illegal action that makes the difference, though not for the reasons advanced by the conventional view.[66] Illegality is not an appropriate element in the action. However, in cases of this kind, illegality affects the nature of the facts. It can determine whether the defendant was merely trying to live his own life or to strike at the plaintiff. And note that, on this view, there can be no rule as to which forms of illegality are relevant. We cannot say that only torts and breaches of contract count, for instance. What will make the difference will turn on the circumstances of the case.

We turn now to *Lonrho v Shell*.[67] The defendant and other parties constructed an oil refinery and pipeline in Southern Rhodesia. The understanding was that oil would be shipped to Mozambique and piped to the refinery, and the plaintiff would be expected to profit from that shipping. The refinery and the pipeline were completed in January 1965. In November, Southern Rhodesia declared unilateral independence and, in response, the UK government made it a criminal offence to supply oil to Southern Rhodesia. No further oil was supplied and the plaintiff suffered loss as a result. The plaintiff alleged that, before the offence came into being, the defendant and associated parties had assured the government of Southern Rhodesia that supply would be maintained and, in fact, did indirectly ensure that it was maintained. This both encouraged the declaration of independence and prolonged the period during which oil could not be shipped, leading to loss to the plaintiff.

The House of Lords found for the defendant on the ground that it was seeking to protect its own interests. Certainly, the defendant's actions (may have) caused loss to the plaintiff, but the defendant did not attempt to control the plaintiff's business. The defendant was merely trying to live its own life.

[65] *Morgan v Fry* [1968] 2 QB 710 (CA).

[66] And note the difference between this and the pizza case. In *Rookes v Barnard* (n 4), the illegality is the mechanism by which the defendants seek to control the plaintiff. In the pizza case, there is no attempt the control the competitors at all.

[67] *Lonrho v Shell* [1982] AC 173 (HL).

Compare this with *Lonrho v Fayed*. The parties wanted to acquire Harrods department store. The plaintiff made the first bid, but the Minister referred the bid to the Monopolies and Mergers Commission, preventing the plaintiff from proceeding until the Commission had produced its report. The defendant then made a bid. Had this bid been referred to the Commission, the defendant would likewise have been unable to proceed. However, the bid was not referred. According to the plaintiff, this was because the defendant and his advisors deceived the Minister about the defendant's commercial standing and backing. As a result, the defendant acquired Harrods while the plaintiff was prevented from bidding.

The House of Lords found for the plaintiff. The judges accepted that the defendant was pursuing his own business interests, but ruled that (on the facts as presented) he was *also* trying to strike at the plaintiff using unlawful means. To translate this into our language, this meant that the defendant could not claim merely to be trying to operate his own business, living his own life. He was also trying to coerce the plaintiff.

The suggestion is not that all cases neatly fit the model advanced here. It is unrealistic to think that any position will cohere perfectly with the positive law in an area routinely described as a mess. In fact, as we now see, the model leads to the rejection of some important modern cases. But the model also helps us to see that these cases must be rejected.

B. The Modern Cases

We now turn to the most recent cases. We begin with *OBG Ltd v Allan*.[68]

In *OBG Ltd v Allan* itself, the plaintiffs were two companies, the first of which was in serious financial difficulty. An unsecured creditor of that company, acting on the advice of its solicitors, purported to appoint two administrative receivers to the company. These four parties were the defendants. The receivers took control of the company. The plaintiffs brought an action alleging that the receivers had been appointed invalidly and that the appointment and the subsequent decisions of the receivers had caused them loss, specifically that the receivers' handling of the 'run off' of the plaintiffs' contracts resulted in the plaintiffs being left worse off than they would have been under their liquidators. The trial judge held that the appointment was indeed invalid and had caused the plaintiffs' loss. The House of Lords found for the defendant. It maintained that because the receivers took control of the first company in good faith, did not employ unlawful means and did not intend to cause loss, the defendants could not be liable.

The absence of liability in this case fits the thesis of this chapter. The defendants in *OBG Ltd v Allan* did not exercise control over the plaintiffs through a third

[68] *Mainstream Properties Ltd v Young* [2007] UKHL 21, [2008] 1 AC 1 (HL), as involving inducing breach of contract, is not relevant at this point.

party. However, that itself suggests that the absence of liability in this case was very odd. There was no exercise of control through third parties because there were no relevant third parties. There was, however, clearly an exercise of control. The control here was exercised directly, not indirectly. The defendants invalidly took control of the first plaintiff company and used it in a way that caused loss to both plaintiffs. That must surely be a form of unjustified constraint, even if not the commission of an economic tort. The defendants' actions were coercive of the plaintiffs. There ought to have been liability in *OBG Ltd v Allan*.

In practice, the law usually deals with fact patterns of this kind by imposing a trust. In general, receivers in the position of the defendants in *OBG Ltd v Allan* are held to be trustees and thus liable for the loss they occasion. Pursuing this avenue appears to have been unavailable—or at least thought to be unavailable—in this case because of the peculiar nature of the plaintiffs' loss.[69] But that cannot make any difference to our ultimate assessment of liability. The defendants in *OBG Ltd v Allan* wrongly took control of the first plaintiff company and caused loss to it during this period of control. That loss must be actionable.

The decision in *OBG Ltd v Allan* is consistent with the argument of this chapter. There can be no liability in the economic torts as there was no indirect control exerted by the defendants over the plaintiffs. But that is only to say that the liability that ought to have been found in *OBG Ltd v Allan* was not the form of liability analysed here. This is not an essay on the law of trusts, so nothing more will be said now, except to note that, in the light of this argument, it is remarkable to observe that this decision has garnered the level of support that it has.[70]

In *Douglas v Hello! Ltd*, a magazine purchased the exclusive right to publish photographs of the wedding of two celebrities. These were the three plaintiffs. The couple had promised the magazine that they would prevent rival media organisations from gaining access to photos of the wedding. In that regard, the wedding guests were told that photography was prohibited and tight security measures were in place. Nevertheless, a freelance photographer infiltrated the wedding, took photos and sold them to the defendant magazine, which published the photos. The House of Lords held that the defendant was liable for breach of confidence. We are not concerned with that here. A majority also found that the defendant would have been liable for causing loss by unlawful means had it committed a tort or breach of contract—being in breach of confidence not counting as unlawful means for the purposes of this tort in the eyes of this majority.

This cannot be right. Imagine that the defendant had committed a tort or breach of contract with some third party. How could that in itself make a difference (recall the pizza delivery case)? Moreover, this was a wedding, and a celebrity

[69] At least, this avenue was not pursued. *OBG Ltd v Allan* [2005] EWCA Civ 106, [2005] QB 762 (CA) [39].

[70] H Carty, 'The Economic Torts in the 21st Century' (2008) 124 *Law Quarterly Review* 641, 648, for instance, describes it as magnificent.

wedding at that. It occurred in public. Guests were invited. Photographers were hired to photograph it and a magazine paid to publish those photos. There is no way that the defendant publishing these photos could be described as trying to exert control over the couple or the magazine. The Court of Appeal was right to say that the defendant lacked the requisite intention and the House of Lords was wrong to dispute this. The only issue in *Douglas v Hello! Ltd* was confidentiality.

Again, the objection to the position advanced by the House of Lords can be expressed independently of the position advanced in this book. Let us focus on the celebrity couple. What interest did they have in seeing that the photos were not published by the defendant? The obvious answer is that the publication invaded their privacy. But this is scarcely credible in this case, as the couple had contracted with the third plaintiff to publish photographs of the wedding. In any case, the couple's interest in privacy was adequately protected by the action for breach of confidence, given how that action has developed in English law. But if not privacy, then what interest is at stake? Is it is the interest in the couple to control their own celebrity? If so, then we would be right to regard the decision of the House of Lords in *Douglas v Hello! Ltd* as signalling a worrying development in the law, effectively giving celebrities property rights in their celebrity.

In *Total Network*, the defendant was engaged in a conspiracy to defraud the Revenue. In effect, the result was that due VAT was not paid. That description is sufficient to show that the House of Lords was wrong to find for the plaintiff. Of course, this is not to say that the Revenue should be unable to recover for its losses in some other fashion. But failing to pay tax is not an attempt to control the Revenue. Given the powers available to the Revenue, it seems odd to think that it requires the tort of conspiracy to be added to its arsenal. In line with what seems to be the view of the majority of commentators, then, I agree that no economic tort was committed in *Total Network*.

In these modern cases, the law has lost its way. This is the result of searching for rules without a developed understanding of the nature of the action to which they apply. Consequently, I am forced reluctantly to predict another century at least of abiding confusion.

VII. The Form of Liability

We must now address the form of liability found in these torts properly understood. It is tempting to argue that, as the torts require the defendant to have targeted the plaintiff in the sense examined above, these are forms of fault-based liability. In fact, however, it is best not to think of them in this fashion. This is because, though it is natural to think that one who targets harm to another must be at fault, it is the targeting and not the fault that matters. In other words, targeting is relevant because it is targeting, not because it is faulty. Thus, a defendant who appears to conspire against a plaintiff escapes liability if he does so out of selfishness. That is not because his selfishness shows that he was not at fault—an absurd notion. It is because it shows that he was not targeting the plaintiff. Targeting matters, not fault. On the other hand, it is not immediately obvious that targeting another is always faulty, and there is no reason to think that liability is always impossible when it is not faulty. Again, it is the targeting that is legally determinative, not any concomitant fault.

In fact, even if it were impossible to be liable here without being at fault, it remains the case that the targeting determines liability and not fault. Even if only faulty defendants are found liable in fact, fault is not an element in the action.[71] As we will see in Chapter 12, the law of negligence is entirely different in this regard. There, fault is legally determinative. It is an element in the action.

VIII. The Mistake of Inducing Breach of Contract

A. *Lumley v Gye*

The tort of inducing breach of contract, having its origins in the master/servant relationship, was given its modern foundation in *Lumley v Gye*, the case that freed the action from its connection with status. Despite the importance of this case, however, the tort remained a legal backwater until the emergence of the 'unified theory' of the economic torts in *Quinn v Leathem* that led to an expansion of liability culminating in the unfortunate decisions of *Torquay Hotel Co Ltd v Cousins* and *Merkur Island Shipping Corp v Laughton*. That is the story told by the conventional view. Apart from its very beginning, it is a work of fiction.

The facts of *Lumley v Gye* have been discussed. The defendant induced Johanna Wagner to breach her contract to perform for the plaintiff. The Court of Queen's Bench found for the plaintiff. Why? In accordance with the now-dominant view, Earle J argued that the defendant was liable as an accessory to Wagner's breach of her contract.[72] As Coleridge J pointed out, however, that cannot be right. Where a defendant is liable as an accessory:

> [T]he wrongful act done is properly charged to be the act of him who has procured it to be done. He is sued as a principal trespasser [for instance], and the damage, if proved, flows directly and immediately from his act, though it was the hand of another, and he a free agent, that was employed. But, when you apply the term of effectual persuasion to the breach of a contract, it has obviously a different meaning; the persuader has not

[71] In the language of Ch 4, whatever kind of substantive liability is imposed here, formally these torts are strict.

[72] *Lumley v Gye* (1853) 2 El & Bl 216, 118 ER 749, 755–756.

> broken and could not break the contract, for he had never entered into any; he cannot be sued upon the contract; and yet it is the breach of the contract only that is the cause of damage. Neither can it be said that in breaking the contract the contractor is the agent of him who procures him to do so; it is still his own act; he is principal in so doing, and is the only principal. This answer may seem technical; but it really goes to the root of the matter. It shews that the procurer has not done the hurtful act; what he has done is too remote from the damage to make him answerable for it.[73]

This passage anticipates many of the points made in Chapter 8.

Coleridge J dissented. Earle J was with the majority. But the remainder of the majority, Crompton and Wightman JJ, gave quite different reasons for their decision. Though they are very similar to each other, Crompton J's argument is the more detailed and it is the one examined here.

According to Crompton J:

> Whatever may have been the origin or foundation of the law as to enticing of servants … it must now be considered clear law that a person who wrongfully and maliciously, or, which is the same thing, with notice, interrupts the relation subsisting between master and servant by procuring the servant to depart from the master's service, or by harbouring and keeping him as servant after he has quitted it and during the time stipulated for as the period of service, whereby the master is injured, commits a wrongful act for which he is responsible at law.[74]

There are three important features of this passage. First, Crompton J pointed to the existence of liability for enticing a servant away from his master. This is known as the action *per quod servitum amisit*. Second, Crompton J expressed uncertainty as to the basis of that liability. Third, Crompton J nevertheless regarded it as appropriate to extend this form of liability to cover this case.

Our understanding of *Lumley v Gye* will be much aided if we remove Crompton J's uncertainty. What is the basis of the action *per quod*? The answer is that the master was understood to possess property in his servant, a possession that generated multital rights, such that enticing the servant away from the master was conceptualised as a kind of trespass to the master's property.[75] The same principle applied to the action *per quod consortium amisit*, which involved depriving a husband of the comfort and support of his wife, in which he was also held to possess property.

We cannot understand *Lumley v Gye* or the subsequent history without seeing that the plaintiff won the case because Crompton and Wightman JJ were prepared

[73] ibid 761.

[74] ibid 752–53.

[75] For a recent discussion of this, see *Barclay v Penberthy* 2012 HCA 40, (2012) 291 ALR 608; and for criticism of that decision, see A Beever, '*Barclay v Penberthy* and the Collapse of the High Court's Tort Jurisprudence' (2013) 32 *University of Queensland Law Journal* 307.

to extend the action *per quod* to cover the facts in that case. Why were the judges prepared to do this? This was Crompton J's answer:

> [I]t was … said that the engagement, employment or service, in the present case, was not of such a nature as to constitute the relation of master and servant, so as to warrant the application of the usual rule of law giving a remedy in case of enticing away servants. The nature of the injury and of the damage being the same, and the supposed right of action being in strict analogy to the ordinary case of master and servant, I see no reason for confining the case to services or engagements under contracts for services of any particular description.[76]

Notice that there is no suggestion here of creating a new tort, of recognising an implicit tort of inducing breach of contract, or anything of the kind. On the contrary, Crompton J took the action *per quod*—the cases upon which he relied were all of this kind—and extended it to cover the facts in *Lumley v Gye*. The defendant was liable to the plaintiff because:

> A person who contracts to do certain work for another is the servant of that other … until the work be finished. It appears to me that Miss Wagner had contracted to do work for the plaintiff within the meaning of this rule; and I think that, where a party has contracted to give his personal services for a certain time to another, the parties are in the relation of employer and employed, or master and servant, within the meaning of this rule.[77]

The defendant was liable because he enticed the plaintiff's servant away from him, an extension of the action *per quod*.

In this regard, the real issue for the Court was to determine at what point a person becomes the servant of another. And the Court took this issue very seriously. The defendant maintained that it was when the period of employment begins. The consequence of this view was that as Wagner never actually began to perform for the plaintiff, she was never a servant and so an action could not lie. What can be said in support of the idea that this is when the master/servant relationship begins? Here again we see the importance of understanding the proprietary basis of the action *per quod*: the answer is that this is the point of 'delivery'. In principle, there is a distinction between promising to give you something and giving it to you, a distinction that German lawyers know as the principle of separation.[78] Promising to make my horse your property is not the same as making it your property. To make it your property, I must deliver it to you, though of course that delivery can be symbolic. On this view, then, Wagner promised to make herself in the relevant respect the property of the plaintiff, but never actually did so. She never became

[76] *Lumley v Gye* (n 72) 753.
[77] ibid 754.
[78] Which is an element of the more general doctrine of abstraction.

a servant. The plaintiff never had proprietary interests in her. He never had any related multital rights, then, and thus could have no action against the defendant.

But the common law does not operate according to the principle of separation. In our law, I can give you something by promising to give it to you. And this was the position adopted by Compton J. For him, Wagner's promise to perform for the plaintiff itself created in the plaintiff proprietary, multital rights.

Nor was Compton J impressed by the (surely in fact entirely compelling) argument that the relationship between a singer and her theatre company is not correctly categorised as master/servant. For him, the issue was clear. The plaintiff suffered loss and there is an analogy between this case and the decided cases on the action *per quod*: liability must follow.[79] That is deeply unsatisfying. One cannot determine whether any relevant analogy exists between the facts in *Lumley v Gye* and those in the then established cases on the action *per quod* without understanding the nature of that action. Thankfully, however, we need not go any further down this path. It is enough to see that, for Crompton and Wightman JJ, *Lumley v Gye* introduced no tort of inducing breach of contract.

Nor, for that matter, did Earle J advance this view. As noted above, he argued that the defendant was liable as an accessory, and that means that the defendant was liable for breach of contract, not for inducing breach of contract. That, I have argued, is impossible, but even if that were mistaken, it would not follow that Earle J's judgment could be read as supporting the existence of a tort of inducing breach of contract. What is more, Earle J confusedly attempted to reinforce his argument by reference to cases involving the action *per quod*.[80] Thus, Earle J's arguments call for accessory liability under breach of contract or for an extension of the action *per quod*. They do not support the existence of a tort of inducing breach of contract.

There is no support for that tort in any of the judgments in *Lumley v Gye*. That case is not a step on the road from status to contract.[81] On the contrary, it saw an extension of status.[82] The case is about status, not contract.

B. *Bowen v Hall*

Perhaps we can find a beginning for inducing breach of contract in *Bowen v Hall*.[83] In that case, the defendant induced the plaintiff's employee to breach his contract.

[79] *Lumley v Gye* (n 72) 753.

[80] *Winsmore v Greenbank* (1745) ER 576, 125 ER 1330 (enticement of wife); *Bird v Randall* (1762) 3 Burr 1345, 97 ER 866 (enticement of servant).

[81] An expression we owe to HS Maine, *Ancient Law: Its Connection with the Early History of Society and its Relation to Modern Ideas*, 10th edn (London, John Murry, 1920) 26.

[82] That ought not to surprise us, even as late as 1853. As discussed in Beever (n 75) 310–12, English courts continued to struggle with this issue (see, for instance, *Admiralty Commissioners v SS Amerika* [1917] AC 38 (HL)) and the High Court of Australia still does so (see *Barclay v Penberthy* (n 75)).

[83] *Bowen v Hall* (1881) 6 QBD 333 (CA).

The case is interesting because it was argued on the basis that this employer/employee relationship was not a master/servant relationship and so it was clear that the action *per quod* could not apply.[84]

In dissent, Coleridge LJ maintained that liability of this kind must be restricted to the master/servant relationship and that the plaintiff in this case must therefore fail.[85] That view lost and the plaintiff won, but on what basis? This is what Brett LJ said:

> [W]herever a man does an act which in law and in fact is a wrongful act, and such an act as may, as a natural and probable consequence of it, produce injury to another, and which in the particular case does produce such an injury, an action on the case will lie.[86]

Moreover, while the defendant was liable because he induced the breach of contract, the legal significance of this is that he damaged the plaintiff:

> [I]f the persuasion be used for the indirect purpose of injuring the plaintiff, or of benefiting the defendant at the expense of the plaintiff, it is a malicious act which is in law and in fact a wrong act, and therefore a wrongful act, and therefore an actionable act if injury ensues from it.[87]

This is liability, but not for inducing breach of contract. It is liability for what we now know as causing loss by unlawful means.[88] The defendant was found liable because he performed an illegal act with the intention of causing loss to the plaintiff. The breach of the contract is determinative only because of its connection with the plaintiff's loss. The breach does not itself feature in the principles of the action.

Brett LJ's mistake was to argue that his position was the one found in *Lumley v Gye*.[89] It was not. That said, however, the outcome of *Lumley v Gye* may be supported on this basis. The liability in both *Lumley v Gye* and *Bowen v Hall* fits perfectly with the theory advanced here. It is the same liability as found in cases such as *Quinn v Leathem* and *Rookes v Barnard*.

C. Subsequent History

After *Bowen v Hall*, we are told, the tort of inducing breach of contract lived a half-life until *Quinn v Leathem*. We now know why. It was the spirit of an action not yet born. And we now also know why the 'unified theory' appears to have given the action a 'new lease of life'. The theory attached the spirit to a living being.

[84] ibid 337.

[85] ibid 342.

[86] ibid 337.

[87] ibid 338.

[88] The claim is not that Brett LJ's position matches exactly that taken by, say, the House of Lords in *OBG Ltd v Allan* (n 8). The point is that Brett LJ is clearly referring to the same general concept.

[89] *Bowen v Hall* (n 83) 337.

But the real consequence of the unified theory was not to amalgamate the torts of inducing breach of contract and causing loss by unlawful means—it was to create a single tort focused on control over the plaintiff through third parties. The tort of inducing breach of contract is a mistake. It is a remnant of the action *per quod*. Its modern form was invented out of nothing and to nothing it must return.

This is not to say that all cases understood to be inducing breach of contract cases are wrongly decided. On the contrary, I have already supported the outcomes of *Lumley v Gye* and *Bowen v Hall*. And perhaps most telling is that the theory advanced here also supports the outcomes of *Torquay Hotel Co Ltd v Cousins* and *Merkur Island Shipping Corp v Laughton*.

The defendants in *Torquay Hotel Co Ltd v Cousins* were representatives of the Transport and General Workers' Union. The union was in dispute with a third party hotel located in Torbay and had voted to go on strike. The union was not in dispute with the plaintiff; no members of the union were employed by the plaintiff. However, after attending an evening banquet, the manager of the plaintiff hotel was asked by a reporter what he thought of the situation. This was reported in the press:

> Mr Michael Chapman, managing director at Torquay five-star Imperial Hotel, said last night that the Hotels' Association were now determined to stamp out the intervention of the Transport Union into the hotel trade. 'You can only take so much before you have to make a stand, and do something, and this we are going to do.'[90]

This greatly angered the members of the union. The following comments were made:

> We are pleased that Mr Chapman has come out into the open against us because we think he is the real nigger in the woodpile, preventing us from making progress.
>
> He has intervened. *That means sanctions* and every means at our disposal will be used. We can cut off supplies at source and *we are going to do that*. I will put out a public warning now—we are quite prepared to put an embargo on any hotelier who intervenes.[91]

The union 'blacked' the hotel, which threatened to deprive the plaintiff of oil. The defendant asked for a quia timet injunction to lift the blacking. The Court of Appeal found in the plaintiff's favour. Again, the issue is why? Unfortunately, there seem to be two answers.

In line with the conventional understanding of the case, Lord Denning MR maintained that liability was rightly based on *Lumley v Gye*.[92] This caused an immediate problem for the plaintiff. The plaintiff had a supply agreement with a

[90] *Torquay Hotel Co Ltd v Cousins* [1969] 2 Ch 106 (CA), 133.
[91] ibid 134.
[92] ibid 137.

third party that guaranteed deliveries of oil, but a clause in that contract excused the third party from delivering in the event of a labour dispute. Because of this, no relevant party *breached* any contract with the plaintiff. That seemed to show that the defendant could not be liable for inducing *breach* of contract. But Lord Denning argued that this form of liability had been extended in *Quinn v Leathem* 'so that each of the parties has a right to have his "contractual relations" with the other [ie, the third party] duly observed'.[93] He also maintained that liability should be widened even further to cover deliberate and direct '*interference* in the execution of a contract',[94] conditions that were satisfied on the facts before the Court.

Naturally, this supports the conventional reading of the case. However, it is necessary to remember that Lord Denning did not share the conventional understanding of *Lumley v Gye* or of the action that we know as causing loss by unlawful means. On the contrary, he adhered to the 'unified theory', according to which the torts of inducing breach of contract and causing loss by unlawful means are one. For him, then, interference with contract was merely one species of a more general kind of wrongdoing. And if we look elsewhere in his Lordship's judgment, we can see how that wrongdoing was conceptualised.

One question in the case was whether the defendants' behaviour was covered by the Trade Disputes Act 1906. This is what Lord Denning said in that context:

> The only question is whether the acts done by the trade union officials against the Imperial Hotel were done in furtherance of the trade dispute with the Torbay Hotel. I do not think they were. They were done in furtherance of the anger which they felt towards Mr Chapman for having, as they said, 'intervened' in the dispute. They were not furthering a trade dispute, but their own fury.[95]

Similarly, Russell LJ said:

> [I]ndustrial action against the others [such as the Torbay Hotel] is designed to lead to action by the others by way of recognition of the defendant union as a negotiating body: industrial action against the Imperial Hotel could have no such end or aim: it could only be it seems to me to punish Mr Chapman for the expression of views unpalatable to the defendant union.[96]

His Lordship also maintained that the defendants' actions 'demonstrate an attitude on the part of the union officials of willingness directly to induce breaches of contract for the supply of fuel oil to the Imperial Hotel in order to carry out a policy of punishing Mr Chapman for his temerity in being critical of the union'.[97] That this would lead to liability is, of course, in line with the theory presented here.

[93] ibid 138.
[94] ibid.
[95] ibid 136–37.
[96] ibid 143.
[97] ibid.

However the judgments in *Torquay Hotel Co Ltd v Cousins* are best understood, the liability imposed in that case has its proper basis in the fact that the defendants were not merely living their own lives—their interests were not at stake—but were exercising control over the plaintiff's manager. They wanted to prevent him from speaking his mind and to punish him for doing so.

As Russell LJ recognised, it was ultimately for a trial to determine whether this reading of the facts was accurate;[98] however, I submit that if the reading was accurate, then liability must follow. The attempt to silence the plaintiff's manager was a serious violation of his liberty.[99] We must not allow discomfort at Lord Denning's arguments or the desire for clarity in this area of the law to occlude the recognition that a significant wrong was done by the defendant in this case. *Torquay Hotel Co Ltd v Cousins* was rightly decided.

In *Merkur Island Shipping Corp v Laughton*, the plaintiff let his ship to one party, who sub-chartered it to another, who contracted with yet another to have it towed out of port. However, the ship was unable to leave port because, engaged in a dispute with the plaintiff, the defendants persuaded the tugmen, in breach of their employment contracts, not to do the towing. The charter provided that 'the captain shall prosecute his voyages with the utmost dispatch'. This meant that, though no breach of this contract occurred, performance of the contract was 'disrupted'. The trial judge granted an interlocutory injunction and the defendants appealed.

Relying in part on the conventional understanding of the decision of the Court of Appeal in *Torquay Hotel Co Ltd v Cousins*, the House of Lords found for the plaintiff. That strategy cannot be supported. The result can be. The case is like *Rookes v Barnard*. Though one could say that the defendants were trying to protect the interests of their members, they chose to do so by inducing the tugmen to perform illegal actions. That cannot be represented as living their own lives. On the contrary, it must be understood as trying to gain control over the plaintiff.

At this point, and in relation to the argument of this chapter as a whole, it is important to stress that I have not claimed that utilising this form of liability is an appropriate way to deal with industrial disputes. I have taken no stand on that matter whatsoever. In line with the courts' positions, I have simply assumed that the parties in these cases were not engaged in industrial disputes. It may be that, for public policy reasons, it is desirable to permit trade unions and the like to exercise—within limits—control over others. If that is so, then statutory regimes that replace the law of tort in this regard should be implemented. It is highly unlikely that creating mere immunities to liability will be sufficient. But that is another topic.

Suffice it for now to say that, though it is impossible to support the existence of a tort of inducing breach of contract, it does not follow that defendants who induce breaches of contracts should escape liability. Often, they should not. But

[98] ibid.

[99] Note that there was an attempt to silence the plaintiff's manager, and the attempt was carried out by coercing the plaintiff. The liability is not for an attempt per se.

the reason for this is not because they induce breaches of contract per se. It is because, in inducing a breach of contract, they exercise control over the plaintiff. Thus, though the tort of inducing breach of contract must be rejected, the outcomes of even cases such as *Torquay Hotel Co Ltd v Cousins* and *Merkur Island Shipping Corp v Laughton* can be supported.

In fact, it can be said that we feel the need for a tort of inducing breach of contract only because we mistakenly cling to the unlawful means control mechanism in the tort of causing loss by unlawful means. If we come to understand the latter action properly, this will allow us to drop that rule, thereby permitting the action for inducing breach of contract to die a merciful death.

IX. Conclusion

The economic torts are a mess, of that there can be no doubt. They will remain so until the wrongdoing that underlies them is properly understood. Only then can developments in the positive law move that law in the direction of coherence and certainty. This chapter has advanced such an understanding—an understanding that might be described as a new, though restricted, unified theory. The so-called economic torts deal with cases in which one person attempts to control another via the medium of a third party.

It is sometimes said that the economic torts have lacked their Atkin. Some reply that they have rather lacked their Bentham. The position advanced here is that we are really waiting for a bit of both.

10

Interference with Contract in the US

If you were asked to pick the area where US and Commonwealth tort law are most divergent, this may well be the one you would choose.[1] Most fundamentally, this divergence is understood to flow from the flirtation of US courts with the so-called prima facie tort doctrine—the notion that intentionally caused harm is recoverable unless justified—coupled with that doctrine's firm rejection by the House of Lords in *Allen v Flood*.[2] Indeed, in this area especially, Commonwealth lawyers are inclined to regard their law as demonstrably superior. Witness, for instance, Lord Hoffmann's rather dismissive claim in *OBG Ltd v Allan* that the US position 'seems to have created a good deal of uncertainty' and thus that 'we are better off without it'.[3] This is a remarkable criticism given that the law in all jurisdictions has precisely this fault. What is more, this is largely because there is in reality no great difference between the prima facie tort doctrine and the Commonwealth's conventional view. Both hold that intentionally caused loss is prima facie wrongful and that limits on the recovery of that loss must be introduced for policy reasons. Though Commonwealth law has been more confident of its control mechanisms, it is in no position to look down on US law in this regard.

What is more, as we see in this chapter, at the level of theory, US law is very similar to that of the Commonwealth. Naturally, the detail is different. Actions must be pursued in different ways in the different jurisdictions. But the actions are attempts to get at the same thing. Thus, US and Commonwealth law in this area are far from different species; they are rather dizygotic twins.

I. The Structure of US Law

The central problem with US law in this area is that its official structure is the mirror image of what it ought to be. This can be seen most clearly in the first *Restatement*. As examined in Chapter 1, US law begins with the notion that

[1] Other contenders include products liability and the reception and development of *Rylands v Fletcher* (1868) LR 3 HL 330.

[2] *Allen v Flood* [1898] AC 1 (HL).

[3] *OBG Ltd v Allan* [2007] UKHL 21, [2008] 1 AC 1 (HL) [14].

tortious liability is based most fundamentally on the idea that it is wrong to influence others negatively. Because of this, it is forced explicitly to say that one is at liberty to have such influence in contexts in which that influence is unobjectionable, obvious and routine. One such area is business competition. Thus, the first *Restatement* explains that: 'One who causes intended or unintended harm to another merely by refusing to enter into a business relation with the other … is [generally] not liable for that harm.'[4] Similarly, the *Restatement* explains that it is not generally wrongful to compete with another, even though loss may be the intended result.[5]

Think about this for a minute. Imagine that you are walking down the street and pass a store. You could enter the store and purchase something. As it is, however, you choose to walk on. Is that illegal? Your decision has a negative influence on the store owner. Is your action then tortious? The *Restatement* is telling you that it is not. That is no surprise. What is odd is that this needed to be said. Consider also the stated rationale for the second rule:[6]

> The rule … rests upon fundamental assumptions in free business enterprise. Each business enterprise must be free to select its business relations in its own interest. Since it is always subject to actual or potential competition, it must choose well or suffer death. In the struggle of each enterprise for maximum returns, maximum supply is presumably assured. Denial of this privilege to select business relations would interfere, it is thought, with an important factor in the competitive process and might defeat its aim.[7]

This is presented as if it were an excuse or justification for business activity. The implication is that, prima facie, business competition is wrongful, but it can be justified on public policy grounds, and so an exception to the general principles governing this area of the law—ie, a privilege—is created.

But nobody—nobody except indoctrinated lawyers—thinks this way. We do not regard businesspeople as habitual wrongdoers (at least not for this reason) rescued by exceptions to general principles. We do not think that the intention to compete is itself wrongful, justified only by the creation of a privilege. This is only made more plain by the fact that, as discussed in Chapters 1 and 8, competition is of the essence of life. In that light, it is notable that the *Restatement* mentions no equivalent privilege with respect to sporting competition, competing for affection or the like, and yet these are no less likely to cause negative influence.

Remarkably, immediately after the passage quoted above, the first *Restatement* appears to recognise this point, claiming that: 'The privilege is basic also in the politics of individualism. Liberty of the individual is thought to include liberty to acquire property and freedom to engage in business and to exercise one's judgment in the selection of business transactions.'[8] On that understanding, we

[4] *Restatement of the Law of Torts* (St Paul, MN, American Law Institute Publishers, 1934) §762.

[5] ibid §768.

[6] The rationale is, in fact, presented as a justification for the first, but clearly it cannot function in that fashion.

[7] *Restatement of the Law of Torts* (n 4) §762, comment a.

[8] ibid.

are no longer talking about a privilege in the above sense. According to this view, competition is legitimate not because it is an excused or justified exception to general principles, but because the general principles permit it. It is an aspect of human freedom. And so it is.

These sections from the first *Restatement* have been superseded. But that does not defeat the point being made here, which is about the mindset, the structure of analysis, with which these issues have been approached. Nevertheless, it is important to acknowledge that the second *Restatement* presents the relevant form of liability as turning not on a general principle of the illegality of harm, but on the defendant's intentional and improper interference with the plaintiff's business relations, causing harm.[9] Intentionality in this context was much discussed in the previous two chapters. Because of that, our analysis here focuses on interference and impropriety.

It is also important to say that the criticisms raised above do not entail that US law is in this regard to be rejected. It means only that the structure that one finds in the *Restatement*, in the cases and elsewhere is a poor model for understanding that law. In fact, as we see now, despite the inadequacy in the structure of analysis, US law closely fits the model advanced in this book.

Additionally, it does not follow from the fact that a decision cannot be accommodated within the theory of indirect control that the position advanced here is committed to holding that the decision is wrongly decided. On the contrary, the decision may well be able to be explained in alternative ways.

Take *Adler, Barish, Daniels, Levin and Creskoff v Epstein*,[10] for instance. The defendants were former employees of the plaintiff law firm who had decided to leave the firm and set up their own practice. One of the defendants wrote to the plaintiff's current clients, going as far as to provide them with 'form letters which could be used to discharge Adler Barish as counsel, name Epstein the client's new counsel and create a contingent fee agreement'.[11] The Supreme Court of Philadelphia held this to be a tortious interference with the plaintiff's contractual relations.

This decision cannot be justified on the ground that the defendants exercised control over the plaintiff. They did not. As there was no evidence of any attempt to strike at the plaintiff, the conclusion must be that the defendants attempted only to promote their own interests in this regard. Thus, liability cannot be supported on the thesis advanced in Part III of this book. However, this does not mean that the case was wrongly decided. Consider the following argument:

> It is true that, upon termination of their employment relationship with Adler Barish, appellees were free to engage in their own business venture … But appellees' right to

[9] *Restatement (Second) of Torts* (St Paul, MN, American Law Institute Publishers, 1965) §766–766B.

[10] *Adler, Barish, Daniels, Levin and Creskoff v Epstein* 393 A 2d 1175 (Pa 1978).

[11] ibid 1178.

pursue their own business interests is not absolute. '[U]nless otherwise agreed, after the termination of the agency, the agent ... has a duty to the principal not to take advantage of a still subsisting confidential relation created during the prior agency relation.'[12]

Though, given the structure of US law, this means that the plaintiff is able to sue for interference with contractual relations, the basis of liability is the misuse of the information which, as confidential, belonged to the plaintiff. Thus, the wrongdoing in *Adler, Barish, Daniels, Levin and Creskoff v Epstein* is a form of direct, not indirect, control. It is more like trespass than causing loss by unlawful means. Thus, though *Adler, Barish, Daniels, Levin and Creskoff v Epstein* cannot be supported on the basis of the argument presented in this part of this book, it is nevertheless in accord with the general thesis advanced here. Many other cases held to involve interference with contract are of this kind.

II. Interference with and Beyond Contract

For Commonwealth lawyers, the foundational conceptual building block in this area of the law is perhaps the notion of causing loss by unlawful means. For the US lawyer, on the other hand, it is interfering with contract. Thus, unlike Commonwealth law, US law in its entirety is regarded as a development of *Lumley v Gye*.[13] Thus, in *Raymond v Yarrington*, the Court maintained that:

> [W]here a party has entered into a contract with another to do or not to do a particular act or acts, he has as clear a right to its performance as he has to his property, either real or personal; and that knowingly to induce the other party to violate it is as distinct a wrong as it is to injure or destroy his property.[14]

This is strongly reminiscent of ideas examined and rejected in Chapter 8. In that light, it is instructive to observe that, in finding for the plaintiff, the Court described the defendants as having 'conspired to break up the agency business of plaintiff and his brother' and engaging in 'the destruction of the business of the plaintiff and his brother ... all of which are alleged to have accrued from a conspiracy on part of defendants'.[15] In *Raymond v Yarrington*, then, the defendants exercised control over the plaintiff. They did so by inducing a third party to breach his contract, but again I submit that this was the mechanism, not the nature, of the coercion in question.

What is more, as Commonwealth law did for a time, US law has grown out from this beginning. In particular, the tort does not require the defendant to induce breach; interference with performance is sufficient. Thus, it has been held that

[12] ibid 1185, quoting *Restatement (Second) of Agency*, 2nd edn (St Paul, MN, American Law Institute Publishers, 1958) §396(d).

[13] *Lumley v Gye* (1853) 2 El (&) Bl 216, 118 ER 749.

[14] *Raymond v Yarrington* 73 SW 800 (Tex 1903) 803.

[15] ibid 801.

inducing a third party legally to terminate her contract with the plaintiff can be tortious even though no breach occurs.[16] Likewise, it is accepted that a defendant who acts so as to make performance impossible, more difficult or less valuable can be liable even in the absence of breach.[17] This, of course, echoes the decisions of the English Court of Appeal in *Torquay Hotel Co Ltd v Cousins*[18] and the House of Lords in *Merkur Island Shipping Corp v Laughton.*[19] Unsurprisingly, therefore, my claim is the same as the one advanced in Chapter 9. The basis of this liability is not interfering with contract, but using the contractual relationship between the plaintiff and the third party in order to gain control over the plaintiff.

Moreover, US law is prepared to go well beyond defending contractual relations, finding defendants liable who interfere with 'prospective contractual relations'.[20] The hypothetical example mentioned in Chapter 8 in which I drive you out of business by threatening to shoot your potential customers (with whom you do not have contracts) would in US law be decided on this basis. Again, my claim is that the wrong here is best conceptualised as using third parties to gain control over the plaintiff.

Thus, despite the differences between US and Commonwealth law, these laws are similar at the level of theory. US law readily fits the account advanced here, though it is a backwards fit. By that, I mean the following. US law begins with the notion that intentional negative influence is unlawful and then carves out a huge list of exceptions. The thesis advanced here is that the liability regime that results is best understood as preventing the defendant exercising control over the plaintiff through another. US law gets to this position in an unhelpful way (as Commonwealth law also does in its own awkward manner), but at the level of theory, the important point is that it gets there. In this light, it is instructive to turn to US law's understanding of *improper* interference.

III. Improper Interference

A defendant can be liable only if she engages in improper behaviour. The reader is unlikely to be surprised to hear that this has proven to be an elusive concept. As I now argue, the reason for this is that the concept is in fact used to track something quite different: control. We can see this simply by working our way through §767 of the second *Restatement*, which states:

[16] eg, *Alpha Distributing Company of California Inc v Jack Daniel Distillery* 454 F 2d 442 (US 1972).

[17] See, eg, *Pelson v Markegard* 586 P 2d 306 (Mont 1978); *Herman v Endriss* 449 A 2d 9 (Conn 1982); *Piedmont Cotton Mills v HW Ivey Construction Co* 137 SE 2d 528 (GA 1964).

[18] *Torquay Hotel Co Ltd v Cousins* [1969] 2 Ch 106 (CA).

[19] *Merkur Island Shipping Corp v Laughton* [1983] 2 AC 570 (HL).

[20] *Restatement (Second) of Torts* (n 9) §766B.

In determining whether an actor's conduct in intentionally interfering with a contract or a prospective contractual relation of another is improper or not, consideration is given to the following factors:

(a) the nature of the actor's conduct,
(b) the actor's motive,
(c) the interests of the other with which the actor's conduct interferes,
(d) the interests sought to be advanced by the actor,
(e) the social interests in protecting the freedom of action of the actor and the contractual interests of the other,
(f) the proximity or remoteness of the actor's conduct to the interference and
(g) the relations between the parties.

It will be instructive to consider these in turn.

A. The Nature of the Actor's Conduct

In this connection, the *Restatement* mentions physical violence, misrepresentation, prosecution of civil or criminal suit and generally unlawful conduct. This, of course, fits with the theory advanced here. A defendant who intentionally causes the plaintiff loss by subjecting either the plaintiff or a third party to such exercises control over the plaintiff. Of more interest is the notion that improper action includes creating economic pressure and violating business ethics and customs. This is interesting because these would not normally constitute unlawful means in English law, supporting the claim made in Chapter 9 that unlawful means ought not to be a precondition of liability. Let us take some examples.

In *Smith v Ford Motor Company*,[21] the plaintiff held a contract of employment with a third party. That contract was terminable at will. The defendant put economic pressure on the third party to terminate the contract, which was done without illegality on the part of the third party—ie, there was no breach of contract. The defendant did this because it was unhappy that the plaintiff continued to retain business relationships with some of the defendant's competitors. The Court held for the plaintiff. In reaching his decision, Lake J quoted the following passage from Hughes J's judgment in the US Supreme Court's decision in *Truax v Reich*.[22] 'The fact that the employment is at the will of the parties, respectively, does not make it one at the will of others'.[23] Thus, though the third party was entitled to terminate the contract at will, the defendant was not. Why not? My answer is that this exercise of will was an assertion of control over the plaintiff.

Also significant are the handful of cases that involve a fact pattern of the following kind. *A* negligently injures *B*. *P*, a lawyer, enters into a contingency arrangement with *B* to represent her in her suit against *A*. *D*, *A*'s insurance company,

[21] *Smith v Ford Motor Company* 221 SE 2d 282 (NC 1976).
[22] *Truax v Reich* 239 US 33 (US 1915) 38.
[23] *Smith v Ford Motor Company* (n 21) 291.

convinces *A* to settle and thus interferes with (though not necessarily breaches) the contract between *A* and *P*. *P* successfully sues *D* for his loss.[24]

To a Commonwealth lawyer, this may seem a surprising result. After all, it is likely to be thought desirable to have insurance matters settled in this way rather than relying on the reality or threat of litigation. It may also appear to clash with the theory advanced here, because it initially seems that the insurance company is merely protecting its own interests. However, as always, these decisions must be understood in their cultural context. As the courts make plain in these cases, particularly in *Herron v State Farm Mutual Insurance Co*,[25] the decisions are motivated by a great deal of mistrust about the intentions of insurance companies. The main concern is that, in the absence of legal representation, *B* is likely to be unduly influenced by *D* to *B*'s substantial detriment. It is for this reason that the defendant's behaviour violates the relevant codes of professional ethics. Thus, the relationship between *P* and *A* is seen as a valuable one, one that *D* must not be permitted to undermine. Now, while those considerations can, and in the cases do, justify *D*'s liability to *P* for breach of contract and deceit, it cannot on its own justify liability to *P*. But the point is this. If one views the relationships between *A* and *P* and *A* and *D* in this manner, then *D*'s communications to *A* will also naturally appear (though not most importantly) to constitute an attack on *P*. And that is the basis of the liability.

B. The Actor's Motive

Consider the words of the *Restatement* in this context:

> In determining whether the interference is improper, it may become very important to ascertain whether the actor was motivated, in whole or in part, by a desire to interfere with the other's contractual relations. If this was the sole motive the interference is almost certain to be held improper.[26]

If the defendant's aim is to damage the plaintiff, then clearly the defendant is attempting to exercise control over the plaintiff.

However, the *Restatement* does not understand the matter in this way. Its justification for the rule now under examination is that: 'A motive to injure another or to vent one's ill will on him serves no socially useful purpose.'[27] This is yet another consequence of US law's false start in this area. As we saw in the first section of this chapter, because we have begun with the notion that intentional negative influence is prima facie wrongful, we are forced to hold that the routine

[24] eg, *Herron v State Farm Mutual Insurance Co* 363 P 2d 310 (Cal 1961); *Jackson v Travelers Insurance Co* 403 F Supp 986 (US 1975).

[25] *Herron v State Farm Mutual Insurance Co* (n 24).

[26] *Restatement (Second) of Torts* (n 9) §767, comment d.

[27] ibid.

creation of negative influence in business contexts is justified by an exception to the general principle instituted for public policy reasons. Given this picture, the rule now under examination is viewed as an exception to that exception. The position is that the normal exception does not apply because that exception is based on public policy concerns and, in these circumstances, the defendant's behaviour does not advance those concerns. Here, then, we get the right result, but through unnecessarily circuitous and confusing reasoning.

The *Restatement* goes on to say that:

> The desire to interfere with the other's contractual relations need not, however, be the sole motive. If it is the primary motive it may carry substantial weight in the balancing process and even if it is only a casual motive it may still be significant in some circumstances. On the other hand, if there is no desire at all to accomplish the interference and it is brought about only as a necessary consequence of the conduct of the actor engaged in for an entirely different purpose, his knowledge of this makes the interference intentional, but the factor of motive carries little weight toward producing a determination that the interference was improper.[28]

Again, though this is advanced in ways that cannot be supported here, the results are appropriate. If the defendant is trying to achieve a number of things, including exercising control over the plaintiff, then that is wrongful. On the other hand, if the defendant has negative influence on the plaintiff, but is pursuing his own self-interest or the interests of others and not striking at the plaintiff, then this is not wrongful.

The plaintiff in *Russell v Croteau* was employed by a company. He alleged that though 'he was considered efficient and that he had received an award for meritorious service', the defendant 'consistently complained of the quality and quantity of the plaintiff's work, that the defendant ridiculed him in the presence of customers, threatened "to get rid of" him and generally made conditions difficult for the plaintiff by making various charges and complaints about the plaintiff to the general manager and other employees'.[29] The plaintiff was eventually dismissed by the general manager. In his defence, the defendant maintained 'that he had no animosity toward the plaintiff, that he never made any complaints or charges or statements about the plaintiff and that he had done nothing to cause the plaintiff's dismissal "in any way, shape or manner"'.[30] The Supreme Court of New Hampshire held that if the plaintiff's allegations of fact were correct, then he was entitled to succeed. There, the defendant would have exercised control over the plaintiff. On the other hand, the Court held that if the defendant's allegations were true, then the defendant must succeed. There, the defendant would not have exercised control over the plaintiff.

[28] ibid.
[29] *Russell v Croteau* 94 A 2d 376 (NH 1953) 377.
[30] ibid.

In *Byars v Baptist Medical Centers Inc*,[31] the plaintiff nurse successfully sued the defendant hospital in negligence for a personal injury that she suffered on its premises. The plaintiff then asked to be placed on the registry held by the hospital used by patients to obtain the care of private nurses. The defendant refused, thus depriving the plaintiff of the opportunity to obtain this employment. In order to understand the nature of this case, at least in the eyes of the Supreme Court of Alabama, the registry was no mere marketing device or source of information, but the sole practical means of obtaining employment of the relevant kind. The Court held as follows:

> If it is true that the defendant's conduct was based upon a negative assessment of the plaintiff's physical ability to perform her nursing duties, the defendant's conduct would not be actionable, for the hospital would have a legal right to establish, publish and apply reasonable standards of fitness, including physical fitness, for private duty nurses.[32]

In these circumstances, the defendant would be protecting the interests of patients rather than exercising control over the plaintiff:

> If, on the other hand, the defendant's conduct was based upon the successful exercise by the plaintiff of her legal right to seek redress in the courts for injury due to the defendant's negligence, that conduct would not justify the interference with plaintiff's future employment opportunities with defendant's patients, but would violate her right as one qualified under the Nurses Registry to be referred to patients seeking her services.[33]

That, of course, would be an exercise of control over the plaintiff: an act of revenge for her successful negligence suit.

C. The Interests of the Other with which the Actor's Conduct Interferes

The *Restatement* rather cryptically holds that:

> Some contractual interests receive greater protection than others. Thus, depending upon the relative significance of the other factors, the actor's conduct in interfering with the other's prospective contractual relations with a third party may be held to be not improper, although his interference would be improper if it involved persuading the third party to commit a breach of an existing contract with the other.[34]

Let us examine a case said to illustrate this rule.

The parties in *Fury Imports Inc v Shakespeare Company*[35] were rival companies that sold fishing rods. They both had arrangements with a third party company,

[31] *Byars v Baptist Medical Centers Inc* 361 So 2d 350 (Ala 1978).
[32] ibid 356.
[33] ibid.
[34] *Restatement (Second) of Torts* (n 9) §767, comment e.
[35] *Fury Imports Inc v Shakespeare Company* 554 F 2d 1376 (US 1977).

Omori, to produce reels for the rods. After some period of time, the third party informed Fury that it would no longer be able to supply it with reels. The question was why. According to Fury: 'Shakespeare had bought into Omori and made it a sizeable interest-free loan on the condition that Omori would quit making Spinmaster reels for Fury, with the purpose of eliminating Fury as a competitor to Shakespeare in the market to sell fishing reels.'[36] According to Shakespeare, on the other hand, 'its purpose for buying into Omori, making it the loan, and requiring that Omori stop supplying reels to Fury, was to save Omori from bankruptcy and preserve it as a steady supplier of reels to Shakespeare'.[37]

The Court held that if the plaintiff's allegations were correct, then it was entitled to recover. In those circumstances, the defendant would have been exercising control over the plaintiff. On the other hand:

> In this case, Shakespeare argues that it had two kinds of 'existing economic interests' in Omori that justified its inducement to breach the Fury-Omori contract. First, it relies on its 'permanent order' of reels from Omori, which predated Fury's contract with Omori, as creating a 'contractor's privilege'. Second, it relies on its purchase of one-sixth of Omori's stock and $200,000 interest free loan to Omori as creating an 'owner's privilege' or 'investor's privilege'. In order to protect these 'existing economic interests', Shakespeare tells us, it was privileged to induce Omori to breach its contract with Fury. The district court, recognizing the principle 'that one who has a financial interest in the business of another is privileged to interfere with a contract between that business and a third person provided that the purpose is to protect its own interest'.[38]

If this is what occurred, then the defendant was not trying to exercise control over the plaintiff but was attempting only to protect its own position. Here, as it were, the defendant was trying only to live its own life, albeit in a way that had a negative influence on the plaintiff.

D. The Interests Sought to be Advanced by the Actor

The *Restatement* holds that:

> The correlative of the interest with which the actor interferes … is the interest that his conduct is intended to promote. Both are important in determining whether the interference is improper. And both are to be appraised in the light of the social interests that would be advanced by their protection.[39]

Let us turn to the cases.

One of the defendants in *Nitzberg v Zalesky*[40] issued a loan to a third party company. This company encountered considerable financial difficulties and this

[36] ibid 1378–79.
[37] ibid 1379.
[38] ibid 1383.
[39] *Restatement (Second) of Torts* (n 9) §767, comment f.
[40] *Nitzberg v Zalesky* 370 So 2d 389 (Fla 1979).

defendant refused to extend more credit unless the company improved its financial position. The company agreed to this and, as a result, the officers of the company all took salary cuts. The plaintiff was one of these officers and brought suit against the defendant for his losses.

This claim was unsurprisingly rejected:

> The requirement of FMI that CIC reduce its overhead before additional operational funds were lent was reasonable and justified. … [The company's manager's] activities, carried out in order to save the corporation, are privileged under Florida law. The law recognizes that a contracting party has a privilege to interfere with a contractual or business relationship, where the interference is necessary to protect his own contractual rights provided that such interference is without malice …
>
> If a person has a present existing economic interest to protect, such as ownership interest or a prior contract right of his own, he is privileged to prevent performance of a contract of another which threatens it.[41]

The reasoning is backwards, but the result is correct. The defendant was protecting its own position rather than attempting to exercise control over the plaintiff.

The defendant in *Leo Spear Construction Company Inc v The Fidelity and Casualty Company of New York*[42] was the surety of a construction company that contracted with a third party university to undertake some construction. The plaintiff subcontracted with the construction company. The construction company defaulted on its contract with the third party and that party terminated. Moreover, though the defendant contracted with another company to complete the construction, this company declined to contract with the plaintiff. The result was that the plaintiff was placed under significant financial distress, in particular because of its debts to its suppliers. The plaintiff decided to take physical possession of building materials that it had brought to the site. This produced a dispute as between the plaintiff and the new construction company over title to these materials. Legal action was taken. The result was that the legal status of this material was unclear. The defendant eventually paid the plaintiff's suppliers, but not until these matters had been clarified. The plaintiff alleged that this was unlawful and caused it loss. Though the plaintiff succeeded at trial, the Court of Appeal reversed the decision:

> In this case, we think that F (&) C was privileged to withhold payment to Spear's suppliers pending determination as to Spear's status and resolution of the controversy as to who was entitled to possession of the material Spear had left on the construction site …
>
> Recovery … based on the delay in paying subcontractors is also inappropriate because there is no proof that F (&) C acted for the purpose of preventing Spear from dealing with third parties. F (&) C had no interest in so doing but it did have an interest in effecting payment to the materialmen in such a way as to foreclose any future claims of liability against it by the materialmen and by Spear for the material involved. This was

[41] ibid 391.

[42] *Leo Spear Construction Company Inc v The Fidelity and Casualty Company of New York* 446 F 2d 439 (US 1971).

> complicated by the fact that some of this material for which payment to the materialmen was delayed was removed by Spear from the construction site. Indeed, it might well be inferred that F (&) C's conduct in delaying payment was merely to induce Spear to return the material which Spear had removed from the site to 'protect ourselves' … which presumably was to deter defendants from engaging another subcontractor to finish Spear's part of the job. It is clear then with respect to the delay in payment that F (&) C acted to protect its legitimate interests and not for the purpose of injuring Spear's relations with third parties.[43]

All of this shows that the defendant was trying to protect its own interests and not take control of the plaintiff.

E. The Social Interests in Protecting the Freedom of Action of the Actor and the Contractual Interests of the Other

The *Restatement* then throws down the gauntlet, maintaining that: 'Appraisal of the private interests of the persons involved may lead to a stalemate unless the appraisal is enlightened by a consideration of the social utility of these interests.'[44] Let's see.

The plaintiff in *Bledsoe v Watson*[45] was a lawyer engaged by the City of Seal Beach to investigate irregularities in some petitions that had been presented to the city and to represent the city and members of the city council in proceedings brought by third parties attempting to force an election to recall members of the city council. The plaintiff alleged that the defendant improperly persuaded the city treasurer to repudiate the contract by writing to the treasurer alleging that retention of the plaintiff was an inappropriate use of the city's funds.

In finding for the defendant, Fleming J said that: 'As a general rule interference with contractual relations is justifiable when a person seeks to protect an interest of greater social value than that attached to the stability of the contract involved.'[46] It was said to be readily demonstrable in this case that the defendant's interest was of greater social value, because California law went out of its way to encourage citizens to question the spending priorities of its public bodies.[47] Thus: 'In our view protection of the means appropriate to prevent an illegal expenditure of public funds and to achieve fiscal integrity in local government carries a greater social value than protection from challenge of plaintiff's employment contract with the city and its council members.'[48]

[43] ibid 445.
[44] *Restatement (Second) of Torts* (n 9) §767, comment g.
[45] *Bledsoe v Watson* 106 106 Cal Rptr 197 (Cal 1973).
[46] ibid 198.
[47] ibid 198–99.
[48] ibid 199.

That argumentation was not necessary. As Fleming J had just pointed out:

> The citizen-resident taxpayer who prevents an illegal expenditure of public funds not only safeguards his private interest in the amount of taxes he pays but upholds the general public interest in the fiscal integrity of his local government. Correspondence with the public officer responsible for the disbursement of the funds under question appears to us an appropriate means of petition and instruction.[49]

This shows that the defendant's representations were in the public interest, but it also more fundamentally shows that the defendant's actions were not an attempt to exercise control over the plaintiff. On the contrary, they were attempts to promote the public interest. On this view, that the defendant was performing his civic duty does not mean that he is entitled to a defence that constitutes an exception to a general rule; rather, it reveals that he did not have the intention necessary to conduct wrongdoing of the relevant kind.[50]

Cal-Medicon v Los Angeles County Medical Association[51] is similar. The plaintiffs were a corporation and a physician associated with the corporation that assisted the Los Angeles County Department of Public Social Services in obtaining medical examinations for recipients of an aid programme. The Los Angeles County Medical Association (LACMA) sent a letter to the physician noting that he had links with Cal-Medicon and stating that:

> It is the opinion of the Committee on Ethics that, by such agreement, you have been in violation of the Code of Ethics of the American Medical Association and the Los Angeles County Medical Association by engaging in the solicitation of patients. In addition, it is the opinion of the Committee on Ethics that there may be a violation of Section 2399 of the Business and Professions Code of the State of California which covers 'cappers and steerers'.[52]

The plaintiffs' allegation was that this letter made other physicians wary of associating with Cal-Medicon, creating a risk of the corporation's insolvency, and that this constituted tortious interference with contractual relations.

In finding for the defendant, Fleming J said:

> Assuming that LACMA's action is sufficient to constitute an interference with Cal-Medicon's business, justification appears on the face of the complaint. LACMA is an organization of medical doctors formed to protect and advance the interests of both its member doctors and the public. A special relationship exists between the Association and its members concerning conduct of the member within the Association's ambit … That special relationship justifies the association's interference in the conduct of its members …

[49] ibid.

[50] See also *Scott v McDonnell Douglas Corp* 112 Cal Rptr 609 (Cal 1974); *Rudoff v Huntington Symphony Orchestra Inc* 397 NYS 2d 863 (NY 1977).

[51] *Cal-Medicon v Los Angeles County Medical Association* 97 Cal Rptr 530 (Cal 1971).

[52] ibid 532.

> LACMA is justifiably concerned with the ethical conduct of its member, Dr. Dorfman. LACMA's actions toward him give rise to no cause of action for 'business interference' incidentally resulting from those actions.[53]

Again, this shows that the defendant's actions were not an attempt to exercise control over the plaintiff. On the contrary, they were attempts to protect the members of the LACMA and the public.[54]

A more interesting case is *GMC Inc v Chrisofolli*.[55] The plaintiff was the owner of adult bookstores that were picketed by the defendants, who were opponents of pornography. The plaintiff maintained that the picketing amounted to a tortious interference with his business. The trial court permitted the picketing to continue, but limited the total number of picketers to 20. It did so partly because the picketers were behaving in an orderly fashion.[56]

The case is interesting because the picketers were, of course, attempting to influence the plaintiff in the sense that they would have desired the closure of his businesses. But it must also be recognised that the picketers did this not in order to control the plaintiff per se, but in pursuit of their vision of the good. It is important to stress that the picketers were not pursuing a merely external preference, ie, a preference as to how others live their lives. Rather, they did not wish to live in a community that contained pornography. Thus, in *GMC Inc v Chrisofolli*, there was a clash between the way in which the plaintiff wished to live his life and the way in which the picketers wished to live theirs. It is in this light that we must consider Judge Whiteside's claim, made in support of the defendants, that:

> A most effective way to eliminate the sale of vulgar (but not legally obscene) publications is to persuade that portion of the general public who support such sales by their purchases to refrain from purchasing such publications. Defendants have a right to attempt to accomplish this purpose by peaceful picketing.[57]

Because the picketers were demonstrating peacefully and because their numbers were limited, their actions were viewed as directed primarily towards changing the attitudes of the plaintiff's potential customers. And as explained in Chapter 8—and revisited in Chapter 13—the plaintiff can have no rights to these attitudes. Thus, in these circumstances, it was appropriate to find for the defendant. But it would have been different had the picketers been trying to teach the defendant a lesson for sinning, for example. Then the case ought to have been decided the other way.[58]

[53] ibid 533.

[54] See also *Masoni v Board of Trade of San Francisco* 260 P 2d 205 (Cal 1953); *Middlesex Concrete Products and Excavating Corp v Carteret Industrial Association* 181 A 2d 774 (NJ 1962).

[55] *GMC Inc v Chrisofolli* 381 NE 2d 217 (Ohio 1978).

[56] ibid 218.

[57] ibid 219.

[58] The *Restatement* refers to *New Negro Alliance v Sanitary Grocery Co* 303 US 552 (US 1938), but that case is irrelevant here. It turned on the applicability of a statute. The court did not need to determine which party's position accorded with the public interest. It needed to determine only whether the Norris-La Guardia Act, 29 USCA applied. The *Restatement* also mentions *Cincinati Bengals Inc v*

F. The Proximity or Remoteness of the Actor's Conduct to the Interference

This matter can be dealt with speedily. The *Restatement* maintains:

> One who induces a third person not to perform his contract with another interferes directly with the other's contractual relation. The interference is an immediate consequence of the conduct, and the other factors need not play as important a role in the determination that the actor's interference was improper. The actor's conduct need not be predatory or independently tortious, for example, and mere knowledge that this consequence is substantially certain to result may be sufficient.[59]

Yes. This is because, in these circumstances, the defendant will have exercised control over the plaintiff:

> If, however, A induces B to sell certain goods to him and thereby causes him not to perform his contract to supply the goods to C, this may also have the effect of preventing C from performing his contractual obligations to supply them to D and E. C's failure to perform his contracts is a much more indirect and remote consequence of A's conduct than B's breach of his contract with C, even assuming that A was aware of all of the contractual obligations and the interference can be called intentional. This remoteness conduces toward a finding that the interference was not improper.[60]

The conclusion is correct, but it has nothing to do with remoteness. In this case, *A* is not exercising control over *D* or *E*. The *Restatement* continues:

> The weight of this factor [ie, remoteness], however, may be controverted by the factor of motive if it was the actor's primary purpose to interfere with C's obligation to D and E, or perhaps by the factor of the actor's conduct if that conduct was inherently unlawful or independently tortious.[61]

That is because, in those circumstances, the defendant will have exercised control over the plaintiff.

G. The Relations Between the Parties

We can also deal quickly with this clause. The *Restatement* provides an example:

> [I]f A is C's business advisor, it is proper for him to advise C, in good faith and within the scope of C's request for advice, that it would be to his financial advantage to break

Bergey 453 F Supp 129 (US 1974). The court held in favour of the defendant for many reasons, including that the plaintiff had failed to show that its position was not in violation of the public interest. But it was quite clear that, that issue aside, the plaintiff had no case. Finally, the *Restatement* cites *Edwards v Travelers Insurance of Hartford, Connecticut* 563 F 2d 105 (US 1977). This is a case of a kind already examined. See the text accompanying n 24 above.

[59] *Restatement (Second) of Torts* (n 9) §767, comment h.

[60] ibid.

[61] ibid.

> his contract with B, while it would be improper if he were a volunteer … Again, it is important whether the relationship between B and C is that of a prospective contract, an existing contract or a contract terminable at will.[62]

It is important to attend to the relationship between the parties, but not because this is properly a determinant of liability per se. Rather, it is because that relationship can reveal whether the defendant was exercising control over the plaintiff. In the example in the *Restatement*, it is clear that the business advisor is not doing so.

IV. Conclusion

The US law of interference with contract or prospective contractual relations begins in a quite different place from the Commonwealth law of causing loss by unlawful means. But it is based on the same notions. In some ways, the nature of US law is more obscured by its structure than Commonwealth law, but in other ways the reverse is true. Nevertheless, though of course there are cases that constitute exceptions, the law generally instantiates the theory advanced here.

[62] ibid §767, comment i.

11

Injurious Falsehood and Malicious Prosecution

This chapter briefly examines two torts of relatively minor significance that also fit the pattern of analysis examined earlier in this part of the book: injurious falsehood and malicious prosecution.

I. Injurious Falsehood

In the Commonwealth, it is said that a defendant who makes a statement 'maliciously' to a third party is guilty of injurious falsehood if the statement causes loss to the plaintiff. The key notion in this regard is malice. The general consensus is that it is unclear what this means. It has been defined as the intent to injure,[1] but also as knowledge that the statement is false or recklessness in that regard.[2] Though frequently lamented,[3] this lack of clarity is due to an only slight misunderstanding. In fact, the tort requires both elements, a fact recognised in the US.[4]

The basis of injurious falsehood is the same as the one we have been examining. In making her statement as she does, the defendant exerts control over the plaintiff via the mechanism of the party to whom the statement is made.

A clear example is the American case *Al Raschid v News Syndicate Co*.[5] The defendant allegedly told the immigration authorities that the plaintiff was an illegal immigrant, knowing that information to be false. The result, according to the plaintiff's version of the facts, was that the plaintiff was deported from the US. Here, on the assumption that the allegations were true, the giving of the information was an exercise of control over the plaintiff achieved by the defendant via the intervention of the immigration authority.

[1] *Steward v Young* (1870) LR 5 CP 122, 127.

[2] *Greers Ltd v Pearman and Corder Ltd* (1922) 39 RPC 406, 417.

[3] For two different ways of dealing with it, though they come to the same thing, see WVH Rogers, *Winfield and Jolowicz on Tort*, 18th edn (London, Sweet (U&0026) Maxwell, 2010) 666–67 (the analysis is not repeated in the 19th edn) and J Murphy, C Witting and J Goudkamp, *Street on Torts*, 13th edn (Oxford, Oxford University Press, 2012) 386–87.

[4] *Restatement (Second) of Torts* (St Paul, MN, American Law Institute Publishers, 1965) §623A.

[5] *Al Raschid v News Syndicate Co* 191 NE 713 (NY 1934).

Another case is *Ratcliffe v Evans*.[6] The defendant published a statement in a newspaper claiming that the defendant had ceased to trade, knowing the statement to be false and with the aim of causing loss to the plaintiff. Again, the wrong is clear. In publishing the statement, the defendant exerted control over the plaintiff via the medium of those who learnt of the claim made in the statement.

This immediately reveals why the tort requires loss. Because control is exerted through a third party, in the absence of loss, there can have been no coercion of the plaintiff. It also reveals why the defendant's statement must be untrue, though there is an important exception to this that must be discussed first. As WVH Rogers helpfully put it:

> [E]ven if the defendant does believe the untrue statement there will still be malice if he is actuated by some indirect, dishonest or improper motive, which seems here to mean the purpose of injuring the claimant rather than defending his own interests or pushing his own business.[7]

The negative claim here reflects notions expressed above, particularly in Chapter 9. A defendant who tells the truth to a third party does not thereby wrong that party (as was argued in Chapter 7), but he may wrong the plaintiff if he were trying to and succeeds in exercising control over the plaintiff via the mechanism of the third party. On the other hand, a defendant motivated to protect his own interests has no such intention.

We can also support the view that a defendant who believes the false statement can nevertheless be liable if he exercises control over the plaintiff by means of that statement, but not in this tort. If the defendant's statement is true and is not made in order to injure the plaintiff, then, as it merely represents the world as it is, it cannot be regarded as an exercise of control over the plaintiff even if it causes the plaintiff loss. Similarly, if the defendant believes the false statement to be true, he is not attempting to gain control over the plaintiff through making a false statement.

II. Malicious Prosecution

In *Martin v Watson*,[8] the defendant complained to the police that the plaintiff had indecently exposed himself to her. This led to the plaintiff being prosecuted. The English Court of Appeal held that, as the defendant did not take part in the decision to prosecute, she could not be liable. The House of Lords reversed this decision. Lord Keith said:

> Where an individual falsely and maliciously gives a police officer information indicating that some person is guilty of a criminal offence and states that he is willing to give

[6] *Ratcliffe v Evans* [1892] 2 QB 524 (CA). See also *Dudley v Briggs* 6 NE 717 (Mass 1886).

[7] Rogers (n 3) 667 (the passage has been omitted from the 19th edn). Rogers referred in this connection to *Dunlop v Mason Talbot* (1904) 20 TLR 579.

[8] *Martin v Watson* [1996] AC 74 (HL).

> evidence in court of the matters in question, it is properly to be inferred that he desires and intends that the person he names should be prosecuted. Where the circumstances are such that the facts relating to the alleged offence can be within the knowledge only of the complainant, as was the position here, then it becomes virtually impossible for the police officer to exercise any independent discretion or judgment, and if a prosecution is instituted by the police officer the proper view of the matter is that the prosecution has been procured by the complainant.[9]

This neatly fits the pattern of liability found throughout this part of this book. In these situations, the defendant exercises control over the plaintiff through the medium of a third party, here officers of the legal system. In this case, the defendant gave information to the police in circumstances in which they were required to believe her, with the result that they acted so as to constrain the plaintiff. Their constraint can be justified, but hers cannot.[10] As Lord Steyn said in *Gregory v Portsmith CC*: 'A distinctive feature of the tort is that the defendant has abused the coercive powers of the state.'[11] The abuse is conducted by getting the state to exercise coercion against the plaintiff.

On the other hand, in *H v B*,[12] the court found in favour of a defendant who had testified against the plaintiff to the police only under considerable pressure from the police to do so and long after the alleged offence. As this defendant did not seek the plaintiff's prosecution, she was not attempting to exercise control over him and was not found liable.

This is why the development of the Crown Prosecution Service in the UK, the District Attorney's Office in the US and similar institutions elsewhere has led to a decline in the significance of this tort.[13] These authorities exercise considerable independent judgement and, if the prosecuting authority can be said to be making its own judgement in deciding to prosecute, then it is impossible to say that *the defendant* succeeds in exercising control over the plaintiff. Thus, as the English Court of Appeal maintained in *H v B*,[14] it becomes necessary to show that the defendant somehow 'manipulated' events, so that, at least, the prosecution proceeded in ways that it would not otherwise have done.

It is also for this reason that the tort requires the defendant to have been motivated by malice, which here seems to mean that she possessed the predominant purpose of injuring the plaintiff.[15] That intention is an essential element of any attempt to exercise control over the plaintiff in the relevant circumstances.

[9] ibid 86–87.

[10] See also *Blair v Shoulz* 7 NW 2d 904 (Iowa 1943); *Lemke v Anders* 53 NE 2d 436 (Wis 1952); *Wood v Palmer Ford Inc* 425 A 2d 671 (Md 1981); *Schleicher v Western State Bank of Devils Lake* 314 NW 2d 293 (ND 1982)

[11] *Gregory v Portsmith CC* [2000] 1 AC 419 (HL), 426.

[12] *H v B* [2009] EWCA Civ 1092, The Times (28 October 2009).

[13] For discussion, see WE Peel and J Goudkamp, *Winfield and Jolowicz on Tort*, 19th edn (London, Sweet (U) Maxwell, 2013) 625–27.

[14] *H v B* (n 12) [47], [58], [84]. Note that the decision in *Scott v Ministry of Justice* [2009] EWCA Civ 1215 is entirely consistent with this view. See also *Grimes v Greenblatt* 107 P 1111 (Colo 1910); *Meraz v Valencia* 210 P 255 (NM 1922).

[15] Peel and Goudkamp (n 13) 627–29; *Restatement (Second) of Torts* (n 4) §668.

In order to understand this tort, it is also necessary to see that the law cannot regard the giving of information that leads to a just conviction as coercion[16]—remembering here that coercion is *wrongful* constraint. This is why these causes of action cannot be dealt with as deceits, injurious falsehoods and the like. Giving information that provides 'reasonable and probable cause' to believe that the plaintiff is guilty of an offence must be viewed not as an attempt to exert control over the plaintiff, but the performance of a legal duty that the defendant owes to society at large.

This is also why the plaintiff can succeed only in the absence of an incriminating finding by a court supporting the defendant's allegations.[17] It has been argued that the justification for this rule is due to 'the risk of diverse determinations by different courts on the same facts and between the same parties',[18] but that cannot be right. The reason why a plaintiff convicted of an offence cannot sue a defendant who accused the plaintiff of the offence is not so as to save the legal system from embarrassment. It is because the conviction indicates that the defendant was performing his legal duty. Thus, as the New Zealand Court of Appeal and the US *Restatement* have recognised, conviction is in this sense a complete defence.[19]

In *Crawford Adjusters v Sagicor General Insurance (Cayman) Ltd*,[20] the Privy Council decided by a majority that this tort would be available in cases where the defendant had brought civil proceedings, reversing the former view that the tort applied only in criminal proceedings, following the position adopted in most of the US.[21] That decision receives support from the argument presented here, though the support can only be cautious.

The Vice President of the defendant company, Mr Delessio, declared 'that he intended to drive Mr Paterson [the plaintiff] out of business and to destroy him professionally ... To one witness Mr Delessio seemed obsessed by a desire to damage Mr Paterson'.[22] As a result of Delessio's actions, Patterson suffered considerable losses and 'massive damage to his reputation and to the willingness of third parties to employ him'.[23]

The dispute between the majority and dissent in *Crawford Adjusters* was fought over two battlegrounds. The first related to the historical basis of the action and the second to a set of policy concerns said to argue against liability. Most telling is what is missing. The fundamental weakness with the position of the majority and of the dissent is that though each side accepts that an injustice was committed by

[16] *Restatement (Second) of Torts* (n 4) §§657, 669.

[17] See especially *Van Heeren v Cooper* [1999] 1 NZLR 731 (CA); *Restatement (Second) of Torts* (n 4) §§657, 658–61.

[18] Rogers (n 3) 929. See also Peel and Goudkamp (n 13) 628.

[19] *Van Heeren v Cooper* (n 17); *Restatement (Second) of Torts* (n 4) §657.

[20] *Crawford Adjusters v Sagicor General Insurance (Cayman) Ltd* [2013] UKPC 17, [2013] 3 WLR 927.

[21] *Restatement (Second) of Torts* (n 4) §§674, 677, 680. See also *Little v Law Institute of Victoria (No 3)* [1990] VR 257.

[22] *Crawford Adjusters v Sagicor General Insurance (Cayman) Ltd* (n 20) [14].

[23] ibid [19].

Delessio against Patterson, no one explains what that injustice was.[24] Because of this, the argument of neither side can be convincing.

The chief arguments of the dissent are that the tort should be restricted to cases of criminal prosecutions because the alternative has the potential to deter legitimate plaintiffs from bringing suit and that the 'primary' litigation must be understood to settle the legal issues. As Lord Sumption expressed these ideas:

> All of this derives from two developed legal instincts ... The first is a concern about the deterrent effect of potential liability upon litigants, who may be inhibited from invoking the jurisdiction of the courts; and upon witnesses, who may be inhibited from freely assisting in the administration of justice ... The second instinct reflects a concern, in the interests of the efficient deployment of resources, to discourage secondary litigation in which the parties complain of the conduct of earlier litigation in what is potentially an unending sequence of actions upon actions.[25]

These arguments are not compelling. For one thing, it is unclear why they do not also apply in the criminal context. More importantly, this position would insulate from liability those who coerce others through the mechanism of the law in order better to pursue those who coerce others in different ways. But it is the same wrongdoing that we are dealing with in each case. There is no justification for protecting one group over the other. Perhaps this view is motivated by the notion that coercion though the bringing of civil proceedings is impossible due to the relevant legal protections. This view appears to receive some support in Lord Sumption's judgment.[26] I submit, however, that the view is naïve and, what is more, the facts of *Crawford Adjusters* demonstrate this.

The purpose of the law of tort, if we must speak of purpose at all, is to respond to acts of coercion. If we accept that the civil law can itself be a mechanism through which coercion occurs, then we cannot support any immunity for malicious prosecution based on civil proceedings.

That said, however, it is important to remember that the tort ought to be available only when the plaintiff has been coerced. It is not sufficient that the plaintiff has merely suffered loss. Thus, contrary to the expectations of the majority and the fears of the dissenters, it is not itself a tortious act to sue someone. Standardly, these are not coercive acts.[27]

[24] Perhaps Lady Hale expresses the view that the injustice was causing loss; see ibid [86]–[87].
[25] ibid [126].
[26] ibid [132].
[27] They are akin to acts of self-defence. For the discussion of self-defence, see Ch 6.

Part IV

Injury

This part deals with a single area of the law: the law of negligence. This is because that law is protean and now encompasses at least the vast majority of liability for injury. As I have already written an overly long book on the law of negligence, this material is more cursory than what has gone before. It focuses solely on providing a theoretical framework for the law. Those with more detailed questions can be directed to my earlier work.[1]

[1] A Beever, *Rediscovering the Law of Negligence* (Oxford, Hart Publishing, 2007).

12

The Law of Negligence

As noted in Chapter 2, constraint takes two forms. First, I constrain you if I put you or your property to my purposes without your consent. We have labelled this control. Second, I constrain you if I deprive you of the means, to which you are entitled, to realise your purposes. This is labelled injury and is the focus of this chapter.

I. The Nature of the Wrongdoing

It is first important to clarify the difference between this kind of wrongdoing and that explored in previous chapters. Let us begin by distinguishing trespass from negligence. The crucial difference is this. A trespasser puts the plaintiff or the plaintiff's property to her purposes. As we saw, this is so even if the trespasser's purpose is self-sacrificing and is to benefit the plaintiff. This occurs because of the intention that the trespasser possesses. Because she intends to touch the plaintiff, to be on the plaintiff's land and to make contact with the plaintiff's chattel, she puts the plaintiff, the plaintiff's land and chattel to her purposes. But things are different where she does not possess this intention. In cases of negligence,[1] the defendant is not putting the plaintiff or the plaintiff's property to her purposes. Rather, she is pursuing her own purposes in a way that interferes with the plaintiff's pursuit of his purposes. The wrongdoing, then, is quite different and the structure of liability dealing with it is also different. In negligence, the plaintiff's complaint is that in the course of pursuing the defendant's own purposes,[2] the defendant injured him, undermining his ability pursue his purposes.

If I crash into your car intentionally, then you can justifiably complain that I was putting your car to my purposes. I exercised control over the car. But if I crash only negligently, as my contact with your car was accidental, you cannot make the same complaint. Making contact with your car was not part of my purpose. I did

[1] For convenience, I assume that in all cases discussed, the defendant is merely negligent in the sense that she did not have the relevant intention and was not reckless. I do not, in fact, believe that it is impossible to be liable in the tort of negligence for intentional wrongdoing. There is simply nothing in the tort of negligence to prevent this.

[2] Which may, in principle, involve a trespass to a third person. That matter is irrelevant here.

not use your car. Rather, your complaint must be that, in pursuing my purposes, I wrongly interfered with your ability to pursue yours.

This immediately reveals why recklessness in the sense examined in Chapter 4 is sufficient for liability in trespass, but irrelevant in negligence. Because recklessness involves a choice to place another or another's property at a risk of which one was aware, it indicates that the defendant's purpose extended to the plaintiff or the plaintiff's property. As we saw in Chapter 4, recklessness involves taking a risk *with* someone or someone's property. The person or the property features in the defendant's purpose. But that is not the case when the interference is inadvertent.

This discussion also reveals a crucial difference between trespass and negligence that is essential for understanding both torts. In trespass, the defendant puts the plaintiff or the plaintiff's property to her purposes. There is what we might describe as an 'asymmetry' in this relationship that makes it immediately obvious that it is one of inequality. But in negligence, the defendant deprives the plaintiff of the means to pursue his purposes in the course of pursuing her own purpose. This is more 'symmetrical'. Thus, it is not immediately clear whose purpose should take precedence. The law took a long time to work that out.

II. Factual Causation and Loss

Unlike trespass, the tort of negligence requires proof of damage. This is because a plaintiff who has not been damaged has not been deprived of the means to pursue his purposes and thus has not been constrained. Therefore, unlike an intentional touching, an accidental mere touching is not actionable because it neither exerts control over the plaintiff nor deprives the plaintiff of the means of achieving his purposes.

It is important to stress that the concept of a purpose is broad. So, for instance, when I hang a painting on my wall, my purpose is simply to look at it, to have it brighten up the room or whatever it is. It need not be any specifically defined financial, practical or even amenable goal. Thus, for instance, if I spill acid on your car, damaging its paintwork, but leaving the drivability of the car unaffected, then if like most people your purpose in possessing the car is partly aesthetic, I interfere with your purposes, even though we are normally inclined to say that *the* purpose of a vehicle is transport.[3]

It is also important to note that this kind of wrongdoing occurs when the defendant deprives the plaintiff of the means to realise his purposes, not merely when the defendant deprives him of the means to realise the purposes he actually chooses to pursue. So, for instance, if I damage the drivability of your car, I deprive you in the relevant sense even if you have decided never to use the car again. The

[3] That, of course, is only one possible purpose with which I interfere. Another purpose would be to retain the car as a valuable asset.

point is that my action deprived you of the ability to use the car for a purpose, not for a purpose you actually have or will have.

Though less familiar and more complex, this notion provides a better explanation for the operation of the law than the received wisdom that the law of negligence is focused on compensation for loss, ie, negative influence. Consider the following examples:

Example 1: D negligently damages the paintwork of *P*'s car. The damage has no effect on the utility of the vehicle. Moreover, though the car loses market value, *P* actually prefers the look of the damaged car.

Example 2: D negligently damages the paintwork of *P*'s car. Though this has no impact on the utility of the vehicle, *P* wishes to have the damaged paintwork repaired. *D* is a celebrity and as a result of the fact that it was *D* who damaged the car, the market value of the car has increased and will decrease when it is repaired.

Example 3: D conducts surgery on *P*'s leg. The aim of the operation is to allow *P* to walk again. Though *D* conducts this operation negligently, the remarkable outcome is that *P*'s leg is so improved that *P* is able to run. However, for reasons of her own, *P* regrets this improvement.[4]

In the first two examples, it is clear that the plaintiff can recover. It also seems clear that the plaintiff in the third case cannot.[5] But why is this?

On the one hand, we might focus on the plaintiff's objective gains and losses. On this view, the question is whether the change instituted by the defendant is valued or disvalued by people generally, usually indicated by a rise or fall in the market value of the object when such is available. This approach can explain why the plaintiff recovers in the first but not the third example: the plaintiff suffers an objective loss in Example 1, but realises an objective gain in Example 3. However, it cannot explain why the plaintiff in Example 2 can recover when she too realises an objective gain.

On the other hand, one might emphasise the plaintiff's subjective gains and losses. On this approach, the question is whether the change instituted by the defendant is valued or disvalued by the plaintiff. Unlike the approach just examined, this one can explain Example 2: there the plaintiff suffers a subjective loss for which she can recover. But it founders on the other two examples. In Example 1, the plaintiff makes a subjective gain and yet recovers. In Example 3, the plaintiff suffers a subjective loss but cannot recover.

The better explanation is the one provided above. The issue is neither objective nor subjective loss. The issue is rather deprivation of the means to the plaintiff's actual or potential purposes. So, the plaintiff can recover in Example 1 because, in

[4] The focus in these cases is on damage rather than liability, in contradistinction with the theme of this book. But that is not inappropriate, as in this area of the law, liability requires damage.

[5] This situation seldom arises, but this conclusion is implied by cases such as *Reibl v Hughes* [1980] 2 SCR 880, in which it is said that the existence of the plaintiff's loss is to be determined objectively. See also *White v Turner* (1981) 120 DLR (3d) 269; *Wallace v Kam* 2012 NSWCA 82, (2012) Aust Torts Reports ¶82–101, [25], [118], [120]–[121].

damaging the car's paintwork, the defendant deprives the plaintiff of the means to realise a potential purpose, eg, taking aesthetic interest in the vehicle or realising its proper value by selling it on the market. Likewise, the plaintiff can recover in Example 2, as there the defendant deprives the plaintiff of the means to realise an actual purpose: taking that same interest. In the third example, however, the plaintiff cannot recover. This is because *D*'s action *increased P*'s means to realise her purposes[6]—a conclusion unaffected by her disappointment. Though that can be characterised as a loss, it is not constraint of the plaintiff and so cannot be wrongful.

On the model advanced here, a wrong can be committed only if the plaintiff was entitled to the means of which she was deprived. That, as was stressed in Chapter 2, is essential to constraint. Accordingly, though I alas cannot use my body to win the 100 metres final at the Olympic Games, that is not because I have been deprived of something to which I was entitled. Similarly, though I would constrain you if I cut the power cable to your television, with the result that you cannot watch TV, I would not constrain you if I cut an electricity cable owned by another that supplies electricity to your house, even though it has the same effect. In the first case, I damage something that belongs to you. In the second case, I do not. This is why pure and relational economic loss is not recoverable in negligence.[7] It is the loss of something to which the plaintiff had no entitlement. It is not therefore constraining or coercive.

III. The Standard of Care

A. The Basis of the Fault Standard

Depriving someone of the means to their purposes, to which they are entitled, is a form of constraint. But that does not mean that it is necessarily coercive. As we saw in Chapter 2, not all constraint is wrongful. This is where the 'symmetry' noticed in the first section of this chapter becomes crucial. In negligence, the defendant deprives the plaintiff of the means to pursue his purposes in the course of pursuing her own purposes. Permitting this allows the defendant to constrain the plaintiff. Prohibiting it constrains the defendant. What must be determined, then, is when one person is entitled to pursue his purposes at the expense of another.[8]

[6] However, it is important not to discount the possibility that *P* may be able to reveal a purpose that he can no longer pursue in this or in like cases. To deny *P* recovery, it is not enough to show that most people would not choose to pursue any such purpose.

[7] *cf Spartan Steel & Alloys Ltd v Martin & Co (Contractors) Ltd* [1973] QB 27 (CA); *Robins Dry Dock & Repair Co v Flint* 275 US 303 (US SC 1927); *East River Steamship Corp v Transamerica Delaval Inc* 476 US 858 (US SC 1986); *Murphy v Brentwood District Council* [1991] 1 AC 398 (HL). For discussion, see A Beever, *Rediscovering the Law of Negligence* (Oxford, Hart Publishing, 2007), ch 7.

[8] In the abstract, it is plausible to suggest that one is never entitled to pursue one's purposes in ways that damage others. See, eg, RA Epstein, 'A Theory of Strict Liability' (1973) 2 *Journal of Legal*

We have seen that the interests of the parties are 'symmetrical'. The defendant deprives the plaintiff of the means to pursue his purposes in the course of pursuing her own purposes. Accordingly, the solution to this difficulty must take the parties' positions equally into account. It must preserve equal maximum freedom. This consideration leads to the default rule that we know as the ordinary reasonable person standard or the law of negligence's objective standard of care.

Recall that the defendant in *Vaughan v Menlove*[9] built a haystack next to the plaintiff's barn and the hay caught fire and destroyed the barn. The court insisted that he be judged according to the standard of the ordinary reasonable person. This approach sets a standard for behaviour that recognises the interest both parties have in pursuing their purposes. It sets the boundary between them in a way that is indifferent to their personal circumstances, realising for each equal freedom of action and equal security. It is an approach that respects the demand for equal maximum freedom.

Accordingly, in principle, the peculiarities of the defendant are irrelevant in determining liability in negligence. The peculiarities of the plaintiff are likewise irrelevant, and not only in the tort of negligence. In the nuisance case[10] of *Rogers v Elliott*,[11] the plaintiff lived close to a church operated by the defendant. The plaintiff claimed that when the bells of the church were rung, he was sent into convulsions due to some odd peculiarity. This was accepted by the Supreme Judicial Court of Massachusetts, at least *arguendo*. The plaintiff alleged that in those circumstances, the ringing of the bells was a legal nuisance and so should be prevented. If this argument had been allowed to succeed, this would have biased the enquiry in favour of the plaintiff. A judgment made on this basis would impose absolute liability, ie, liability that flows from the mere causation of injury. But in *Rogers v Elliott*, the Court ruled that, as an ordinary reasonable person would not have been adversely affected by the bells, the defendant was not guilty of a nuisance.

It is important to note that the so-called 'ordinary reasonable person' is not a person or a statistical average, but a value judgement about how people should behave.[12] Hence, the concept of an ordinary reasonable person has no content in advance of the relevant value judgement. The legal rules for making that

Studies 151. This, however, cannot be accepted as it implies absolute liability. The impossibility of that form of liability was examined in Ch 3. An alternative approach is to suggest that people are entitled to pursue their purposes so long as they take care not to injure others. This subjective approach is also highly intuitive when expressed in the abstract, and has been and continues to be influential. See, eg, the reasoning in *Mansfield v Weetabix Ltd* [1998] 1 WLR 1263 (CA). But again it cannot be accepted. It suggests that liability should be based on personal fault, a notion also rejected in Ch 3. For discussion of *Mansfield v Weetabix*, see Beever (n 7) 79–84. The outcome of this case can perhaps be supported on the ground that the primary tortfeasor was acting as an automaton, however.

[9] *Vaughan v Menlove* (1837) 3 Hodges 51, 132 ER 490.

[10] For my analysis of the law of nuisance, see A Beever, *The Law of Private Nuisance* (Oxford, Hart, 2013).

[11] *Rogers v Elliott* 15 NE 768 (MA SJC 1888).

[12] Beever (n 7) 84–86.

judgement are examined in section III.B below. In consequence, the rule that the defendant's actions are to be judged in the light of the standard of the ordinary reasonable person is negative rather than positive. It tells us that certain concerns are irrelevant, but does not itself tell us what is relevant. The concerns that are irrelevant are the idiosyncrasies of the parties. As we have seen, these are irrelevant because considering them would be unfair as between the parties in circumstances where the parties' interests are 'symmetrical'.

Moreover, the position advanced here also explains why the law sometimes departs from the ordinary reasonable person standard. Imagine that a plaintiff agrees to undergo a medical operation performed by a surgeon. Imagine also that the surgeon performs the operation badly and the plaintiff is injured as a result. Can the plaintiff sue the surgeon in negligence for his injury?[13] If the standard to be applied to judge the surgeon's actions were that of an ordinary reasonable person, then the answer would almost certainly be no. While the surgeon may have performed the operation badly for a surgeon, it is unlikely that she performed it below the standard of the ordinary reasonable person. Unsurprisingly, in these cases the standard applied by the courts is that of an ordinary reasonable surgeon.[14]

The standard is adjusted in this case because the parties form a common purpose, of which the particular idiosyncrasy of the defendant is an essential element. The surgeon holds herself out as possessing a special skill and the plaintiff interacts with her on that basis. Hence, the purpose relevant to the interaction between the parties is such that the surgeon is expected to possess the special skills. This means that in determining whether the surgeon was negligent, the standard to be applied is one that takes into account the fact that the interaction between the plaintiff and the surgeon must be understood in the light of the defendant's representations to the plaintiff that she possessed a special skill.

A parallel case is *Paris v Stepney Borough Council*,[15] which turned on the peculiarities of the plaintiff. The plaintiff was blind in his left eye. While working for the defendant, the plaintiff was injured when he struck a U-bolt with a hammer, dislodging a shard of metal that entered his right eye, causing complete blindness. At the time of the accident, the defendant knew that the plaintiff was blind in his left eye. The plaintiff alleged that the defendant was negligent in failing to provide him with safety glasses.

Crucially, the plaintiff's position was not that all employees conducting such work should have been provided with safety glasses. Rather, it was that, given that he was already blind in one eye, the defendants should have taken into account the seriousness of the injury if the other eye were damaged. Accordingly, the plaintiff's claim was that, while it was not negligent to fail to provide glasses to other

[13] Other causes of action may also be available, such as breach of contract. These are ignored here.

[14] *Bolam v Friern Hospital Management Committee* [1957] 1 WLR 582 (QBD); *Bolitho v City and Hackney HA* [1988] AC 232 (HL); *Restatement (Third) of Torts: Physical and Emotional Harm* (St Paul, MN, American Law Institute Publishers, 2010) §12.

[15] *Paris v Stepney Borough Council* [1951] AC 367 (HL).

employees, the seriousness of the potential injury to him meant that the defendant was obliged to take special precautions to protect his eyesight.[16] The House of Lords agreed and rightly so. The partial blindness of the plaintiff was not decisive in itself, but it was correctly held to have been relevant in determining the standard of care owed by the defendant, as this affected the nature of the interaction between the parties. The defendant employed the plaintiff knowing that he was partially blind and hence knowing of the increased risk posed to the plaintiff, without providing the plaintiff with safety glasses. The plaintiff's partial blindness was an element of the parties' common purpose.

On the other hand, if the defendant is a child and that is relevant to the relationship between the parties, then the standard of care can be lowered in order to take the child's situation into account.[17] Again, the reason for this is clear. If I engage with a child as a child, then I can only expect that child to behave as a child. The age of the child is an element of our common purpose. However, if the defendant is a child and that is not relevant to the relationship between the parties—if I am struck by a child driving a car heading in the opposite direction, for example—then the ordinary adult standard applies.[18] There is no relevant common purpose here.

B. Reasonable Care

We must now turn to the positive side of the standard of care. If the peculiarities of the parties are normally irrelevant, how is it possible to determine whether the defendant was negligent? If we cannot attend to the particular defendant on trial to resolve the appropriate level of care, how can it be decided whether the defendant was legally at fault?

As the above has made clear, the answer to this question must be fair to both parties. What we need is a regime in which people are permitted to act, where action is not itself viewed as wrongful (no absolute liability), but where the legitimacy of action depends on consideration both of the agent's position and of that of the persons whom the agent will affect. Only such a regime can provide equal maximum freedom. And that is the regime that, in the Commonwealth, we at least had.

In *The Wagon Mound (No 2)*,[19] Lord Reid held that a defendant's negligence is to be determined by considering the level of risk she created. The level of risk is decided by taking into account both the likelihood of the risk materialising and

[16] As discussed below, the seriousness of the potential injury to the plaintiff is relevant in determining the standard of care.

[17] *McHale v Watson* (1966) 115 CLR 199 (HCA); *Mullin v Richards* [1998] 1 WLR 1304 (CA); *Restatement (Third) of Torts: Physical and Emotional Harm* (n 14) §10.

[18] *McErlean v Sarel* (1987) 42 DLR (4th) 577 (Ont CA); *Restatement (Third) of Torts: Physical and Emotional Harm* (n 14) §10(c). For analysis, see Beever (n 7) 87–96.

[19] *Overseas Tankship (UK) Ltd v Morts Dock & Engineering Co Ltd (The Wagon Mound (No 2))* [1967] AC 617 (PC).

the seriousness of the consequences if they materialise.[20] Lord Reid further distinguished between risks that are fantastic or far-fetched and risks that are real. His Lordship held that a defendant could be liable only if she created a real risk. Real risks were also divided into two subcategories: substantial risks and small risks. Lord Reid maintained that a defendant is negligent if she creates a substantial risk. On the other hand, if a defendant creates a small risk, then she is negligent unless the burden of eliminating the risk was high.[21]

Here we can see the House of Lords trying to give equal weight to the legally significant interests of the parties. The plaintiff cannot insist that the defendant should have preserved him from all risk: fantastic or far-fetched risks are not actionable. This is because the alternative would mean that the defendant's freedom to pursue his purposes is curtailed to such an extent that he is prohibited from performing any action that posed risk to the plaintiff, even if that risk was unforeseeable or so infinitesimal that no reasonable person would pay attention to it. That would unfairly restrict the defendant's freedom. In practice, it would amount to absolute liability. On the other hand, defendants cannot insist that they are free to fulfil their purposes as they will: the creation of a substantial risk is actionable. Here, the alternative would mean that the plaintiff's ability to pursue her purposes would be severely limited because the defendant would be permitted to perform actions even when it is clear that those actions pose serious risk to the plaintiff's person or property. That would unfairly restrict the plaintiff's freedom. Moreover, as Lord Reid recognised, we frequently create small though not fantastic or far-fetched risks to others. To hold that one cannot be liable for these risks is to allow one too much latitude to constrain others. On the other hand, to hold that one will be liable for the realisation of all of these risks is to constrain one in the interests of others to too high a degree. Instead of adopting either extreme position, then, Lord Reid maintained that one is liable for the creation of a small risk, but not if it would have been unfairly difficult for one to have eliminated that risk. Here, then, the legally significant interests of the plaintiff are protected by not allowing others to create any small risk, but the legally significant interests of the defendant are also protected by not requiring defendants to eliminate all foreseeable risks when doing so would impose a considerable and unfair burden on them.

The position taken in the Commonwealth is usefully compared with that officially taken by US law. In *United States v Carroll Towing*,[22] Learned Hand J said that a defendant is negligent if he creates a risk where the probability of the risk occurring (P) multiplied by the seriousness of the risk if it materialises (L) is

[20] See also *Bolton v Stone* [1951] AC 850 (HL), 867.

[21] It is particularly important to notice that the issue is whether the burden is high—it is emphatically not whether it is higher than the risk. This must be compared with the US approach, which will be examined shortly.

[22] *United States v Carroll Towing* 159 F 2d 169 (US 2nd Cir 1947).

greater than the burden of eliminating the risk (B). Hence, we have the famous 'Hand formula': the defendant is negligent if B<PL.[23]

'The defendant is negligent if B<PL' might be a neat formulation, but what is the purported justification for this approach? The answer is that if B<PL, then it would have been efficient, in the economic sense of that term, for the defendant to have prevented the risk materialising. In these circumstances, the expected social cost of the accident was greater than the expected social cost of the precautions to prevent the accident. On the other hand, if B>PL, then it would have been inefficient for the defendant to have prevented the risk from materialising. Here, the expected social cost of the accident was less than the expected social cost of the precautions to prevent the accident. On this view, then, the enquiry into the defendant's negligence is an attempt to find the 'lowest cost avoider' and the aim of the law of negligence is to maximise economic efficiency by providing incentives for efficient behaviour: those who act inefficiently are required to compensate those who suffer loss as a result of one's inefficient behaviour, while those who act efficiently are not so required and are also permitted to retain their gains.

Unsurprisingly, this 'utilitarian' approach violates the principles enunciated here.[24] It is inconsistent with the plaintiff's innate right, because it permits the defendant to perform actions likely to injure the plaintiff as long as those actions are beneficial to other people. It is also inconsistent with the defendant's innate right, because it allows defendants to be held liable for actions that impose unforeseeable risks if those actions were not socially valuable.[25] In a nutshell, the Hand formula holds the rights of the parties hostage to the interests of others.[26]

In that light, it is important to note that Richard Wright has argued persuasively that, though the Hand formula is officially accepted in the US, US courts generally do not apply it in fact. Remarkably, as Wright points out, Learned Hand J did not apply the formula in *Carroll Towing* itself.[27] In reality, the approach actually followed in the US is much closer to that of Commonwealth courts than might at first appear. That is not surprising. In order to avoid injustice, US courts have found themselves abandoning their official position to decide cases more in line with the theory presented here.

Unfortunately, due in part to the dominance of instrumentalism and consequentialist thinking in legal academia, legislatures in some parts of the Commonwealth

[23] *cf Restatement (Third) of Torts: Physical and Emotional Harm* (n 14) §3.

[24] See, however, SR Perry, 'Responsibility for Outcomes, Risk, and the Law of Torts' in GJ Postema (ed), *Philosophy and the Law of Torts* (Cambridge, Cambridge University Press, 2001).

[25] The fact that other aspects of the law of negligence may prevent this is not to the point here.

[26] And note that, on the assumption that these rights exist, no self-respecting person could accept that she should accept their violation on the ground that, as everyone's rights are being violated in an economically efficient way, she benefits in the long run. Compare L Kaplow and S Shavell, 'Fairness versus Welfare' (2001) 114 *Harvard Law Review* 961.

[27] RW Wright, 'Justice and Reasonable Care in Negligence Law' (2002) 47 *American Journal of Jurisprudence* 143; RW Wright, 'Negligence in the Courts: Introduction and Commentary' (2002)

have adopted a more '*Carroll Towing*-like' position. For instance, s 32 of South Australia's Civil Liability Act 1936 holds that:

> In determining whether a reasonable person would have taken precautions against a risk of harm, the court is to consider the following (amongst other relevant things):
>
> (a) the probability that the harm would occur if precautions were not taken;
> (b) the likely seriousness of the harm;
> (c) the burden of taking precautions to avoid the risk of harm;
> (d) the social utility of the activity that creates the risk of harm.[28]

This was introduced as part of a package of reforms designed to respond to Australia's so-called insurance crisis and was intended to render the law more defendant-friendly than it had been. If my experience is representative, it is now widely recognised that these reforms were ill-advised. In relation to this particular issue, the problem is obvious. How can the fact that an activity is socially useful justify imposing the costs of it on the injured plaintiff, a person who may derive no benefit from the activity? The notion that this is supported even on the basis of distributive justice—which I insist is irrelevant in any case—is extraordinary.[29] I have argued elsewhere that this legislation can and ought to be interpreted narrowly.[30]

IV. Duty and Remoteness

A. The Duty of Care

Recall that in this area of the law, judgements are appropriately made by focusing on the interactions between the parties. In discussing the objective standard of care, we saw that the relevant judgements do not focus on the defendant in isolation, but examine the relationship between the defendant and the plaintiff. Hence, to say that a defendant has been negligent is not to make an ethical judgement about that individual. It is rather to make a judgement about the legitimacy of the defendant's interaction with the plaintiff, judged from the perspective of both parties. As we have also seen, the relevant judgements are interpersonal, not

77 *Chicago-Kent Law Review* 425; RW Wright, 'Hand, Posner, and the Myth of the "Hand Formula"' (2003) 4 *Theoretical Inquiries in Law* 145.

[28] *cf* my discussion of the Compensation Act 2006 (UK) in Beever (n 7) 112–14.

[29] Compare the judgment of La Forest in *Tock v St John's Metropolitan Area Board* [1989] 2 SCR 1181, who insists that liability must fall on those who provide social benefits at cost to the plaintiff, as that liability ensures that the cost is borne by those who benefit. For discussion of that judgment as it relates to the law of nuisance, see Beever (n 10) 143–44.

[30] Beever (n 7) 112–14.

societal. The appropriate perspective is that of the parties taken as a two-person unit.

We have also seen that a defendant is negligent if she creates a substantial risk of injury to another or a small risk where the burden of eliminating that risk is not high. According to the two most famous cases in the law of negligence, *Donoghue v Stevenson*[31] and *Palsgraf v Long Island Railroad Co*,[32] a defendant owes a plaintiff a duty of care if and only if the defendant's actions place the plaintiff at a reasonably foreseeable risk of injury. Specifically, in order to be liable to the plaintiff, the defendant must have been negligent for creating a risk of injury to that person. As Cardozo CJ put it in *Palsgraf*: 'The risk reasonably to be perceived defines the duty to be obeyed.'[33]

In *Donoghue v Stevenson*, the defendant produced ginger beer for sale without ensuring that the ginger beer was safe to drink. The plaintiff drank the ginger beer and was injured. The House of Lords ruled that the defendant owed the plaintiff a duty of care. The risk created by the defendant that led to the finding that the defendant was negligent was a risk to the plaintiff (amongst others).[34] Hence, the defendant was negligent, not or not only in the irrelevant sense that he had acted unethically, but in the significant sense that his interaction with the plaintiff was illegitimate.

Palsgraf, however, was different. Persons for whom the defendant was responsible pushed a man onto a moving train as the train was pulling out of a station. This dislodged a package the man was carrying. The package was wrapped in newspaper. It contained fireworks. When the package hit the ground, the fireworks exploded, causing scales far down the platform to fall onto the plaintiff, injuring her. In finding that the defendant owed the plaintiff no duty of care, Cardozo CJ said:

> The conduct of the defendant's guard, if a wrong in its relation to the holder of the package, was not a wrong in its relation to the plaintiff, standing far away. Relatively to her it was not negligence at all. Nothing in the situation gave notice that the falling package had in it the potency of peril to persons thus removed.[35]

In other words, the risk that led to the finding of negligence was the risk that the owner of the package would be injured. It is negligent to push people onto a moving train because they might be injured. There was also a risk of injury to the plaintiff, of course, as evidenced by her injury. But it was not negligent to create

[31] *M'Alister (or Donoghue) (Pauper) v Stevenson* [1932] AC 562 (HL Sc). See also *MacPherson v Buick Motor Co* 111 NE 1050 (NY CA 1916).

[32] *Palsgraf v Long Island Railroad Co* 162 NE 99 (NY 1928). See also *Bourhill v Young* [1943] AC 92 (HL).

[33] *Palsgraf v Long Island Railroad Co* (n 32) 100.

[34] Strictly, all this should be expressed in the hypothetical, as the case was brought to the House of Lords on a strike out application. To do so, however, would require such convoluted language that it would obscure the point.

[35] *Palsgraf v Long Island Railroad Co* (n 32) 99.

that risk. It is not negligent to push someone onto a moving train because people standing at the other end of the platform might be injured. In the language of the law of the Commonwealth, the risk to the plaintiff was fantastic or far-fetched. In *Palsgraf*, then, the people who were negligent did not wrong the plaintiff (though they may have wronged the person carrying the package). As between them and the plaintiff, there was no negligent act. The plaintiff therefore failed. Again, all this is in line with the position advanced here.

B. Remoteness (Scope of Liability/Proximate Causation)

The approach to remoteness is virtually identical. In *The Wagon Mound (No 1)*,[36] persons for whom the defendant was responsible (the defendant's employees) negligently allowed a large quantity of bunkering oil to spill into the harbour. This caused two injuries to the plaintiff. First, the oil fouled their slipways. Second, the oil caught fire, causing damage to the plaintiff's wharf. The Privy Council ruled that the plaintiff could recover for the first injury, but not for the second as the fire was unforeseeable. As Viscount Simonds explained:

> It is a principle of civil liability … that a man must be considered to be responsible for the probable consequences of his act. To demand more of him is too harsh a rule, to demand less is to ignore that civilised order requires the observance of a minimum standard of behaviour … For, if it is asked why a man should be responsible for the natural or necessary or probable consequences of his act (or any other similar description of them), the answer is that it is not because they are natural or necessary or probable, but because, since they have this quality, it is judged, by the standard of the reasonable man, that he ought to have foreseen them.[37]

Though some of this language unfortunately suggests ethical judgement, in fact it is perfectly in accord with the position advanced here.

The defendant's employees were negligent for creating a risk of fouling the slipways. The risk of that occurring was substantial. Therefore, when that risk materialised, the defendant's employees wronged the plaintiff. The plaintiff could therefore recover for the materialisation of that risk. But the defendant's employees were not negligent for creating the risk of fire. There was a risk of fire, but that risk was fantastic or far-fetched.[38] Hence, the defendant's employees did not wrong the plaintiff in causing the fire. Accordingly, the plaintiff could not recover for that injury.

[36] *Overseas Tankship (UK) Ltd v Morts Dock & Engineering Co Ltd (The Wagon Mound (No 1))* [1961] AC 388 (PC).

[37] ibid 422–23.

[38] Note that this judgement is to be made by placing oneself in the position in which the agents were; it is not to be made with hindsight. Of course, after the fire had occurred, the risk of similar future events was far from fantastic or far-fetched. See, eg, *Doughty v Turner Manufacturing Co Ltd* [1964] 1 QB 518 (CA).

Another clear example is presented in the third *Restatement*:

> Richard, a hunter, finishes his day in the field and stops at a friend's house while walking home. His friend's nine-year-old daughter, Kim, greets Richard, who hands his loaded shotgun to her as he enters the house. Kim drops the shotgun, which lands on her toe, breaking it. Although Richard is negligent for giving Kim his shotgun, the risk that makes Richard negligent is that Kim might shoot someone with the gun, not that she would drop it and hurt herself (the gun was neither especially heavy nor unwieldy). Kim's broken toe is outside the scope of Richard's liability, even though Richard's tortious conduct was a factual cause of Kim's harm.[39]

Nothing need be added.

A similar, though more complicated, case is *McKew v Holland*.[40] The defendant negligently caused injury to the plaintiff's left leg that left it in a weak state. Three weeks later, the plaintiff was standing at the top of a flight of stairs when he felt a sudden weakness in his leg and decided to jump a number of steps to the next landing. As a consequence, he suffered serious injury to his right leg, for which he attempted to sue the defendant. The House of Lords ruled that the plaintiff could not recover for the injury to his right leg. This was because the defendant was not negligent for creating a risk of injury to that leg caused by leaping down a flight of stairs. The defendant was not negligent for producing the risk of the actual injury (to the right leg) that the plaintiff suffered, that risk being fantastic or far-fetched; as such, that injury was not wrongly caused by the defendant (though it was caused by the defendant).

V. The Defences

The most important defences in this context are voluntary assumption of risk, contributory negligence and illegality.[41] These can be dealt with very briefly.

The reason for the first defence is clear. If the plaintiff consented to undergo the risk that resulted in his injury, then the defendant's creation of that risk cannot have wronged the plaintiff. This is because, for reasons that mirror those examined in Chapter 6, in the presence of the plaintiff's consent, the risk taking was part of the parties' shared purpose.

The second defence is also unproblematic. Contributory negligence occurs when the plaintiff's injury was caused both by the defendant's and the plaintiff's

[39] *Restatement (Third) of Torts: Physical and Emotional Harm* (n 14) §29, illustration 3.

[40] *McKew v Holland* 1970 SLT 68 (HL).

[41] In the US, what is here called contributory negligence is known as comparative negligence. Alabama, Maryland, North Carolina, Virginia and the District of Columbia have retained the old common law approach to contributory negligence exemplified in cases such as *Butterfield v Forrester* (1809) 11 East 60, 103 ER 926 and *Davies v Mann* (1842) 10 M & W 546, 152 ER 588.

negligence. According to statute in the Commonwealth and much of the US, in these circumstances, 'a claim in respect of that damage shall not be defeated … but the damages recoverable in respect thereof shall be reduced to such extent as the Court thinks just and equitable having regard to the claimant's share in the responsibility for the damage'.[42] This also fits with the theory advanced here. If the defendant is responsible to the plaintiff because he was negligent, then if the plaintiff was himself negligent, that fact ought to play a role in determining the extent of the defendant's responsibility.[43]

Illegality is more complicated, but the principle is simple to state. If the means to the plaintiff's purpose of which the defendant deprived the plaintiff, or the plaintiff's purpose itself, was illegal, then the defendant's action cannot constrain the plaintiff. This is because, in these circumstances, the defendant will not have deprived the plaintiff of the means to his purposes to which he is entitled or interfered with the purpose that he is at liberty to pursue. Thus, if a plaintiff suffers an injury that prevents him from continuing an illegal activity, then recovery for that loss should not be permitted. A 'professional' bank robber cannot recover for loss of future 'earnings' as a bank robber as a result of being negligently injured.[44] In the same way, if a defendant's negligence causes the destruction of a plaintiff's house in which the plaintiff had a heroin stash, the plaintiff can recover for the house, but not for the heroin.

VI. Conclusion

Because it deals with differently structured fact patterns or approaches them from a different perspective, the law of negligence is quite unlike the torts examined earlier in this book. It deals with injury, not control. What is more, unlike the other torts, negligence is protean. It has grown to cover almost the whole sphere of coercion through injury. Ironically, that means that it can be dealt with more quickly. Of more difficulty is what we must turn to next.

[42] Law Reform (Contributory Negligence) Act 1945 (UK) s 1. Identical or similar legislation exists elsewhere. For the position in the US, see *Restatement (Third) of Torts: Apportionment of Liability*, 3rd edn (St Paul, MN, American Law Institute Publishers, 2000).

[43] For a full analysis, see Beever (n 7) 341–45.

[44] EJ Weinrib, 'Illegality as a Tort Defence' (1976) 26 *University of Toronto Law Journal* 28, 42; *Hall v Hebert* [1993] 2 SCR 159, 174–75

Part V

Miscellaneous Issues Involving Control, Injury and Loss

The final part of this book examines three miscellaneous issues concerning the relationship between coercion, control, injury and loss (negative influence). Chapter 13 examines the law of defamation. It argues that this area of the law is an uncomfortable attempt to deal with both control and injury under a single head of liability. Chapter 14 explores the law's attitude to the mind and mental injury. It maintains that, in part because of the distorting focus on loss rather than coercion, the law is seriously deficient in recognising the importance of the intellectual life and must be revised in this regard. Chapter 15 deals with the issue of patient consent and specifically with the rule advanced in the Commonwealth that a patient who consents to an operation wrongly uninformed of the attendant risks can have an action in negligence, but not in battery. It demonstrates that this position relies on the false conception that the wrongdoing in these cases is injury and loss when it is in fact control. Again, the demand is for reform.

Consequently, then, all three chapters of this part call for legal reform. This contrasts with what has come before, which on the whole approves of the outcomes reached in the case law while calling for a revision of our understanding of that law. It is again important to note that the theory advanced here is interpretive rather than descriptive or prescriptive. In particular, the impetus for reform arises out of the normative structure of the law itself—at least as this book understands that structure to be. In that delightfully old-fashioned phrase, reform of this kind used to be called the law working itself pure.

13

The Law of Defamation

This chapter seems at first to be something of a *da capo al fine*, with '*fine*' written in bold at the end of Chapter 11. In fact, it is a recapitulation in which the two themes of the development are repeated. I cannot, however, promise a reduction in tension because the law of defamation as it stands is a discordant attempt to present its divergent themes at one moment, like a bungled version of the finale of Mozart's 'Jupiter' Symphony. Our job, then, is reconstruction. The themes must be separated and played independently.

It is perhaps comically understated to say that the law of defamation is untidy and that, though most agree that some form of liability in this area is desirable, the legitimacy of the law of defamation as it stands is questionable. Tony Weir memorably wrote that:

> Defamation is arguably the most difficult of all torts. It is certainly the oddest … [D]efamation is odd at the very core. Here is a plaintiff complaining of being misrepresented. Well, we know what must be shown in a normal claim for *mis*representation: *Hedley Byrne*[1] told us. The plaintiff must prove (a) that the statement was false, that it was a misrepresentation; (b) that the defendant was wrong to say it, in breach of a duty (not so easy to establish); (c) that the plaintiff suffered proven harm as a foreseeable result. Now change just one thing. Suppose that the representation is *critical of the plaintiff*: 'Untune one string', as Shakespeare nearly says, 'and hark what discord follows!' In the case of *such* a representation the plaintiff need prove *none* of the above: he can get damages (swingeing damages!) for a statement made to others without showing that the statement was untrue, without showing that the statement did him the slightest harm, and without showing that the defendant was in any way wrong to make it (much less that the defendant owed him any duty of any kind). Are we still in the law of tort?[2]

Well, I think that we are still in the law of tort, but consider also the following, this time from the US:

> It must be confessed at the beginning that there is a great deal of the law of defamation which makes no sense. It contains anomalies and absurdities for which no legal writer ever has had a kind word, and it is a curious compound of a strict liability imposed on innocent defendants, as rigid and extreme as anything found in the law, with a blind and almost perverse refusal to compensate the plaintiff for real and very serious harm.[3]

[1] *Hedley Byrne (&) Co Ltd v Heller (&) Partners Ltd* [1964] AC 465 (HL).

[2] T Weir, *A Casebook on Tort*, 8th edn (London, Sweet (&) Maxwell, 1996) 519.

[3] WP Keeton et al, *Prosser and Keeton on the Law of Torts*, 5th edn (St Paul, MN, West Group, 1984) 771 (footnote omitted).

At times this area of the law is indeed blind and perverse, but the problem is not so much that defamation is out of tune with the rest of the law, but that it is itself out of tune. This first becomes apparent when we consider the right thought to underlie the tort of defamation.

I. The Right

Analysis of the law of defamation characteristically begins with the assertion that this tort protects the right to reputation. That is a bad start. There is no such thing.

As I write, Usain Bolt has the reputation as the world's fastest man. One day, however, his performances will be eclipsed by a younger athlete. When that happens, Bolt's reputation as the world's fastest man will be no more. But there can be no suggestion that Bolt will be able to sue for this.

The example reveals two important points. The first is that, as discussed in more detail below, a defamation consists of some kind of utterance. In the language of the law, there must be a defamatory statement. But there are many ways to damage someone's reputation without making a statement. The future champion will destroy Bolt's reputation as the world's fastest man by running faster, not by making any statement. The second point is the more general one that reputations are frequently damaged in ways that are not even remotely actionable. To stick with sporting examples, losing his heavyweight boxing crown appears to have cost George Foreman the boxing reputation he ought to have had, at least temporarily—and note that one could hardly suggest that there was any shortage of utterances from Muhammad Ali relating to this—but there can be no question about this being actionable, despite the fact that the damage was intended by Ali.[4]

Again, the notion that we have a right to reputation is a product of the loss model. The loss characteristically suffered as a consequence of a defamatory statement is damage to reputation. This has led to the view that the law of defamation must protect a right to reputation. In fact, however, a right to a reputation is an impossibility in any system that recognises freedom of thought. You cannot have a right to your reputation, because your reputation is constituted by the beliefs that other people have about you. Your reputation is in their heads. The alleged right to reputation is therefore a non-starter. We must begin again.

In reply, one might suggest that while there is no right to reputation *simpliciter*, there is a right to the reputation that one ought to have, to one's correct reputation or to some such notion. However, while adopting this view may be useful for

[4] It is not reasonable to argue that this was because, though Ali violated Forman's right to reputation, Ali had some defence to fall back on. This is like trying to fix a shattered glass with glue. It is what one might call a defensive defence.

legal analysis, it is no good for legal theory. These definitions tell us little without an account of what 'ought to have' or 'correct' means in this context. Evidently, that would require a developed theory. Moreover, it remains the case that the reputation one ought to have etc can be attacked in ways that are not relevant to the law of defamation. Most fundamentally, there can be no right to the reputation one ought to have or the like consistent with freedom of thought. Mozart's reputation seems irreparably damaged by his father's conviction that he remained mentally a child, needing his paternal guidance. Were there a right to the reputation he ought to have, only his death would prevent Mozart from being able to sue the generation of moviegoers influenced by film *Amadeus* that so enthusiastically kowtowed to Leopold's distorted vision of his son. Similarly, though I would revel in the ability to take legal action against anyone not recognising the genius of Leonard Cohen on his behalf, unfortunately it cannot be done. And as for some of the reviewers of my writings and the readers of those reviews ... Alas, there is no such right.

II. Defamation as Control

I claimed above that the tort of defamation is itself out of tune. Primarily, this is because, on its surface, it looks for all the world to be a tort dealing with control. Indeed, a coherent law of defamation could be so constructed. The problem is that control-based liability is frequently inappropriate in this area and so the law has been forced to find mechanisms that bring it closer to liability based on injury. Even then there are exceptions. But understanding the law of defamation theoretically is primarily a matter of seeing both its commitment to and departure from liability based on control.

A. The Nature of a Defamatory Statement

The law of defamation requires the plaintiff to prove that a defamatory statement was published by the defendant that identifies the plaintiff. We are here concerned with the first of these requirements. What is a defamatory statement?

Unfortunately, there is no clear answer to this question. The case law contains many different definitions and commentators tend to list them rather than choose between or improve on them.[5] Leading definitions are that a defamatory

[5] See, eg, J Fleming, *The Law of Torts*, 9th edn (Sydney, LBC Information Services, 1998) 580–85; WE Peel and J Goudkamp, *Winfield and Jolowicz on Tort*, 19th edn (London, Sweet (&) Maxwell, 2013) 360–65; J Burrows, 'Defamation' in S Todd (ed), *The Law of Torts in New Zealand*, 6th edn (Wellington, Thompson Reuters, 2013) 813–22.

statement is one that tends to lower the plaintiff in the eyes of right-minded members of society,[6] is false and to the plaintiff's discredit,[7] tends to make others shun the plaintiff[8] or, leaving out only the kitchen sink, 'which tend[s] to expose one to public hatred, shame, obloquy, contumely, odium, contempt, ridicule, aversion, ostracism, degradation, or disgrace, or to induce an evil opinion of one in the minds of right-thinking persons, and to deprive one of their confidence and friendly intercourse in society'.[9]

A particularly noticeable feature of the last two of these 'definitions' is the focus on the impact on third parties. The idea is not merely that the statement causes people to think less of the plaintiff, ie, that it damages the plaintiff's reputation, it is that the statement causes people to think less of the plaintiff, triggering them to alter their behaviour towards the plaintiff in a way that is detrimental to that person. This is well captured in the second *Restatement*'s assertion that: 'A communication is defamatory if it tends so to harm the reputation of another as to lower him in the estimation of the community or to deter third persons from associating or dealing with him.'[10] This indicates, contrary to the general impression given by the *Restatement*,[11] that the right involved is not a right to reputation, but a right somehow tied up with being able to associate with others that is violated by having one's reputation attacked. Reputation is not the right protected. Rather, the attack on reputation is the mechanism for violating the right protected, whatever that right is.

There are two key features of this position. The first is that the plaintiff's reputation must be damaged. It is not sufficient that the plaintiff suffer loss as the result of damage to someone else's reputation, even though such can cause significant negative influence. Damage to the reputation of one's children or business partners, for instance, can be devastating and, from the defendant's perspective, entirely foreseeable; nevertheless, that loss is not recoverable. Again we see the irrelevance of negative influence.

The second point is that liability for defamation is premised on the notion that the defamatory statement will affect the behaviour of third parties towards the plaintiff in ways that are detrimental. This suggests that defamation is a form of constraint. It involves exercising control over another's life by getting third parties to think ill of that person. Take a paradigm case. Imagine that I say on national television that you are a paedophile. It is not difficult to see this act as constraining you, not because of the direct effect that the statement has on you—it is not like a punch in the face—but because of the impact that my statement will have on the way that others will behave towards you. Because of what they think of you,

6 *Sim v Stretch* [1936] 2 All ER 1237 (HL), 1240.
7 *Yossoupoff v MGM* (1934) 50 TLR 581, 584.
8 ibid 587. See also Peel and Goudkamp (n 5) 360.
9 *Kimmerle v New Your Evening Journal* 186 NE 217 (NY 1933) 218.
10 *Restatement (Second) of Torts* (St Paul, MN, American Law Institute Publishers, 1965) §559.
11 eg, ibid ch 24, defines defamation as involving 'invasions of interest in reputation'.

you will no longer be able to express yourself in the world as you would have been able to, so much so that it is natural to regard my statement as coercive. Again, the point is not that my statement will have a negative influence on your life, though it surely will. The point is rather that in making the statement, I exercise control over you through others.[12] In that way, the tort is most like the torts of indirect control examined in the third part of this book, a point to which we will return.

In *Peck v Tribune Co*,[13] the defendant published an advertisement containing a photograph of the plaintiff accompanied by the words: 'Nurse and Patients Praise Duffy's. Mrs. A. Schuman, One of Chicago's Most Capable and Experienced Nurses, Pays an Eloquent Tribute to the Great Invigorating, Life-Giving, and Curative Properties of Duffy's Pure Malt Whisky.' The advertisement further attributed the following statement to the plaintiff: 'After years of constant use of your Pure Malt Whisky, both by myself and as given to patients in my capacity as nurse, I have no hesitation in recommending it as the very best tonic and stimulant for all local and run-down conditions.'[14] In fact, the plaintiff was not named Mrs Schuman, was not a nurse, did not drink alcohol and made no such comments. In finding for the plaintiff (meaning that the case was to be returned to trial), Holmes J said:

> [O]bviously an unprivileged falsehood need not entail universal hatred to constitute a cause of action. No falsehood is thought about or even known by all the world. No conduct is hated by all. That it will be known by a large number, and will lead an appreciable fraction of that number to regard the plaintiff with contempt, is enough to do her practical harm. Thus, if a doctor were represented as advertising, the fact that it would affect his standing with other of his profession might make the representation actionable, although advertising is not reputed dishonest, and even seems to be regarded by many with pride ... It seems to us impossible to say that the obvious tendency of what is imputed to the plaintiff by this advertisement is not seriously to hurt her standing with a considerable and respectable class in the community.[15]

As the discussion of the doctor helps to make clear, the issue is not the plaintiff's reputation per se; it is the impact of the statement on the behaviour of third parties that is in question. And the suggestion is that this is in question because that impact can amount to control of the plaintiff by the defendant via those third parties.

Consider also *Kirk v AW Reed*.[16] In the 1960s, a photograph appeared in a book entitled *The New Zealanders in Colour*. The photograph, in the words of the judge, 'depicts the plaintiff dressed in what I might call "Saturday morning clothes" holding a flagon of beer and a bottle that contains wine or beer leaning against what both counsel have described as a rubbish receptacle in a main street of a

[12] At least, this may be the case. This example is examined in more detail below.
[13] *Peck v Tribune Co* 214 US 185 (US 1909).
[14] ibid 188.
[15] ibid 190.
[16] *Kirk v AW Reed* [1969] NZLR 801.

typical New Zealand town'.[17] The photograph was accompanied by the caption 'Christmas beer. A reveller with his Christmas beer supply waits for the bus at High Street, Lower Hutt'.[18] According to the plaintiff's testimony, he posed for these photographs in a small New Zealand town[19] because the photographers pretended that they were tourists who wanted a photo of 'A typical New Zealander on the booze'.[20] This is significant, because it means that the plaintiff's consent to having the photographs taken did not mean that he consented to the photograph appearing in the book and hence the defendants could not escape liability on the ground that the plaintiff consented to their actions. The judge held that, together with the caption, the photograph 'could well be said to hold the plaintiff up to contempt or ridicule'.[21] Moreover, the judge said that the publication was capable of suggesting one or all of the following ideas: that 'the plaintiff was drunk and dissolute on a Sunday afternoon in the main street of the city of Lower Hutt … that the plaintiff was addicted to alcohol and dissolute in his ways … [and] that the plaintiff was idle and disorderly in his ways'.[22]Accordingly, the judge ruled that the defendant could have been guilty of defaming the plaintiff.[23]

Bearing in mind that this happened in the 1960s in a small town in a then relatively conservative society (this was not San Francisco or Carnaby Street in London), we can understand this decision as being grounded on the notion that the publication of the photograph and the caption was an exercise of control over the plaintiff. This is because it would have had a significant impact on the plaintiff's ability to relate to others on his and their own terms (rather than on the defendant's terms). Given what other people were likely to think of the plaintiff in the light of the publication and given how this would make them respond to the plaintiff, the plaintiff might no longer have been able to associate, conduct business etc with those with whom he would otherwise have been able to do so. On this understanding, the publication did not merely have a negative influence on the plaintiff's life—it was a violation of his freedom. The plaintiff was constrained through the mechanism of the opinions of others by the defendants' choice to publish the photograph with the caption. The publication, in other words, was coercive.

One might also think of *Charleston v News Group Newspapers Ltd* in this regard.[24] The defendant published the English newspaper, the *News of the World.*

[17] ibid 802.

[18] ibid.

[19] Today, Lower Hutt is regarded more as a suburb of the somewhat bohemian city of Wellington. Things were different in the 1960s.

[20] *Kirk v AW Reed* (n 16) 802.

[21] ibid.

[22] ibid.

[23] Some explanation of the relevant procedure may here be in order. Though jury trials are increasing rare outside of the US, they remain available in defamation cases. If jury trial is selected, then it is for the judge to decide whether the statement made *is capable of bearing* a defamatory meaning. It is for the jury to decide whether the statement *was defamatory*.

[24] *Charleston v News Group Newspapers Ltd* [1995] 2 AC 65 (HL).

The plaintiffs were actors in the well-known television soap opera, *Neighbours*. The defendant published what was described by Lord Bridge as:

> [A] large photograph of a man and a woman nearly naked. The woman is leaning forward over some piece of furniture and the man is standing behind her apparently engaging in an act of intercourse or sodomy with her. Superimposed over the lower part of their bodies is an outline map of Australia bearing the words 'Censored down under'. To the right of this is another smaller photograph of a woman wearing a tight-fitting blouse or jacket with holes cut to expose her bare breasts. The face of the man in the large photograph is the male plaintiff's and the face of the woman in both photographs is the female plaintiff's.[25]

The headlines of the article read 'Strewth! What's Harold up to with our Madge?' and 'Porn Shocker for Neighbours Stars'. In fact, the faces of the plaintiffs had been superimposed onto the bodies of porn stars. The article as a whole made this clear and also revealed that the plaintiffs had not been involved in any way in the making of the photograph or in what it depicted.

The House of Lords ruled that there was no defamatory statement of the plaintiffs in this case because, read as a whole, the article revealed that the plaintiffs had not been involved. This was despite the fact that, as their Lordships conceded, many people would have seen the photograph and headlines without reading the article. We return to this matter below. The crucial point now is that the House of Lords would have accepted the plaintiff's claim that the photograph and the headline were defamatory had the photograph and the headline been unaccompanied.

Again, this publication—ie, the photograph and the headline—was coercive. In publishing, the defendant exercised control over the plaintiffs. Given the impact of the publication and given the kind of people that the plaintiffs were—eg, actors playing a respectable married couple—this publication would seriously have affected their ability to live the life that they ought to have been free to live. The wrong, then, is not simply the loss of the plaintiffs' reputation, it is not mere negative influence, but it is the loss of freedom that accompanies the particular kind of loss of reputation that would have been caused by the publication.

A similar case is *Cassidy v Daily Mirror Newspapers Ltd*.[26] The defendant published a photograph of a man and a woman. The caption to the photograph read 'Mr. M.C., the race horse owner, and Miss X, whose engagement has been announced'. The statement was not intended to imply that Miss X was engaged to Mr MC. However, the English Court of Appeal held that the publication was capable of bearing a defamatory meaning to Mr MC's wife, as it suggested that she was not legally married. It is important to note that the relevant events occurred in 1928. Given the social mores of the time, the implication that the plaintiff was not legally married could have had a very significant impact on her life, thus justifying the notion that the publication coerced the plaintiff.

[25] ibid 68.

[26] *Cassidy v Daily Mirror Newspapers Ltd* [1929] 2 KB 331 (CA).

Perhaps the clearest examples are the now highly controversial cases in which white plaintiffs who lived in the Southern US during the slavery or 'Jim Crow' eras successfully recovered for the publication of suggestions that they were non-white.[27] Naturally, if we understand the law of defamation as protecting one's reputation from statements likely to lower one in the eyes of right-minded members of society, then these decisions can only be notorious. However, we have seen that this is not the best way to conceptualise the action. Rather, we should say that, given the laws in force and the social mores, the claim that one was non-white would seriously undermine one's freedom. In those circumstances, the suggestion that one was non-white would clearly be a constraint of one through the mechanism of the opinions of others by the defendant's choice.[28] No doubt, on occasion these statements were made for precisely that reason.

At this point, it is important to note that the argument has been that the cases examined are most usefully interpreted as involving constraint, as they involve an effect on the plaintiff consistent with such. The argument has not been that these cases actually involve constraint, however. That is because, for reasons that will become clear, it is also important to consider the intention of the defendant, and that matter has not been broached.

B. Identification and Publication

This analysis also reveals the basis of the second requirement for defamation: that the defamatory statement identify the plaintiff. Unless the statement identifies the plaintiff, it cannot have the effect of coercing the plaintiff via the actions of third parties. The same is true of the third requirement: the rule that the tort is committed by the publisher of the statement, where publishing means making the statement available to a third party. If I make a defamatory statement about you without publishing it—say by writing it in my diary—then I do not exercise control over you in any way. But if Sally then publishes the contents of my diary on the internet, it is that publication that results in control.

None of this is to be taken as unconditional support for the rules relating to identification or publication. In fact, in the following, we see that to a degree,

[27] See, eg, *Natchez Times Publishing Co v Dunigan* 72 So 2d 681 (MS SC 1954).

[28] It should go without saying that none of this is to be taken as an endorsement of these circumstances. The Jim Crow laws and the surrounding social mores clearly violate Kantian moral principles. But the issue here is the understanding of the law of defamation given those laws and mores. Incidentally, this shows that those who argue that the suggestion that a woman has been raped cannot constitute a defamatory statement as no right-minded person would think less of such a woman mislocate the issue. Of course, it is true that no right-minded person would think any less of a person who has been raped, but if people are not right-minded in this way, then such women may find themselves coerced. If so, they deserve to be compensated.

the rules must be rejected. The claim now is only that the theory advanced here explains why identification and publication are required.

C. Truth (Justification)

Truth is a complete defence to a claim for defamation.[29] Notoriously, truth is for the defendant to prove. Though this is often thought to be deeply problematic, it is supported by the theory advanced here.

Before that can be demonstrated, however, it is first necessary to deal with developments in US law, where it is now controversial where the burden of proof lies.[30] For our purposes, the important point is that this controversy is not over the law of defamation per se. Rather, it is about the consequences of the Supreme Court of the United States' decision in *Herbert v Lando*,[31] which decided, as a matter of constitutional law (which is why it is binding on state courts), that in relevant circumstances, it is incumbent on the defendant to prove fault regarding the truth of the defamatory statement. As a matter solely of common law, solely of the law of tort, it is clear that US law supports the position that the burden of proof is on the defendant,[32] though that now *may* be of little practical relevance. So, we are left with the following question: why, as a matter of common law, does the defendant face the burden of proving that the statement was true?

First, a defamation is an exercise of control over the plaintiff achieved via the mechanism of affecting the plaintiff's reputation. Prima facie, this is achieved if a defamatory statement is published that identifies the plaintiff. The allegation that the statement was true does not deny that the statement constrained the plaintiff. Rather, it maintains that the constraint was not ultimately wrongful as the reputation the plaintiff obtained was the one that he ought to have had. As has been insisted earlier in this book, this does not mean that true statements cannot coerce. The point is only that true statements cannot ground liability in this tort.

It is interesting to note that this analysis supports the otherwise baffling language of the second *Restatement* on this matter: 'although [in principle] the plaintiff must allege falsity in his complaint, the falsity of a defamatory communication is presumed. It has been consistently held that truth is an affirmative defense which must be raised by the defendant and on which he has the burden of proof'.[33] For the reasons just enunciated, a statement cannot genuinely be defamatory unless it is false. But given that even a true defamatory statement constrains the plaintiff,

[29] For some American exceptions, see *Restatement (Second) of Torts* (n 10) §581A, comment a.

[30] Compare, eg, *Farnsworth v Tribune Co* 253 NE 2d 408 (Ill 1969) and *Meiners v Moriarity* 563 F 2d 343 (US 1977).

[31] *Herbert v Lando* 441 US 153 (US 1979).

[32] See, eg, *Palmer v Adams* 36 NE 695 (Ind 1893); *Age-Herald Pub Co v Waterman* 81 So 621 (Ala 1919).

[33] *Restatement (Second) of Torts* (n 10) §581A, comment b.

the assumption is that it is false unless shown to be otherwise. Thus, at common law, the burden of proof is on the defendant.

D. Honest Opinion (Fair Comment)

If the defamatory statement made by the defendant expresses an opinion concerning the plaintiff where that opinion is presented as an observation or inference from the facts, then the defendant is entitled to rely on the defence of fair comment or honest opinion.[34] Let us take a paradigm case.

Imagine that an author publishes a novel that is accurately described but harshly evaluated by a critic. No doubt, the criticism can have a deep impact on the author's life. However, because the critic presented her criticisms to the public as comments on facts, she allows the members of the public to reach their own conclusions and thus does not exercise control over the author.[35] This is why the distinction between fact and comment in the statement must be sufficiently clear. In order to attract the defence, the potentially defamatory aspects of the statement must be presented in such a way that it is clear that they are the opinion of the defendant, indicating to the reader that she is to formulate her own conclusions. As it were, the critic is saying 'This is what I think about the book', inviting the reader to make her own judgements.

No doubt, there is a fine line to be drawn in many cases, but take the following example. Imagine that the novel in question is an historical novel set in the twelfth century. If the critic falsely states that the characters in the novel are wearing wristwatches, then this cannot be fair comment because the critic makes a factual allegation about the book that the reader of the review is entitled to and usually will take at face value, an allegation that implies that the author is incompetent. On the other hand, if the critic states that 'the characters in the book have motivations that do not ring true in the historical context. It is as if they were wearing wristwatches', then this can be fair comment, as the critic will be read as expressing her contestable (I do not say subjective) opinion about the merits of the book and the reader of the review is expected to understand that this is contestable. Thus, if the reader decides that the author is incompetent, that is her doing and not the critic's.

Again, this is not to be taken as an unconditional endorsement of the law's position on fair comment. The issue for now is only the fundamental basis of this defence and its relationship with control.

[34] It is also sometimes said that the comment must be on a matter of public interest, but that is not universal. See eg Defamation Act 1992 (NZ) ss 9–10; Defamation Act 2013 (UK) s 3. For the US position at common law, see ibid §566, comment a.

[35] The reason why the readers do not exercise control is examined below.

E. Conclusion

In these ways, the law of defamation plays in C. On the face of it, it is concerned with control. But only half the orchestra is so tuned. Other instruments treat defamation as wrongdoing for injury. We turn to examine these shortly. For the moment, however, we must examine a deep problem with the law of defamation, even as it relates to control.

III. The Form of Control in Defamation

Recent developments in US law prompted by constitutional concerns aside, most would agree that defamation is a tort of strict liability. What is more, this particular brand of strict liability most closely resembles that found in the law of trespass. At common law, a defendant is liable for defamation if he publishes a defamatory statement that identifies the plaintiff. He does not have to target the plaintiff in any way or, when dealing with libel, cause loss. On the face of it, the argument of this chapter has provided some support for this position. Both trespass and defamation deal with control and so it is appropriate that these liability regimes are similar.

In fact, they are far too similar. Like trespass, defamation is concerned with control, but not with the same kind of control. The circumstances of defamation are quite unlike those of trespass. Even given what has been said, those circumstances more closely resemble those relevant to the economic torts. As in those torts, in defamation the defendant exercises control over the plaintiff via third parties. And that means, for the reasons examined in Chapter 9, that the defendant ought to be liable only if he targeted and harmed the plaintiff.

A defendant who uses the plaintiff's body without the plaintiff's consent puts that person to her purposes and thereby coerces her even if she does not intend to do so and causes the plaintiff no injury. But when the allegation is that that defendant has done something to third parties that has caused those persons to act in ways that result in coercion of the plaintiff by the defendant, the allegation can be true only if the third parties did in fact act in the ways they are said to act (ie, there is loss to the plaintiff) and the defendant intended to act on the plaintiff in that way. In the context of defamation specifically, a defendant exercises control over a plaintiff via the making of a statement to third parties only if the statement affects the third parties in a way that constrains the plaintiff and the defendant intends that constraint. Targeting and loss ought to be necessary conditions of this form of liability.

This also accounts for the fact that persons influenced by the defendant's defamatory statement cannot be liable in these cases, though they are as much causes of the negative influence to the plaintiff as the defendant. These parties cannot be liable as they do not have the relevant intention. They are trying to live their own lives, not to control the plaintiff's. Their actions therefore cause negative influence, but are not coercive.

To the extent that defamation is concerned with control, it ought to be a tort of strict liability. But because defamation exerts control only indirectly, it ought to be the kind of strict liability that requires targeting and damage, as per the economic torts. Yet we have nothing like this. The law of no jurisdiction comes close to requiring targeting in the relevant cases. Moreover, some jurisdictions have abolished the distinction between libel and slander in such a way that extends rather than contracts the ability to sue without proof of harm.[36]

To that last rule, the UK is an exception. Section 1 of the Defamation Act 2013 tates that: 'A statement is not defamatory unless its publication has caused or is likely to cause serious harm to the reputation of the claimant.' This is a large step in the right direction, but several problems remain.

First, of course, this amendment does nothing to introduce a requirement of targeting. Second, there is no requirement to prove harm, only to prove that harm is likely. However, this could possibly be supported by noting that it can be difficult to prove harm in this context and hence perhaps to maintain that, in this area, a requirement to show only that harm is likely is fair as between the parties. Third, the focus on reputation is strictly speaking inappropriate. The issue is whether the defendant's statement causes harm to the plaintiff by effecting the actions of third parties. That will be achieved by the statement influencing the reputation of the plaintiff in the eyes of the third parties. Nevertheless, what ultimately matters is whether the plaintiff is harmed in the requisite manner. The type of harm that the plaintiff suffers is not important. Finally, the harm should not need to be serious—though it will take some time for the courts precisely to define the nature of 'serious harm' in this context (if that is not being too optimistic). What we see here is something that will come to the fore in the discussion that follows, something that plagues the law of defamation: the attempt to deal with a problem in one area not by fixing that area, but by introducing something else in another area, a something else that creates its own problems.

The position, then, is that when defamation deals with cases of control, those cases involve control that is indirect. The form of liability appropriate in those cases, then, ought to require targeting and harm. What is perhaps even more important is that defamation is not always concerned with control. Often it deals with injury. That is our topic now.

[36] eg, Defamation Act 1992 (NZ) s 4; Defamation Act 2005 (NSW) s 7.

IV. Defamation as Injury

A. The General Difficulty with Defamation as Control

In cases of control, the defendant puts the plaintiff or the plaintiff's property to his purposes either directly or indirectly. When that occurs, strict liability is called for, because putting another or another's property to your purposes is warranted only if that person consents or the action is justified on other grounds. This was contrasted with the law of negligence in Chapter 12. In a negligence case, the defendant pursues his own purposes in a way that interferes with the purposes of the plaintiff. There, an appropriate standard for determining liability must mediate between the legal interests of the parties, the fault standard being a standard of that kind. Returning to defamation, the problem here is that it is very often the case that the only plausible claim against the defendant is for injury rather than for control.

If I say on national television that you are a paedophile because I want to destroy your life, then I exercise control over you indirectly. But if I make the same statement in the same context, but do so because I am a children's rights campaigner seeking to protect children from paedophilia and use your name by mistake, confusing it with that of a well-known offender, then I do not exercise control over you. No doubt, your life is adversely affected and it may well be correct to conclude that I coerced you and must be liable. But if so, the wrong in this case is injury. I am not using you or what is yours, putting you to my purposes. I am pursuing my purposes in a way that injures you in the pursuit of yours. This is more like negligence.

Consider *E Hulton (&) Co v Jones*.[37] The defendants were an author and a newspaper who published a fictional account of a character named Artemus Jones, stating that Jones was engaged in shady dealings in France. The plaintiff, a real Artemus Jones, claimed that he was identified in the publication. Though the plaintiff accepted that the defendants did not intend to refer to the plaintiff, the Court found in the plaintiff's favour. In support of this decision, Lord Loreburn LC said:

> Libel is a tortious act. What does the tort consist in? It consists in using language which others knowing the circumstances would reasonably think to be defamatory of the person complaining of and injured by it. A person charged with libel cannot defend himself by shewing that he intended in his own breast not to defame, or that he intended not to defame the plaintiff, if in fact he did both. He has none the less imputed something disgraceful and has none the less injured the plaintiff … Just as the defendant could not excuse himself from malice by proving that he wrote it in the most benevolent spirit, so

[37] *E Hulton (&) Co v Jones* [1910] AC 20 (HL).

> he cannot shew that the libel was not of and concerning the plaintiff by proving that he never heard of the plaintiff.[38]

This is at least dangerously close to absolute liability. Lord Loreburn appears to have said that the fact that the plaintiff was injured is in itself decisive. That cannot be accepted.

Let us focus on the defendant author. Given the facts as accepted by the Court, that person did not attempt to exercise any control over the plaintiff. He wanted only to write a work of fiction that contained a character that he unfortunately named Artemus Jones. No doubt, his actions affected the plaintiff, but that is another matter. The claim against the author, then, cannot have been that he put the plaintiff to his purposes. It must rather be that, in pursuing his purposes, he interfered with the plaintiff's purposes.

It is in that light that we must consider Lord Loreburn's remark that the defendant's 'remedy is to abstain from defamatory words'.[39] The point is that an author can protect himself from liability by not making statements defamatory of any person, whether real or imagined. This reveals how one-sided the positive law is in this regard. Lord Loreburn advised the author not to write anything containing any defamatory statements whatsoever and indicates that anyone who fails to heed this advice opens herself up to the possibility of liability. But that prevents people living their lives. In this case, the author must be per se entitled to write fictional accounts of negative characters, including ones living in France engaged in nefarious activities. Are we to say that prima facie Shakespeare was a wrongdoer, but got lucky that there was no living King of Denmark named Claudius, no Venetian named Iago etc? And what are we to say of all those men with the surname Cornwall? Something has gone seriously wrong here.

In *E Hulton (&) Co v Jones*, the author of the story interfered with the plaintiff's purposes. However, he did so not by putting the plaintiff to his purposes, but in the course of pursuing his own purposes: writing a story. It is inappropriate to deal with this conflict by imposing strict liability. Instead, a standard is called for that mediates between the interests of the parties.

In that light, it is interesting to observe Lord Loreburn's comments regarding the extent of the damages awarded to the plaintiff, comments that turned on the fact that the plaintiff was a former employee of the defendant newspaper:

> The damages are certainly heavy, but I think your Lordships ought to remember two things. The first is that the jury were entitled to think, in the absence of proof satisfactory to them (and they were the judges of it), that some ingredient of recklessness, or more than recklessness, entered into the writing and the publication of this article, especially as Mr. Jones, the plaintiff, had been employed on this very newspaper, and his name was well known in the paper and also well known in the district in which the paper circulated. In the second place the jury were entitled to say this kind of article is to be condemned.

[38] ibid 23–24.
[39] ibid 24.

> There is no tribunal more fitted to decide in regard to publications, especially publications in the newspaper Press, whether they bear a stamp and character which ought to enlist sympathy and to secure protection. If they think that the licence is not fairly used and that the tone and style of the libel is reprehensible and ought to be checked, it is for the jury to say so.[40]

This lends support to the suggestion that the defendants' liability in fact turned in part—perhaps unconsciously on the part of the Court—on the idea that the defendants were negligent or even that, though it could not be proven, they had intentionally identified the plaintiff, thus exercising control.

Unfortunately, the notion that there is a right to reputation inevitably clouds this issue. It is tempting to argue that the defendants in *E Hulton (&) Co v Jones* used the plaintiff, ie, the plaintiff's reputation, for the purposes of the story. Likewise, one might maintain that in the second case presented at the beginning of this section, I use you, again your reputation, to advance the protection of children. But this is wrong. There is no right to reputation. You have a right not to be controlled or injured by me. In the first case outlined above, I control you by affecting your reputation. In the second case, I affect your reputation, but I do not exercise control over you. If this is actionable, it ought to be as injury.

Let us take another example. Imagine that you and I are leading theorists of tort law and are engaged in a public debate. Adopting contrasting theoretical positions, our argument is cordial but forceful. What are we doing here? Well, one of the things that we are doing is, often implicitly but also occasionally explicitly, attacking each other's reputations. I am saying that those who think that you have constructed the best theory of tort law ought to change their minds and think less of you as a result. Why is this not actionable? Perhaps one is tempted to argue that our debate is covered by the fair comment defence or a privilege. As it stands, that is fine, but the more fundamental point is surely that this kind of speech is not even prima facie wrongful. It should not need to be defended. What we require, then, is a theory that explains the rightfulness of this speech, and not one that treats its permissibility as an exception to general principles that would otherwise hold the speech to be wrongful.[41]

The reason this speech is rightful is fundamentally that it is not an exercise of control. Though I am intending to make people think less of you, I am not intending to control you. If I succeed, then I damage your reputation intentionally, but I do not control you. On the contrary, in arguing with you, if anything I eliminate control over you. In addressing you as a rational person in this way, I promote your freedom.[42]

[40] ibid 24–25.

[41] *cf* ss 3(7)(b) and 6 Defamation Act 2013 (UK), which protects similar statements through the operation of defences. But these statements surely ought not to need defending.

[42] I am not suggesting that all, or even much, academic debate actually does this. For instance, in order to promote your freedom, I have to engage with your ideas. If I am simply using your work as a tool to advance my agenda or if my own agenda blinds me so that I am unable even to appreciate what your ideas are, then this promotion cannot occur.

Accordingly, the thesis is the following. The tort of defamation is constructed as a form of liability dealing with direct control. In fact, however, it never deals with that form of control. It deals only with indirect control and injury. This means that though the tort of defamation is built as a form of trespass-like liability, that form of liability is never here appropriate. Rather, liability ought to be determined in accordance with targeting or fault as the case may be.

Though it can be misleading to put it this way, the problem can nevertheless usefully be expressed as follows. There are three possible torts of defamation: one resembling trespass, one resembling the torts of indirect control and one resembling negligence. The problem is that we have only the first when that is the only one that we should not have. The two that we do not have are the ones that we need. In practice, as we now see, this difficulty is ameliorated by the fact that elements of liability for injury are imported into the law through the back door. But the result is an incoherent form of liability that is unable to deal properly with either indirect control or injury.

B. Defamatory Statement

Consider first the rule found in *Charleston v News Group Newspapers Ltd*. Recall that in this case, the defendant newspaper published a photograph which depicted two people having sex, the faces of the plaintiffs being superimposed onto the models. The photograph was accompanied by a headline that indicated that the plaintiffs were involved, though the body of the article made it clear that they were not. The House of Lords ruled that the publication was not actionable as the article as a whole indicated that the plaintiffs were uninvolved, even though many people would encounter the photograph and the headline without reading the article.

The basis of this rule can be revealed by considering a hypothetical case. Imagine that I am standing at a bus stop talking to Sarah. As people alight and disembark from busses that arrive while we talk, people catch segments of our conversation. Taken out of context, some of these segments are defamatory. However, in context, it is clear that they are innocent. Imagine, for instance, that I say 'Sally is going back on the game' and that this is heard by Serena, a passer-by, and Sarah. On the face of it, I have defamed Sally to Serena and Sarah. But Sarah knows that 'The Game' is the name of a yacht that our friend Susan owns and what I am saying is that, though Sally often gets seasick, she has resolved to go back on board. The problem is that while that may save me from the claim that I defamed Sally to Sarah, it cannot show that I did not defame Sally to Serena. But the rule in question prevents me from being sued in these circumstances. That outcome is supported by the position advanced here. In conducting my conversation with Sarah, I am pursuing my own purposes. I am not and am not trying to put Sally to my purposes. Strict liability in this area is inappropriate.

Note the law's response, however. It does not say that, in this context, liability is to be determined in accordance with fault. It says that there can be no liability because of the rule under discussion. That is the wrong approach. Let us imagine, for instance, that I know that Serena will hear me, that Serena will think that Sally has become a prostitute and that this will harm Sally. Here, I ought to be liable because I have wrongly injured Sally. Or imagine that I intend Serena to think that Sally has become a prostitute and to harm Sally thereby. In this case, I ought to be liable because I have exerted control over Sally. The rule wrongly prevents this from happening. In fact, it is readily arguable that *Charleston v News Group Newspapers Ltd* was wrongly decided for exactly this reason. It is highly probable that the defendant published the photograph and the headline with the intention of making potential readers—ie, potential purchasers of the newspaper—believe that the plaintiffs were involved. On this view, the defendant did in fact exercise control over the plaintiffs. It intended the statement to have this effect on third parties.

This problem is characteristic of the law of defamation. We start with a regime of strict liability that is far too plaintiff-friendly. The response is to create defences (whether technically labelled defences or not) such as the rule just examined, because this problem is recognised. But these defences are too defendant-friendly. The rule in question has a place, but it is drawn too broadly. It is relevant only to injury, not to control, and it is only partially relevant there.

In circumstances where strict liability is inappropriate, the response is not to move towards fault (though that sometimes occurs, as we will see). Rather, it is often to rule out liability altogether. That is a mistake. No doubt, if we encounter a fact pattern that makes this clear, a court will make another rule that restricts the application of the first rule—a rule that creates an exception to an exception—but this is the wrong way to proceed. We do not need an overreaching strict liability tempered with overreaching defences even with the addition of exceptions to the defences, when what is aimed at is really, in relevant cases, a regime of fault-based liability.

It is useful to compare *Charleston v News Group Newspapers Ltd* with *Burton v Crowell*.[43] The defendant published an advertisement that contained a photograph of the plaintiff that, in the fantastic language of Learned Hand J:

> [R]epresented him coming from a [horse] race to be weighed in; he is carrying his saddle in front of him with his right hand under the pommel and his left under the cantle; the line of the seat is about twelve inches below his waist. Over the pommel hangs a stirrup; over the seat at his middle a white girth falls loosely in such a way that it seems to be attached to the plaintiff and not to the saddle. So regarded, the photograph becomes grotesque, monstrous, and obscene; and the legends, which without undue violence can be made to match, reinforce the ribald interpretation. That is the libel.[44]

[43] *Burton v Crowell* 82 F 2d 154 (US 1936).
[44] ibid 154.

The defendant argued that this could not be defamatory because, while at first glance someone seeing the picture might think that the plaintiff was exposing himself in public and was deformed: 'Nobody could be fatuous enough to believe any of these things; everybody would at once see that it was the camera, and the camera alone, that had made the unfortunate mistake.'[45] Hand J accepted that argument. Nevertheless, he held that the publication was defamatory. This was because the publication:

> [E]xposed the plaintiff to overwhelming ridicule. The contrast between the drawn and serious face and the accompanying fantastic and lewd deformity was so extravagant that, though utterly unfair, it in fact made of the plaintiff a preposterously ridiculous spectacle; and the obvious mistake only added to the amusement.[46]

We can understand this to mean that though every viewer of the publication would realise the truth, the publication nevertheless constrained the plaintiff.[47] That reasoning is directly applicable to *Charleston v News Group Newspapers Ltd*.[48]

C. Publication

The defendant in *Huth v Huth* received a tradesman's account addressed to his estranged wife:

> Captain Huth sent the account in an envelope … and on the account wrote the words complained of in this case. 'Mrs. Huth' was struck out, and in the defendant's handwriting appear 'Not known. Try Miss Edith Greaves'; that was the maiden name of Mrs. Huth. Later there appear on the same document addressed to the saddler: 'The woman known as "Mrs. Huth"'—'Mrs. Huth' was in inverted commas—'will henceforth take her maiden name of Miss Edith Greaves. Yours truly, P. S. Huth'. Again on the same document was written: 'The woman in question has forfeited all claims to the title of "Mrs. Huth"'—'Mrs. Huth' was again in inverted commas—'and I hereby and herewith disown her. P. S. Huth'. That account, with that writing upon it by the defendant, was enclosed in the envelope addressed to the lady in her maiden name, under cover of a half-penny stamp, and consequently in an envelope which was neither sealed nor gummed.[49]

The plaintiffs were the children of Captain Huth and his wife. They alleged that the defendant's statement implied that they were illegitimate.

[45] ibid 155.

[46] ibid.

[47] However, it must be admitted that Hand J immediately went on to say that: 'Had such a picture been deliberately produced, surely every right-minded person would agree that he would have had a genuine grievance; and the effect is the same whether it is deliberate or not' (ibid). That is in accordance with the established legal rules, but is, I submit, unjustified.

[48] Of course, on the theory advanced here, to be actionable, the publication must cause ridicule that rises to the level of constraint.

[49] *Huth v Huth* [1915] 3 KB 32 (CA), 37.

The issue of concern here is publication. Had the defendant's wife opened and read the letter, then there could have been no defamation (by the defendant). This is because of the rule that a defamatory statement made to one's spouse is not actionable.[50] In fact, however, the letter was opened by a butler.

Lord Reading CJ maintained:

> It must of course be borne in mind that however insulting and offensive the matter might be which the husband wrote to his wife, if it was addressed to the wife and only intended for her, and she alone saw it, no action for libel could be brought by her: an action for libel can only be brought if there is publication to some third person. In my judgment there was no evidence of publication to the butler.[51]

Before we can get to the crucial issue, it is necessary to deal with a confusion introduced in this passage. Lord Reading's argument assumes that the plaintiff was the defendant's wife. That is incorrect. The defendant's wife was the plaintiffs' mother. It is right to say that, had she opened the letter, she would have been unable to sue. That is because, in those circumstances, the letter would not have been published to a third party. In this action, however, she is a third party. In fact, what would have prevented the plaintiffs succeeding in those circumstances is the rule that a defamatory statement made to one's spouse is not actionable.[52]

For our purposes, the crucial point is that, as the butler opened the letter, the defendant was not held to have published the defamatory statements it contained and so escaped liability. But why? What is the basis of this position?

The simplest answer is that the defendant did not publish the letter. The butler did it. That is fine as far as it goes, though in the US it has been argued that this indicates that the law is concerned with fault in this context,[53] a conclusion that of course supports the argument presented here. But let us put that aside. The problem is that, even as a matter of Commonwealth orthodoxy, it is also clear that if the defendant ought to have realised that the butler would open the letter, then he would have been held to have been a publisher. As Harman LJ said in *Theaker v Richardson*:

> In *Huth v Huth* the publication was said to be to the butler who opened the letter out of mere inquisitiveness, and the claim failed because this was a breach of the butler's duty not to be anticipated by the defendant. In *Sharp v Skues*[54] the jury answered in the

[50] *Wennhak v Morgan* (1888) 20 QBD 635. See also *Restatement (Second) of Torts* (n 10) §592. This rule can be supported on the ground that, as it were, one's spouse is, *as regards others*, part of one's own space. Hence, making a statement to one's spouse is not crossing over into the plaintiff's space.

[51] *Huth v Huth* [1915] 3 KB 32 (CA), 39.

[52] In response, it is possible to argue that the effect of the rule is that the wife of the defendant is not considered at law to be a third party, in which case Lord Reading does not commit the error attributed to him. In that case, the objection is that this position wrongly denies spouses proper legal personality. It is one thing to protect inter-spousal communication, but another to do so by denying the legal personality of one of the spouses.

[53] Keeton et al (n 3) 802–03.

[54] *Sharp v Skues* (1909) 25 TLR 336 (CA).

negative a question as to knowledge on the defendant's part of the likelihood of the letter being opened by a clerk or partner of the plaintiff. Lord Cozens-Hardy M.R. said this:

> ' It would be a publication if the defendant intended the letter to be opened by a clerk or some third person not the plaintiff, or if to the defendant's knowledge it would be opened by a clerk; but the jury had negatived this in the clearest terms, and under these circumstances it was impossible to hold that some act done by a partner or a clerk of the plaintiff by his direction and for his own convenience when absent from the office could be a publication by the defendant under circumstances which the jury have found … the defendant knew could not possibly happen.'[55]

It thus appears that the answer to the question of publication of a libel contained in a letter will depend on the state of the defendant's knowledge, either proved or inferred, of the conditions likely to prevail in the place to which the libel is destined.[56]

Notice here the reference to two concerns, neither of which fits liability based on direct control. The first is the intention of the defendant. The issue is not whether the defendant performs an intentional action that results in wrongful publication, the issue parallel with the law of trespass; it is whether the defendant intends the wrongful publication. That resembles the torts of indirect control rather than trespass and that is appropriate as, when we are dealing with control at all in the law of defamation, the control is indirect. The second concern is the defendant's negligence. The position is that if the defendant did not intend publication, he can nevertheless be liable if he ought to have foreseen that publication would occur.

The claim is not that this reveals that the law of defamation is in fact a regime of indirect control and negligence liability. It is not. In other circumstances, it is clear that a defendant who neither intended publication nor was negligent in this regard can be liable. The point is that we see here the law crawling away from its official position in the direction of a more appropriate one.

A paradigm example of what I am calling inappropriate law in this regard is a defendant who broadcasts on live television a defamatory statement made by a third party when the defendant had no reason to believe that the statement would be made. As the publisher of the statement, the broadcaster has characteristically been held strictly liable in these circumstances. But it is notable that here again, significant exceptions to this approach have now been created.[57]

D. Honest Opinion (Fair Comment)

The basic nature of the defence of fair comment was examined above. There are, however, elements of this defence that suggest liability for injury rather than for

[55] ibid 337.

[56] *Theaker v Richardson* [1962] 1 WLR 151 (CA), 157–58.

[57] eg, Defamation Act 2005 (SA) s 30; Defamation Act 2005 (NSW) s 32; Defamation Act 2005 (Vict) s 32; Defamation Act 1996 (UK) s 1. See also Defamation Act 1992 (NZ) s 21.

control.[58] Consider, for instance, the decision of the New Zealand Court of Appeal in *Awa v Independent News Auckland Ltd*.[59] The case involved a dispute between the immediate and extended families of the entertainer,[60] Billy T James. When James died, his body was forcibly taken from his home against the wishes of his immediate Pakeha (ie, European) family so that he could lie on the local marae, the Maori public home of James' extended family, in order for him to be buried in accordance with the custom of his tribe on Taupiri mountain. The defendant newspaper published an article containing the following:

> In an extraordinary graveside speech Billy's 'body snatching' Uncle [the plaintiff] Bill Awa spoke directly to a tearful Cherie [James' adopted daughter]:
>
> > I look to you and bless you in the honour of your dad. I hope your mother will find it in her heart to join us in the future. We will take you home when you are ready. I want to thank you on behalf of the Waikato … and other people for letting us bring your dad here.
>
> Mr Awa and helpers spirited Billy T from his Murawai [sic] home, claiming he belonged to the people because he gave to the people and his taonga had to be shared. Billy's grieving widow didn't agree and boycotted her husband's burial.[61]

In holding that the defence of fair comment applied, Blanchard J said something quite incredible—that readers of the newspaper:

> [W]ould have known, indeed the article itself indicated, that there was nothing improper in the appellant's purpose in removing the body. The word 'spirited' would not have been understood to have been used in the narrow sense of taking something by stealth, perhaps to a secret destination. It was obvious that the newspaper was not saying that there had been secrecy or concealment. It would have been equally obvious to readers that Mr Awa's motivation was that Maori custom should be observed. The real issue in the public mind was the manner in which he had gone about achieving that purpose and the effect of his conduct on the widow. It was not being suggested that he had acted dishonestly or dishonourably.[62]

That is entirely implausible. I submit that, on the contrary, the impression of the passage is precisely that the plaintiff acted dishonourably. What is more, though 'spirited' cannot be taken to imply secrecy—the body was said to have been removed forcibly after all—in context it both suggests underhanded behaviour and appears to constitute a sneer at the values, ie, *spiritual* values, that motivated the plaintiff. Furthermore, if nothing improper had been imputed to the plaintiff, then what is the need for the defence of fair comment? What, in these circumstances, would the defamatory statement be?

[58] In that light, we might ask whether s 3(4) of the Defamation Act 2013 (UK) in effects imports a fault standard.

[59] *Awa v Independent News Auckland Ltd* [1997] 3 NZLR 590 (CA).

[60] That is a slight simplification, as James' family circumstances were complex, but the simplification is of no moment here.

[61] *Awa v Independent News Auckland Ltd* (n 59) 594.

[62] ibid.

What was motivating the Court of Appeal? The answer is contained in the following:

> From the perspective of a non-Maori New Zealander, the opinion that Mr Awa acted wrongly towards Mrs James was certainly possible, as is demonstrated by the views expressed by others in the contemporaneous public debate. Such an opinion might be deprecated by Maori as Eurocentric but a significant section of the public seems to have considered that the widow's wishes should have been respected; that she should not have been placed in a position of being required to submit to the will of the appellant and his party. Those who honestly thought so had the right to express that opinion publicly. A newspaper was entitled to reflect it. Hypothetically, assume that the position had been that Mrs James had successfully prevented the body being taken and had declined to permit any Maori element in the funeral arrangements. Maori would surely have been legally justified in stating in colourful terms their views of a Pakeha who sought to exclude them from mourning Billy T in their own way. They too would have been able to say that they expressed their opinion honestly on a matter of public concern.[63]

This involves a recognition of something said above. As long as he is not seeking control over the plaintiff, the defendant must be entitled to live his own life and to pursue his own purposes. His interaction with the defendant must be judged according to a standard that mediates as between their interests. Strict liability is not appropriate here. In this case, the defendant is entitled to express and defend his values in a public forum, even if they damage the reputation of the plaintiff. This is why the Court held the defence of fair comment to apply even though it was clear that the defamatory statements in question were not comment at all.

Having said that, it is at least arguable that *Awa* was wrongly decided. As has been maintained, the dispute ought to have been determined by adopting a standard that mediated between the interests of the parties, not by applying an overreaching defence. It is hard to see how labelling the plaintiff a body snatcher could be justified based on such an approach. And despite Blanchard J's assurances, one must wonder what would have happened had the races of the parties been reversed.

E. Qualified Privilege

In *Boston v WS Bagshaw (&) Sons*,[64] a man calling himself 'Boston of Rugeley' purchased three pigs at an auction. He managed to take the pigs away without paying for them. The defendant auctioneers sent the following letter to 34 or 35 other auctioneers in the area:

> Dear Sirs, Yesterday, September 20, we held an auction sale at Rolleston Grange, Tutbury, where a person purchased three pedigree Wessex Saddleback Gilts and gave the name

[63] ibid 595.

[64] *Boston v WS Bagshaw (&) Sons* [1966] 1 WLR 1135 (CA).

> 'Boston' of Rugeley when these pigs were 'knocked down' to him. Subsequent to the sale this person did not pay and at the time of writing this letter we have been unable to trace this purchaser.[65]

The plaintiff was a man named Alfred Robert Boston and he lived in Rugeley. He maintained that he was identified in the letter as people thought that it referred to him.

Lord Denning MR, however, said:

> I am clearly of opinion that the occasion was privileged. The rogue who stole the pigs would try to dispose of them as soon as he could. He would not wish to be caught with them in his possession. He would probably take them off to some other market and sell them. It was, I should have thought, the public duty of Mr Naylor to warn other auctioneers of the position so that they should not be induced to handle the pigs. It might indeed help catch the thief. At any rate it was a matter in which the auctioneers had a common interest fit to be protected.[66]

This case illustrates the nature of the defence of qualified privilege. The defence applies if the defamatory statement is made by a person who has a duty to make it and the statement is made to a person or persons who have an interest in receiving it. Importantly, this duty need not be a legal duty. It is sufficient if the defendant was under a moral or social duty to make the statement.[67]

The reason for this is the one we have been examining. The defendant must be entitled to pursue his own purposes as long as he does so in ways that do not undermine the more fundamental interests of the plaintiff. The defendant in *Boston v WS Bagshaw (&) Sons* was not trying to exercise control over the plaintiff; he was merely trying to do his civic duty as an auctioneer.

This also fits with the notion that the defence of qualified privilege is defeated by 'malice',[68] here meaning lack of an honest belief on the part of the defendant in the truth of the defamatory statement, a position also reached in US law.[69] The defence is unavailable in these circumstances because the defendant in such cases is not merely pursuing his own purposes.

But again, the defence is not well formed. Imagine, for instance, that the defendant in *Boston v WS Bagshaw (&) Sons* knew about the existence of the plaintiff, knew that he was likely to be affected by the letter and could easily have made it clear that the plaintiff was not the 'Boston of Rugeley' in question. Then, I submit, he ought to have been liable. In that case, the defendant would have wrongly injured the plaintiff.

[65] ibid 1130.

[66] ibid 1131.

[67] *Adam v Ward* [1917] AC 309 (HL).

[68] See, however, s 19 of the Defamation Act 1992 (NZ). In fact, the position advanced in this Act is in line with that presented here, though it achieves it in a different way.

[69] *Restatement (Second) of Torts* (n 10) §§599–600.

Consider also the defence of responsible journalism now available in some jurisdictions.[70] Journalists must be permitted to pursue their own purposes, as long as they do so fairly, ie, non-negligently, to those they affect. This brings us to our next topic.

F. Public Issues in Defamation

This chapter has not dealt with the defence of absolute privilege or various special issues, for example, the defamation of public figures such as politicians.[71] This is because these issues take us beyond the scope of the investigation conducted in this book. In these cases, the defendant is not acting in a private capacity, but is performing a public role, and so the conflict between the parties is rightly settled in part in terms of public law rules and values. Of course, this raises important issues, but they are not ones under examination in this book. Thus, they will not be discussed here. Suffice it to say, however, that all of these developments have introduced elements of fault into the law of defamation.

V. Conclusion

As we already knew, the law of defamation is deeply problematic. This chapter has presented a diagnosis of this difficulty. There are two related errors. The first is that, as we might say, there is one law of defamation and one regime of liability, where there should be two. In making a statement, one can exercise control over another or injure that person. Different approaches to liability are appropriate in each case. The second problem is that the law adopts the wrong form of liability: trespass-like strict liability. This is inappropriate because defamation cases do not involve one person directly exercising control over another. Rather, when control is an issue, the control is exercised via third parties.

Of course, this calls for a major overhaul of the law of defamation. But what is the alternative? For how long will we be content to live with a law that can be described as Weir did at the beginning of this chapter?

[70] *Jameel v Wall Street Journal Europe SPRL* [2006] UKHL 44, [2007] 1 AC 359; *Cusson v Quan* 2009 SCC 62, [2009] 3 SCR 712; Defamation Act 2013 (UK) s 1(1)(b).

[71] eg, *New York Times Co v Sullivan* 11 L Ed 2d 686 (US SC 1964); *Reynolds v Times Newspapers* [2001] 2 AC 127 (HL); *Lange v Atkinson* [1998] 3 NZLR 424 (CA); *Lange v Atkinson* [2000] 1 NZLR 257 (PC); *Lange v Atkinson* [2000] 3 NZLR 385 (CA); *Lange v Australian Broadcasting Corp* (1997) 189 CLR 520 (HCA). See also *Gertz v Robert Welch* 418 US 323 (US 1974); *Herbert v Lando* 441 US 153 (US 1979).

14

The Mind

Chapter 1 maintained that our most basic right is the entitlement to be independent of the choices of others. Chapter 4 argued that, when applied to the body, this most fundamentally entails a right to control over our own bodies. But something is clearly missing. Where in the law do we find recognition of the equally fundamental right over our minds? Where is the tort that does for the mind what the torts of assault, battery and false imprisonment do for the body? The answers are: nowhere and there isn't one.

Practicalities help to explain this fact. Most importantly, while it is not difficult to put another's body to one's purposes, it is much harder to do this with another's mind. Moreover, it is extremely difficult to do this without also using the other's body, meaning that the law of battery and other areas of the law also serve to protect the mind. Because of reasons of this kind, the law has managed without torts that specifically deal with the mind. It is nevertheless the case that the law of tort neglects the importance of the mental and should be criticised for doing so.

This issue is usefully examined by telling the story of US law in regard to recovery for mental injury in the law of negligence, and comparing that story with the law in the Commonwealth. We begin with the decision of the Supreme Court of California in *Dillon v Legg*.[1]

From the porch of her house, Margery Dillon watched as her daughter Erin, attempting to cross the road, was run down and killed by David Legg, who was alleged to be driving negligently. Unsurprisingly, Margery suffered mental distress as a result of the incident, for which she sued Legg. The Court ruled that although Margery was a bystander—meaning that she was not herself placed at risk of physical injury by Legg's driving—she could recover for her 'emotional shock' in accordance with the ordinary principles of the law of negligence. The crucial issue was whether Margery's emotional distress was foreseeable. In that regard, the Court in *Dillon v Legg* said that three factors need to be taken into account in cases of this kind: whether the plaintiff was near the scene of the accident, whether the emotional harm resulted from a direct impact on the plaintiff (eg, witnessing the event rather than, say, hearing or reading about it afterwards) and whether the plaintiff and the person physically injured by the tort were closely related.[2]

[1] *Dillon v Legg* 441 P 2d 912 (CA 1968).
[2] ibid 920.

It must be stressed that the Court intended these only as considerations to be taken into account when determining whether the plaintiff's injury was foreseeable. As Tobriner J said:

> The evaluation of these factors will indicate the Degree of the defendant's foreseeability: obviously defendant is more likely to foresee that a mother who observes an accident affecting her child will suffer harm than to foretell that a stranger witness will do so. Similarly, the degree of foreseeability of the third person's injury is far greater in the case of his contemporaneous observance of the accident than that in which he subsequently learns of it. The defendant is more likely to foresee that shock to the nearby, witnessing mother will cause physical harm than to anticipate that someone distant from the accident will suffer more than a temporary emotional reaction. All these elements, of course, shade into each other; the fixing of obligation, intimately tied into the facts, depends upon each case.[3]

Though *Dillon v Legg* is widely regarded as a leading case in this area, the view that it opens the floodgates to too much potential liability in bystander cases is nevertheless widespread. As a result, modern US law in fact resembles *Dillon v Legg* only rather distantly. In particular, the passage of time has seen the considerations listed in *Dillon v Legg* harden into exclusionary rules.

Thus, 21 years after *Dillon v Legg*, the Supreme Court of California ruled in *Thing v La Chusa*[4] that a mother who suffered mental harm as the result of hearing that her son had been injured, having rushed to the scene to see him lying bloody and unconscious in the roadway and believing him to be dead, could not recover because she had neither seen nor heard the accident itself. It is quite plain, however, that her injury in the circumstances was foreseeable. Likewise, in *Bird v Saenz*,[5] the same Court again ruled that family members who witnessed their mother's death in hospital due to medical negligence had no cause of action because they had not witnessed the medical negligence itself. These two decisions surely reveal that the law in this area is an ass.

The guidelines relating to direct perception[6] and family members have also hardened in this way. So, in *Grotts v Zahner*,[7] the Nevada Supreme Court denied recovery to a woman on the ground that it was 'only' her fiancée who was killed, a decision that confirms the equid character of this law.

In this regard, US law closely resembles the law of England. But the leading case in that jurisdiction dealing with bystander plaintiffs—there referred to as cases involving secondary victims—only makes the problems more evident. The plaintiffs in *Alcock v Chief Constable of the South Yorkshire Police*[8] were the friends and relatives of persons who had died in the Hillsborough football stadium disaster

[3] ibid 920–21.
[4] *Thing v La Chusa* 771 P 2d 814 (CA 1989).
[5] *Bird v Saenz* 51 P 3d 324 (CA 2002).
[6] See, eg, *Roitz v Kidman* 913 P 2d 431 (WY 1996).
[7] *Grotts v Zahner* 989 P 2d 415 (NV 1999).
[8] *Alcock v Chief Constable of the South Yorkshire Police* [1992] 1 AC 310 (HL).

who developed mental illnesses as a result. They all failed. The House of Lords ruled that in order to recover, a plaintiff must have been proximate in time and space to the accident,[9] must either see or hear the accident or be present at its immediate aftermath[10] and, at least ordinarily, must be related to the accident victim. Particularly hideous was the suggestion that no duty of care was owed to the plaintiff Robert Alcock because, as Alcock had lost 'only' his brother-in-law, 'h[e] was not … reasonably foreseeable as a potential sufferer from shock-induced psychiatric illness'.[11]

Scandalised perhaps even more by these arguments than the outcomes for which they argue, academics in England have tended to maintain either that these 'control mechanisms' should be abandoned[12] or that recovery in this area should be abolished entirely.[13] But the law has responded to neither suggestion, revealing it to be Buridan's ass.

In a similar fashion, US law has seen fit to restrict recovery for the intentional infliction of emotional distress by demanding that defendants can be liable only if their conduct was 'extreme and outrageous'.[14] No one will be surprised to hear that the courts have determined that this is a highly fact-sensitive issue that must be decided on a case-by-case basis.[15] In other words, the rule is an entirely unprincipled 'control mechanism' designed to prevent recovery from getting out of hand.

But there is one significant difference between English and US law in relation to the recovery of mental harm. In the former jurisdiction, a plaintiff can recover only if she suffers a recognised psychiatric injury. This is a point of much importance.

In US law, it is never entirely clear how the plaintiff's injury is conceptualised. Thus, §45 of the third *Restatement* speaks of liability (only) for 'severe emotional disturbance', but the fifth such draft contained the following discussion:

> It was suggested that the Reporters should not use the term 'emotional disturbance' and that instead they should use the term 'emotional tranquility'. The Reporters responded that they are thinking seriously about substituting the term 'emotional harm' for 'emotional disturbance' throughout the draft. It was suggested that this Section has narrowed its tort more than is reflective of what courts are doing.

This is very odd. The notion that one has a right to be free of emotional disturbance is unsupportable. I am emotionally disturbed when I wake to find it cloudy. It is even odder to think that I have a right to emotional tranquillity. In

[9] ibid 397 (Lord Keith), 404–05 (Lord Ackner).

[10] ibid 398 (Lord Keith), 400–01, 405 (Lord Ackner).

[11] ibid 406.

[12] eg, M Jones, 'Liability for Psychiatric Damage: Searching for a Path between Pragmatism and Principle' in JW Neyers, E Chamberlain and SGA Pitel (eds), *Emerging Issues in Tort Law* (Oxford, Hart Publishing, 2007).

[13] eg, J Stapleton, 'In Restraint of Tort' in P Birks (ed), *The Frontiers of Liability* (Oxford, Oxford University Press, 1994).

[14] *Restatement (Third) of Torts: Physical and Emotional Harm* (St Paul, MN, American Law Institute Publishers, 2010) §45.

[15] See, eg, *Almy v Grisham* 639 SE 2d 182 (VA 2007).

that regard, emotional harm is preferable, but it remains quite unclear what it means. Am I emotionally harmed to discover that my car has broken down, that my favourite sports team has failed in this year's competition, that my articles have been rejected for publication or that my workplace has become a nest of vipers?

In that light, we can see why US law has been so determined to restrict the class of plaintiffs who are able to sue. If mere emotional disturbance, interference with emotional tranquillity or even undefined emotional harm is sufficient injury to ground a cause of action, then it is clear that 'control mechanisms' must be introduced in order to restrict recovery or liability will be out of hand.

In that regard, it is instructive to note that, unlike US law, English law does not feel the need to restrict recovery for intentionally caused psychiatric injury by insisting that a defendant's conduct must have been 'extreme and outrageous'. Even more significant is that fact that, with regard to mental injury across the board, Australian law, while accepting that the plaintiff must have suffered a recognised psychiatric injury, has no time for the 'control mechanisms' found in English and US law (though it seems as if legislation has unfortunately complicated matters[16]).[17]

So far, all we have learnt is that English and Australian law's more restrictive approach to mental injury has allowed it (ie, English and Australian law with respect to intentionally caused mental injury and Australian law regarding negligently caused mental injury) to develop a more principled approach to recovery. That, of course, does not on its own prove that English and especially Australian law is superior on this point. But that is my task now.

It must be clear that there can be no right to mental tranquillity or to be free of mental disturbance. There is simply too much disturbance and not enough tranquillity in the world to think that one has a right in this regard. It is no better to talk of mental harm unless that term is defined in accordance with what is said below. And it does not solve things simply to put epithets such as 'severe' before these terms. If there can be no right to be free from mental disturbance, for instance, then if severe mental disturbance is wrongful, the fact that it is severe does not explain why it is wrongful.

Psychiatric illness is another matter. Though I will criticise this notion in the following discussion, it is plausible to think that the requirement that the plaintiff have suffered a psychiatric illness is an (unconscious) attempt to connect the law with the innate right. The idea is relatively simple. If I cause you to have a psychiatric illness, then I have interfered with your freedom. This is because psychiatric illnesses debilitate one mentally in a way that affects one's freedom of choice.

[16] For discussion, see K Barker et al, *The Law of Torts in Australia*, 5th edn (Melbourne, Oxford University Press, 2012) 476–79.

[17] *Tame v New South Wales* 2002 HCA 35, (2002) 211 CLR 317; *Gifford v Strang Patrick Stevedoring Pty Ltd* (2003) 214 CLR 269 (HCA).

I have no right to be free of mental disturbance. You do not violate my freedom by making me sad or even by making me grieve.[18] Of course, I do not want to live in a world where facts are such that I have to grieve. But grieving as such does not undermine my free will. Causing me to have a psychiatric illness is another matter, however.

The English and Australian approach in this regard is therefore to be preferred over that found in the US. But it is still far from perfect. The main reason for this is that English and Australian law demands that the plaintiff have suffered a *recognised* psychiatric illness, and it looks in the wrong place for the recognition. As Michael Jones has emphasised,[19] lawyers tend to look for recognised psychiatric illnesses in publications such as the American Psychiatric Association's *Diagnostic and Statistical Manual of Mental Disorders*. This is not the place to summarise Jones' persuasive reasons for holding that this material must be treated with caution. For our purposes, the point is that such manuals are not aimed at and only at collecting the names of disorders that affect one in a way that undermines one's freedom.

The claim is not that lawyers should ignore material of the sort under discussion. On the contrary, lawyers need to pay close attention to the findings of psychiatrists and the like. The problem is that they are not paying sufficiently close attention. They tend to borrow without considering context. It is significant to note that not only is not enough attention being paid to why psychiatrists etc are classifying as they are, lawyers are generally at a loss to know why they want the information in the first place. If the question is 'Why do we want to know whether the plaintiff suffers from a recognised psychiatric illness?', the only answer is likely to be: 'Because the courts have said that this is what the plaintiff must have.' 'But why do the courts say this and are they right to do so?' The theory presented here has helped us to answer these questions.

The control mechanisms that we have examined cannot be justified on the ground that they reflect foreseeability concerns. It is entirely foreseeable that a plaintiff who is far from the scene of an accident, who fails to witness the accident as it is occurring and who is distantly related to the primary victim may suffer psychiatric injury. These control mechanisms should therefore be abolished. On the other hand, in negligence cases, we must recognise that defendants should be liable only if they were negligent for causing an unreasonable risk of the psychiatric injury that the plaintiff suffers in the circumstances that she suffers it. It is not possible to justify liability to a defendant who is negligent for different reasons. Thus, in *Dillon v Legg*, the fact that the defendant was driving in a way that imposed an unreasonable risk to pedestrians is not sufficient to show that he ought to have been liable to the plaintiff. On the contrary, the plaintiff needed to

[18] Unless, of course, that was your purpose. In those circumstances, you may be liable for exerting indirect control over me.

[19] M Jones, 'Liability for Psychiatric Damage' in Neyers, Chamberlain and Pitel (n 12).

show that the defendant created an unreasonable risk of causing psychiatric injury to bystanders. In this case, there is no difficulty—protecting others from psychiatric injury is not the main reason one should drive carefully, but it is a reason—yet this observation blocks the suggestion that the position under examination opens up the floodgates. Under this proposal, defendants will be liable only if they, as reasonable people, can foresee that their actions will have an impact on the plaintiff's mental states that will undermine the plaintiff's freedom. I can see no justification for limiting liability beyond this rule.

Perhaps there is a concern for those in the broadcast media, for example, who are called on to report natural disasters and the like. But this concern seems overblown. In combination with what has been said above, the defence of voluntary assumption of risk coupled with proper advertising, warning and the like appears to be a more than adequate protection.

We have been discussing examples of a kind that have challenged courts in recent times. The argument has been that they reveal that the law places inadequate importance on the mind. Hypothetical cases of control make this point even more clearly, despite the fact that they have not come before the courts. In the past, defendants have lacked the technology easily to realise examples of these kinds, at least frequently to do so. But those days are over. With developments in technology, the positive law requires reform in this area in order to keep up with its own principles. Let us begin with a relatively mundane case.

Imagine that I hypnotise you with your consent. While you are under hypnosis, and without your consent, I implant a suggestion of some kind. Say that I cause you to desire a product with which I am connected or to lose your affection for your spouse to whom I am attracted. Is this tortious? As far as the positive law is concerned, it seems that, unless the tort is negligence, the answer must be no. But that is the wrong answer. This is the violation of your freedom of the order of a battery: a direct exercise of control over you. It must be actionable as such.

Naturally, cases of this kind are unlikely to be common, but consider the placing of subliminal messages in television programmes or films. And consider the ability of organisations, most significantly governmental organisations, to collect data about us—internet usage, mobile phone usage, shopping patterns, recreational preferences etc—and the ability of those organisations and others to use that information in order to control us in ways about which we may not even be aware. The best protection we can have against this is likely to be a developed law of tort. But that law will not develop until we throw off the loss model and refocus our understanding on individual liberty. This book is intended to aid that change.

15

Patient Consent and the Right to Self-determination

As explored in Chapter 4, a patient who receives an operation to which she did not consent has a cause of action for battery. This chapter examines a related issue: the treatment of a patient who ostensibly consents to an operation, but was improperly informed of the attendant risks. In particular, the chapter is concerned with evaluating the rule adopted in Australia, Canada and England that in such circumstances, the patient can sue not in battery, but only in negligence.[1] For convenience, this is labelled the *disclosure rule*.

It is also important immediately to elucidate what this chapter is not about. It is not a comprehensive analysis of any jurisdiction's position on patient consent. Thus, beyond that necessary to make the case against the disclosure rule, the chapter does not seek to place the case law within its broader context dealing with wider issues of patient consent and medical negligence. Moreover, though it argues against the disclosure rule, it does not attempt to elucidate a comprehensive liability regime based on the alternative for which it argues. For instance, though it maintains that actions for battery ought to be available in circumstances where they are currently barred, it takes no stand on where the various burdens of proof should lie in these cases.[2] This is partly in an effort to keep the chapter short and to the point, but it is most fundamentally because of a determination not to lose the wood for the trees. The injustice worked by the modern law in this area ought to be clear to us. As it is, however, it is obscured by the fact that this law is so drenched in detail that its departure from fundamental principle has become difficult to detect. The trees are no doubt important, but this is an attempt to diagnose a disease that has infected the whole wood.

It should also be noted that this chapter does not examine the law's test for determining when a risk ought to be disclosed—though the matter must be touched on in passing.[3] That issue is not relevant here. We are exploring the

[1] *Chatterton v Gerson* [1981] 1 QB 432; *Sidaway v Board of Governors of the Bethlem Royal Hospital* [1985] AC 871 (HL); *Reibl v Hughes* [1980] 2 SCR 880; *Rogers v Whitaker* (1992) 175 CLR 479 (HCA).

[2] *cf*, eg, MA Somerville, 'Structuring the Issues in Informed Consent' (1981) 26 *McGill Law Journal* 740.

[3] For a useful analysis of the legal position in this regard, see D Mendelson, *The New Law of Torts*, 2nd edn (Melbourne, Oxford University Press, 2012) 385–88. The issues here are, of course, complex. To make matters worse, see the issues raised in S Cohen, 'The Nocebo Effect of Informed Consent'

following question: 'When a risk ought to have been disclosed but was not, what is the appropriate response?' We can answer this question without taking a stand on the appropriate test for the duty to disclose.

The reader will not be surprised to hear that there are two models for understanding the pertinent issue: the loss model and the one advanced here that focuses on the patient's freedom. These models understand the problem presented by fact patterns of this kind in very different ways. Moreover, both of these models are found in the case law—indeed, every significant case presents both of them. For this reason, the case law is awash with confusion. It is worth tracing through some of the case law in order to reveal this.

I. *Canterbury v Spence*

Let us begin with the judgment of the US Court of Appeals in *Canterbury v Spence*.[4] The defendant performed an operation on the plaintiff's back. The plaintiff alleged that, as a result of this operation, he was left partially paralysed and that the defendant had wrongly failed to inform him of the risk of this paralysis before the operation. The Court held that:

> The root premise is the concept, fundamental in American jurisprudence, that '[e]very human being of adult years and sound mind has a right to determine what shall be done with his own body…' True consent to what happens to one's self is the informed exercise of a choice, and that entails an opportunity to evaluate knowledgeably the options available and the risks attendant upon each. The average patient has little or no understanding of the medical arts, and ordinarily has only his physician to whom he can look for enlightenment with which to reach an intelligent decision. From these almost axiomatic considerations springs the need, and in turn the requirement, of a reasonable divulgence by physician to patient to make such a decision possible.[5]

Clear here is the focus on protecting the patient's right to control the use of his own body. In this regard, the Court maintained that 'the patient's right of self-decision shapes the boundaries of the duty to reveal',[6] showing that this right is the foundation of the defendant's potential liability. Moreover, as the Court also made clear, a defendant who performs an operation on a patient who is not properly informed of the risks involved commits a battery. This is because 'it is

(2014) 28 *Bioethics* 147, though the argument of this article is too focused on loss prevention and too paternalistic to be directly relevant here. See also *Montgomery v Lanarkshire Health Board* [2015] UKSC 11, [2015] AC 1430.

[4] *Canterbury v Spence* 464 F 2d 772 (US 1972).

[5] ibid 780, quoting *Schloendorff v Society of New York Hospital* 105 NE 92 (NY 1914) 93 (citations omitted).

[6] *Canterbury v Spence* (n 4) 786.

evident that it is normally impossible to obtain a consent worthy of the name unless the physician first elucidates the options and the perils for the patient's edification'.[7]

This position is in line with the argument of this book. Each individual has a right to control the use of his own body. An operation is a use. The fact that the surgeon typically operates in the patient's interests is entirely consistent with this point. The surgeon is entitled to put the patient to her purposes, even to purposes that benefit the patient, only with the plaintiff's consent. But unless the patient is properly informed, he cannot be said even to understand the purposes to which the defendant surgeon will put his body. Thus, his apparent consent cannot be operative as in these circumstances, it cannot show that the touching of the plaintiff is in accordance with a shared purpose.

The Court also recognised an exception to this general approach.[8] This exception:

> [O]btains when risk-disclosure poses such a threat of detriment to the patient as to become unfeasible or contraindicated from a medical point of view. It is recognized that patients occasionally become so ill or emotionally distraught on disclosure as to foreclose a rational decision, or complicate or hinder the treatment, or perhaps even pose psychological damage to the patient. Where that is so, the cases have generally held that the physician is armed with a privilege to keep the information from the patient, and we think it clear that portents of that type may justify the physician in action he deems medically warranted. The critical inquiry is whether the physician responded to a sound medical judgment that communication of the risk information would present a threat to the patient's well-being.[9]

The language here is unfortunately somewhat loose. The last sentence in particular suggests that the surgeon is entitled to withhold information from the patient when she believes that doing so is in the patient's best interests. In context, however, it is clear that this was not the Court's intention. The suggestion is rather that the surgeon is entitled to withhold information that would undermine the patient's capacity to make a rational decision concerning the operation.[10] Again, then, the focus is on the patient's freedom. The patient must be given the relevant information so that he can make an autonomous choice; however, if the receipt of the information would itself undermine the patient's autonomy, then that information can be withheld. In this regard, then, *Canterbury v Spence* is a paradigm for the theory presented here.

[7] ibid 783.

[8] In fact, the Court recognised two exceptions. The first concerns emergency situations of the kind examined in Ch 6.

[9] *Canterbury v Spence* (n 4) 789.

[10] In this regard, the privilege is a consequence of the general approach to treating the mentally incompetent. *cf Re C* [1994] 1 WLR 290. Compare *Montgomery v Lanarkshire Health Board* (n 3) [88], which remains unacceptably paternalistic on this score.

But there is more to *Canterbury v Spence* than this. Consider the following passage dealing with a patient's ability to recover for his specific injury:

> No more than breach of any other legal duty does nonfulfillment of the physician's obligation to disclose alone establish liability to the patient. An unrevealed risk that should have been made known must materialize, for otherwise the omission, however unpardonable, is legally without consequence. Occurrence of the risk must be harmful to the patient, for negligence unrelated to injury is nonactionable. And, as in malpractice actions generally, there must be a causal relationship between the physician's failure to adequately divulge and damage to the patient.[11]

This is a result of US law's emphasis on harm in this area, which was criticised in Part II of this book. The crucial point to realise is that it relies on the loss model and that that model is inconsistent with the basis of the defendant's liability as enunciated by the Court. As the Court explained, that liability is based on the plaintiff's right to self-determination, here the right to control the use of his own body. Causing harm to another is not the only way in which that right can be violated.

According to the facts assumed for the purposes of the appeal in *Canterbury v Spence* and according to the position of the Court:

(1) The basis for liability in this area of the law is the plaintiff's right to self-determination.
(2) That right is violated if the defendant operates on the plaintiff without giving the plaintiff sufficient information about the operation because, in those circumstances, the plaintiff cannot have given his informed consent.
(3) Those circumstances obtained.

It must follow from this that as the plaintiff's right was violated, the right said to underlie liability in this area, the defendant ought to have been liable for performing the operation regardless of any harm to the plaintiff.

In the language of this book, the Court began correctly by identifying liability as responding to control, but then, at a crucial juncture, shifted to analysing liability as responding to injury. In fact, the Court made this all but explicit in two ways. First, though it initially identified the relevant action as being for battery,[12] in the passage above, the Court is speaking of negligence. Second, despite first identifying the plaintiff's right to self-determination as the foundation of liability, the Court then tells us that 'the very purpose of the disclosure rule is to protect the patient *against consequences* which, if known, he would have avoided by foregoing the treatment'.[13] The focus now is not self-determination, but the avoidance of loss.[14]

The position advanced in *Canterbury v Spence* is inconsistent. The judgment sets out an account of liability based on control, but then switches in mid-stream

[11] *Canterbury v Spence* (n 4) 790.
[12] ibid 783.
[13] ibid 790 (emphasis added).
[14] See also the curious first paragraph at ibid 781.

to liability based on injury. My contention is that the Court was right first time. An operation performed without the patient's informed consent ought to be recognised as a battery and, as argued in Chapter 4, that tort ought to be actionable per se.

II. *Sidaway v Board of Governors of the Bethlem Royal Hospital*

Sidaway presents the opposite picture to *Canterbury v Spence*. With the exception of Lord Scarman's judgment, which is more in line with the thesis presented here, the judgments in this case begin with the loss model. The problem again, however, is that they cannot be said to end there.

The defendant surgeon operated on the plaintiff without telling her that the operation carried a risk of damage to her spinal column and nerve roots. As a result of the operation, the plaintiff was left severely disabled. The majority of their Lordships treated the relevant issue not as concerning the patient's right to control her own body, but as ensuring that the patient received the best treatment, where 'best' is defined in terms of a medical assessment of the patient's health outcomes. As Lord Templeman said, 'the objective' of providing information is 'restoring the patient's health'.[15] In other words, the focus is on the avoidance of preventable loss.

This explains why their Lordships treated the duty to inform the patient of risk as merely one aspect of the surgeon's general duty to care for the patient.[16] And that in turn explains why the Court took the plaintiff's suggestion that the *Bolam* test—which determines liability in part in accordance with medical convention[17]—should not apply in this case as an attack on the applicability of that test in general.[18] There is all but no recognition in these judgments that the issue might be not loss prevention, but the protection of the plaintiff's autonomy. Because of this, Lord Diplock was able to say that: 'The only effect that mention of risks can have on the patient's mind, if it has any at all, can be in the direction of deterring the patient from undergoing the treatment which in the expert opinion of the doctor it is in the patient's interest to undergo.'[19] If we assume that the operation was in the patient's best interests in terms of her health *ex ante* and if we assume that the role of the law is to promote the patient's health, then the task is to ensure that the patient has that operation. On this view, then, it is clear that the law should not encourage, let alone require, the surgeon to give the patient

[15] *Sidaway v Board of Governors of the Bethlem Royal Hospital* [1985] AC 871 (HL), 904.
[16] See especially ibid 893.
[17] *Bolam v Friern Hospital Management Committee* [1957] 1 WLR 582 (QBD).
[18] Again, see especially *Sidaway v Board of Governors of the Bethlem Royal Hospital* (n 15) 893–94.
[19] ibid 895.

information that would make it less likely that she would sign the consent forms. That would undermine the purpose of the law.

That, of course, makes sense from the perspective of the loss model, but it is surely distressingly paternalistic. In response to Lord Diplock, one should say that an effect of informing the plaintiff of the risks is that she is able to live her life autonomously and not to have these important decisions effectively made for her by others, a quite objectionable situation even if those others have the patient's best interests at heart.

Consider also the following passage from Lord Templeman's judgment:

> The duty of the doctor in these circumstances, *subject to his overriding duty to have regard to the best interests of the patient*, is to provide the patient with information which will enable the patient to make a balanced judgment if the patient chooses to make a balanced judgment. A patient may make an unbalanced judgment because he is deprived of adequate information. A patient may also make an unbalanced judgment if he is provided with too much information and is made aware of possibilities which he is not capable of assessing because of his lack of medical training, *his prejudices or his personality*. Thus the provision of too much information may prejudice the attainment of the objective of restoring the patient's health.[20]

Though Lord Templeman is awake to the relevance of these matters for the patient's autonomy, most noteworthy is his insistence that such concerns are 'subject' to the demands of the plaintiff's health. For this reason, Lord Templeman suggests that the surgeon is not only permitted to withhold information that might deter the patient from consenting to the operation because of his prejudices or personality, his Lordship insists that this information ought to be withheld.[21] This, as we have seen, is because the overall aim is said to be restoring the patient to health. This position, then, recognises the importance of the patient's freedom, but subordinates it to that of his health.

Consider also Lord Bridge's claim that:

> [A] decision what degree of disclosure of risks is best calculated to assist a particular patient to make a rational choice as to whether or not to undergo a particular treatment must primarily be a matter of clinical judgment. It would follow from this that the issue whether non-disclosure in a particular case should be condemned as a breach of the doctor's duty of care is an issue to be decided primarily on the basis of expert medical evidence.[22]

Why must the decision be a matter of clinical judgement? If the aim is best to ensure that the patient chooses to do what is most likely to conduce to his health, then the answer is obvious. But why is that the aim? It is because of the dominance of the loss model.

[20] ibid 904 (emphasis added).

[21] The first concern mentioned by Lord Templeman can perhaps be justified on the basis of the patient's autonomy, though much care is called for here. Patients are generally capable of understanding a great deal if adequate time is taken to explain matters to them.

[22] *Sidaway v Board of Governors of the Bethlem Royal Hospital* (n 15) 900.

Sidaway, then, is paradigm for the loss model. But recognition of the importance of the plaintiff's autonomy is bubbling beneath the surface of the judgments, though in some rather a long way beneath. After all, if achieving health really is the aim of the law in this area, why is there a need to consult the patient at all? Why the need for any kind of consent? If we were to take their Lordships' pronouncements on the basis of this liability to their logical conclusions, then we would have no liability for the failure to disclose per se. We would simply have liability for loss, the failure to disclose being one possible causal mechanism for that loss to occur. There would be no duty to disclose, merely a duty not to cause loss, including of course a duty not to cause loss by failing to disclose.[23]

III. *Montgomery v Lanarkshire Health Board*

The position taken by the House of Lords in *Sidaway* was rejected by the UK Supreme Court in *Montgomery*. Lords Kerr, Reed, Neuberger, Clarke, Wilson and Hodge maintained that:

> [S]ocial and legal developments ... point away from a model of the relationship between the doctor and the patient based upon medical paternalism. They also point away from a model based upon a view of the patient as being entirely dependent on information provided by the doctor. What they point towards is an approach to the law which, instead of treating patients as placing themselves in the hands of their doctors ... treats them so far as possible as adults who are capable of understanding that medical treatment is uncertain of success and may involve risks, accepting responsibility for the taking of risks affecting their own lives, and living with the consequences of their choices.[24]

Their Lordships went on to insist that:

> [T]his approach entails a duty on the part of doctors to take reasonable care to ensure that a patient is aware of material risks of injury that are inherent in treatment. This can be understood, within the traditional framework of negligence, as a duty of care to avoid exposing a person to a risk of injury which she would otherwise have avoided, but it is also the counterpart of the patient's entitlement to decide whether or not to incur that risk.[25]

However, their Lordships also accepted that the appropriate action in these circumstances was negligence. If we are dealing with cases in which the plaintiff has been operated on without giving a properly informed consent, then it is unclear why that should be so. Moreover, their Lordships accepted that a defendant could

[23] In fact, it might be argued that *Sidaway* is at least very close to adopting this potion. If that is the right interpretation of this case, then I submit that English law was thoroughly unjust in this context, being deeply and unjustifiably paternalistic.

[24] *Montgomery v Lanarkshire Health Board* (n 3) [81].

[25] ibid [82].

be liable only if her failure to inform the patient of risk causes the plaintiff injury—a point to be examined in detail in section V of this chapter. But it is again unclear why this should be so on the assumption that the fundamental value here is the patient's right to choose. That right can be violated without any loss occurring.

In *Montgomery*, then, we see the reverse of *Sidaway* and something much more like *Canterbury v Spence*. The Court begins by focusing on the plaintiff's autonomy, but, bubbling beneath the surface, the loss model remains. Thus, even though the Court insists that the patient's right to self-determination is the paramount value in operation in this context, it nevertheless insists on loss.

IV. Consequences of the Models

Viewed in accordance with the loss model, the fundamental problem in cases of this kind is that the plaintiff is suffering some kind of loss as the result of the defendant's behaviour. This suggests that the appropriate action in response to this problem is negligence. Thus, we get the disclosure rule—the rule according to which a plaintiff wrongly uninformed of risk may have a cause of action in negligence, but not in battery. Furthermore, as this view characterises the potential wrongdoing as the defendant's failure to inform the plaintiff leading to the plaintiff's injury, it maintains that the plaintiff can recover only if the failure to warn did in fact lead to injury. This leads to the notion that if the plaintiff would have consented to the operation had he been informed of the risk, then there can be no liability, as in those circumstances the defendant's negligent action was not a (but-for) cause of the plaintiff's injury. Moreover, because of the focus on negligence, it seems pertinent to ask whether it was reasonable for the defendant to have performed the operation and whether the operation was in accordance with established medical practice.

On the other hand, viewed in accordance with the model advanced in this book, the fundamental problem in cases of this kind is that the plaintiff has been put to the defendant's purposes without proper consent, meaning that the touching was not in accordance with a purpose shared by the parties. Loss, on this view, is incidental to liability. It follows that the appropriate action is battery and not negligence. Thus, this view calls for the abolition of the disclosure rule. As this view holds loss to be irrelevant to liability, it is unconcerned with whether the failure to inform led to injury. Battery being actionable per se, factual causation is in this sense irrelevant. Thus, it does not matter whether the plaintiff would have consented to the operation had she been informed. Moreover, because the concern is with whether the plaintiff has been put to the defendant's purposes without proper consent, enquiry into the reasonableness of the defendant's conduct or of the operation is otiose.

Note that, as in this book in general, the focus here is on liability rather than on damages. Thus, these positions may not be as far apart in practice as they at first seem. Imagine, for instance, a plaintiff who ostensibly consented to an operation uninformed of the attendant risks and who develops an injury as the result of the materialisation of one of those risks, but where we can be sure that he would have consented to the operation even if he had been informed of the risks. The first view holds that there can be no liability, as the defendant's negligent failure to inform the plaintiff of the risk which materialised was not a cause of the plaintiff's injury. The second view holds in contradistinction that there must be liability in this case as the touching of the plaintiff, as not properly consented to, was a battery, but it does not follow from this as a matter of course that the plaintiff will be able to recover for the injury in question. This is because, in this circumstance, the injury *might* be remote in the sense that it does not lie within the ambit of the defendant's wrongdoing.[26] The results here may be more similar than first meets the eye.

That said, however, there is nevertheless a considerable gulf between these two views. Usefully, this conflict came to a head in the judgment of the High Court of Australia in *Wallace v Kam*.[27] Because of this, the case is worth exploring in some detail.

V. *Wallace v Kam*

A. Facts

The defendant neurosurgeon performed an operation on the plaintiff to treat a condition of the plaintiff's lumber spine. For our purposes, the operation carried two material risks. The first was a one in 20 chance of 'permanent and catastrophic paralysis' caused by damage to the plaintiff's nerves.[28] The second was a risk of bilateral femoral neurapraxia caused by lying immobile on the operating table. The second risk materialised; the first did not. The plaintiff sued, claiming damages for the consequences of the neurapraxia, alleging that the defendant wrongly failed to warn him of these risks and that he would not have consented to the operation had he been warned of either one.

The trial judge found that the defendant negligently failed to inform the plaintiff of the risk of neurapraxia. However, he also found that the plaintiff would have consented to undergo the operation had he been aware of that risk alone. That led the judge to conclude that the failure to warn of the risk of neurapraxia

[26] It is sometimes claimed that remoteness does not operate in the tort of battery or in other torts. However, this is simply impossible. Remoteness in some form must operate in all torts. Imagine, for instance, that you batter me as a young adult and 50 years later I perform some action in part because of my memory of that event, and that action causes loss. Are you responsible for this? Of course, remoteness in this area need not match that found in the law of negligence, but all liability must end somewhere.

[27] *Wallace v Kam* [2013] HCA 19, (2013) 297 ALR 383.

[28] ibid [1].

was not a cause of the plaintiff's injury and thus to deny recovery. The trial judge made no finding in relation to the alleged failure to warn of the risk of paralysis. Accordingly, the appeal to the High Court was taken on the assumption that the plaintiff was not informed about that risk and that the defendant was negligent for not doing so.[29]

B. The Basis and Shape of Liability

Why do medical professionals have a duty to disclose risks? This is the High Court's answer:

> The component of the duty of a medical practitioner that ordinarily requires the medical practitioner to inform the patient of material risks of physical injury inherent in a proposed treatment is founded on the underlying common law right of the patient to choose whether or not to undergo a proposed treatment. In imposing that component of the duty, the common law recognises not only the right of the patient to choose but the need for the patient to be adequately informed in order to be able to make that choice rationally. The policy underlying the imposition of that component of the duty is to equip the patient with information relevant to the choice that is the patient's to make.[30]

Similarly, in *Rogers v Whitaker*, Mason CJ, Brennan, Dawson, Toohey and McHugh JJ maintained that:

> [E]xcept in cases of emergency or necessity, all medical treatment is preceded by the patient's choice to undergo it. In legal terms, the patient's consent to the treatment may be valid once he or she is informed in broad terms of the nature of the procedure which is intended. But the choice is, in reality, meaningless unless it is made on the basis of relevant information and advice.[31]

All of this supports the view advanced here. The patient has a right to choose. That right cannot be exercised meaningfully unless the patient is properly informed. Thus, if the patient is not properly informed, then the performance of the operation is wrongful, despite the patient's ostensible consent. That position suggests that the appropriate action is battery rather than negligence and that causation of loss is therefore irrelevant. But that is not the position taken by these courts.

In *Rogers v Whitaker*, when turning to discuss the ability to recover, the same judges maintained that 'nothing is to be gained by reiterating … expressions … such as "the patient's right of self-determination"'.[32] But what were the judges speaking of in the earlier paragraph if not that right? The Court held in favour of the disclosure rule, maintaining that the defendant was able to sue only in

[29] 'On the facts found *and assumed*, Dr Kam breached his … duty … by failing to warn Mr Wallace of two material risks': ibid [28] (emphasis added).

[30] ibid [8].

[31] *Rogers v Whitaker* (n 1) 489.

[32] ibid 490.

negligence. In *Wallace v Kam*, this led the Court to hold that, as the plaintiff would have consented to undergo the risk of neurapraxia had he been informed of it, the defendant's negligent failure to inform him of that risk was not a cause of his injury and thus that the defendant was not liable. But none of this makes sense according to the basis of liability as enunciated by the courts.

The fundamental problem here is this. It is surely clear that the courts ought to recognise that we possess a right to self-determination in these contexts. It is our bodies that are being operated on, so it must be our choices that govern whether these operations occur. The courts feel this requirement and reflect this in their language and decisions. Despite this, however, they remain remarkably timorous in enforcing the right that they claim to recognise. In *Wallace v Kam*, this twofaced character of these judgments became explicit.

According to the decision in *Wallace v Kam*:

(1) The defendant wrongly failed to give the plaintiff information to which the plaintiff had a right.
(2) The plaintiff possessed this right in order to ensure that he had the information necessary to make a rational decision as to whether to undergo the operation.
(3) The plaintiff was entitled to the information necessary for rational decision making because it was for him to decide whether to undergo the operation and that decision could not rationally be made without the information.
(4) The operation was performed without the plaintiff being in the position to make a rational decision as to whether to undergo it.
(5) However, the defendant did not wrong the plaintiff in law, as the risk that materialised was a risk that the plaintiff would have been prepared to accept.

It is important to stress that this description of *Wallace v Kam* is the Court's own view. The problem is (1)–(4) alone is sufficient to generate the conclusion that the defendant legally wronged the plaintiff and therefore ought to be liable. Moreover, (5) in no way alters this. In fact, (5) is irrelevant. To put this another way, the position taken by the Court is that the defendant did not wrong the plaintiff even though he failed to give the plaintiff the information that the plaintiff required in order meaningfully to control the use of his own body, information that the defendant was under a duty to give to the plaintiff. I submit that this cannot be right. It is inconsistent with the Court's own assessment of the basis of the defendant's potential liability.

Remarkably, the Court came as close as it is possible to come to recognising this. As noted earlier, the Court acknowledged that liability in this area is 'founded on the underlying common law right of the patient to choose'.[33] But the Court immediately went on to say:

> However, consistent with the underlying purpose of the imposition of the duty to warn, the damage suffered by the patient that the common law makes compensable is not

[33] *Wallace v Kam* (n 27) [8].

> impairment of the patient's right to choose … The compensable damage is, rather, limited to the occurrence and consequences of physical injury sustained by the patient as a result of the medical treatment that is carried out following the making by the patient of a choice to undergo the treatment.[34]

This means that, though there is nominally a right to choose, the law does not actually enforce this right in these cases. The right enforced is not the right to choose, but some right not to be injured. The right to choose is in some way legally recognised, but it is in these contexts without legal force. Again, the claim is not that this is an implied consequence of this passage. On the contrary, that is what the passage is telling us explicitly. I am merely paraphrasing.

The position, then, is that the defendant has a duty to disclose because of the patient's right to choose, but that if the defendant fails to disclose, then liability is determined in accordance with a right other than the right to choose. If this is not simply incoherent, it is, by failing to give effect to the plaintiff's right to choose, a serious injustice to the plaintiff.

Consider also this passage:

> The duty of a medical practitioner to warn the patient of material risks inherent in a proposed treatment is imposed by reference to the underlying common law right of the patient to choose whether or not to undergo a proposed treatment. However, the policy that underlies requiring the exercise of reasonable care and skill in the giving of that warning is neither to protect that right to choose nor to protect the patient from exposure to all unacceptable risks. The underlying policy is rather to protect the patient from the occurrence of physical injury the risk of which is unacceptable to the patient. It is appropriate that the scope of liability for breach of the duty reflect that underlying policy.[35]

Again, this is to say that, in this area, the right to choose is of no legal consequence.

In both of these passages, the claims before the 'however' concern the plaintiff's rights. Those claims call for liability in the tort of battery. When we reach the 'however', however, we see the consequences of shifting to the law of negligence. As is all but admitted, the law of negligence cannot respect that right. The inescapable conclusion is that the law is not respecting the very right that it regards as both fundamental and as forming the basis of the defendant's liability.

Again, it must be stressed that the claim is not that the courts ought properly to recognise the right to choose (though I would make that claim). The courts themselves say this. The problem is that they do not live up to their own pronouncements.

It is instructive to consider the following passage in the light of this criticism:

> The normative judgment that is appropriate to be made is that the liability of a medical practitioner who has failed to warn the patient of material risks inherent in a proposed

[34] ibid [9].
[35] ibid [36].

treatment 'should not extend to harm from risks that the patient was willing to hazard, whether through an express choice or as found had their disclosure been made'.[36]

This approach does not ask whether the plaintiff consented. It asks only whether the plaintiff would have been willing to undergo the risk had he known about it. This, of course, is for the court to determine. That does not respect the autonomy of the plaintiff. The lawfulness of the use of his body is determined not in accordance with his own decisions, but in the light of judgments made about what he may have wanted in counterfactual circumstances. The point is that even if the plaintiff would have consented, he did not consent, and a proper respect for his autonomy would determine the ambit of his liberty in terms of his decisions. This is why it is not generally a defence to battery to show that the plaintiff would have consented or even that the plaintiff wanted the touching in question. Think of this in the context of sexual battery, for instance. Here the law demands actual consent and is right to do so.

In fact, matters are worse than this. In *Sidaway*, the House of Lords ruled that the defendant's duty to inform the plaintiff is determined in accordance with the practices of the defendant's profession.[37] Thankfully, that has not been accepted in Australia or Canada[38] and has now been repudiated in the UK.[39] However, it remains the case that the causal issue is decided in accordance with an objective test.[40] Thus, placing these cases in the law of negligence has led the courts to the view that the question is not whether the individual plaintiff would have been willing to undergo the risk of which she was not informed, but whether a reasonable person in the plaintiff's position would have been willing. What, now, is left of the idea that there is a 'common law right of the patient to choose whether or not to undergo a proposed treatment', a right that means that the defendant must 'equip the patient with information relevant to the choice that is the patient's to make'?[41] In what sense can we say that the law lives up to the maxim that 'Every human being of adult years and sound mind has a right to determine what shall be done with his own body'?[42] The answer is not encouraging.

[36] ibid [37], quoting *Wallace v Kam* [2012] NSWCA 82, (2012) Aust Torts Reports ¶82–101.

[37] *Sidaway v Board of Governors of the Bethlem Royal Hospital* (n 15).

[38] *Rogers v Whitaker* (n 1) 487; Civil Liability Act 2002 (Tas) s 22(1); Civil Liability Act 2003 (Qld) ss 20(1), 22(1); Civil Liability Act 2002 (NSW) s 50(1); Civil Liability Act 1936 (SA) s 41(1); Wrongs Act 1958 (Vic) s 59(1); *Reibl v Hughes* (n 1); *White v Turner* (1981) 120 DLR (3d) 269.

[39] *Montgomery v Lanarkshire Health Board* (n 3).

[40] *Wallace v Kam* (n 36) [25], [118], [120]–[121]; *Reibl v Hughes* (n 1); *White v Turner* (n 38) 269. Compare *Sidaway v Board of Governors of the Bethlem Royal Hospital* (n 15) 888. This also appears to be the position taken in *Montgomery v Lanarkshire Health Board* (n 3), though the issue was not specifically examined by the Court.

[41] *Wallace v Kam* (n 27) [8].

[42] *Schloendorff v Society of New York Hospital* (n 5) 93. See also *Re F (Mental Patient: Sterilisation)* [1990] 2 AC 1 (HL), 73.

C. Factual Causation

Though not central to our concerns here, it is worth pausing to consider the position of the Court in *Wallace v Kam* in relation to factual causation in this context.

In accordance with the loss model, the High Court maintained that disputes of this kind are to be determined in accordance with the traditional but-for test,[43] the question being whether the defendant's negligence caused the plaintiff's injury. However, as the Court recognised, that results in a difficulty. Precisely what must be the cause of the plaintiff's injury? There are two possibilities.

First, if the defendant's negligence is defined as the failure to warn of the risk of the plaintiff's injury—the neurapraxia—then, given the findings of the trial judge, the defendant's negligence did not cause the plaintiff's injury as he would have consented to the operation had he been warned of that risk. Here, we take the risks separately, ignoring the risk of paralysis. We can refer to this as the *separatist* approach.[44] Second, if the defendant's negligence is defined as the failure to warn of the risks of which the plaintiff ought to have been warned—of the neurapraxia and paralysis—then, given the operative assumptions, the defendant's negligence did cause the plaintiff's injury. Here we take the risks together: a *cumulative* approach.[45] This reveals that the case could not be disposed of in terms of factual causation alone. As the Court stressed, the case turns on a normative rather than a merely factual judgement concerning which of these two approaches is to be preferred.

The Court opted for the first approach. However, though it presented reasons for doing so, all of these reasons tacitly *assume* that the first approach is preferable. Consequently, the Court's decision is in this regard unjustified.

First, the Court maintained that the argument for its conclusion 'can be expressed somewhat glibly in the proposition that Mr Wallace should not be compensated for the materialisation of a risk he would have been prepared to accept'.[46] Of course, it would be wrong to place great emphasis on this passage, but analysis of it is nevertheless useful as it illustrates an error that infects the Court's more considered position in this regard. What was the risk that the plaintiff would have been willing to accept? The risk of neurapraxia is the obvious answer. But the answer is only partly correct. It is true that the plaintiff would have been prepared to accept the risk of the neurapraxia had he remained ignorant of the risk of paralysis. But it is not true to say that he would have been prepared to accept the risk of the neurapraxia had he also been made aware of the risk of paralysis. Hence, the Court's position does not argue in favour of the separatist view. It assumes that this is the appropriate view.

[43] *Wallace v Kam* (n 27) [16].

[44] See Somerville (n 2) 804.

[45] ibid.

[46] *Wallace v Kam* (n 27) [32].

In this context, it is important to clarify the following regarding the plaintiff's attitude to the risk of neurapraxia. Let us begin with two claims. First, had the plaintiff been informed of the risk of neurapraxia but not of the risk of paralysis, then he would have agreed to have the operation. Second, had the plaintiff been informed of the risk of the paralysis but not of the risk of neurapraxia, then he would not have agreed to have the operation. It is important to see that it does not follow from these claims that the failure to warn of the risk of neurapraxia was casually irrelevant. We can see this by imagining a third case in which the plaintiff is informed of both risks and insists that it is his awareness of both risks that leads him to refuse his consent. We might imagine him saying, for instance: 'Of course the main reason I chose not to have the operation was because of the risk of paralysis, but when I also heard about the risk of neurapraxia, that made me all the more certain.'[47] This analysis helps to reveal that the Court's argument begged the question. If the risks are taken separately, ie, if we look at the facts in terms of the first situation envisaged in this paragraph, then the plaintiff was injured as the result of 'the materialisation of a risk he would have been prepared to accept'. But if the risks are taken together, ie, if we look at the facts in terms of the third imagined situation, then the plaintiff was injured as the result of the materialisation of a risk he would not have been prepared to accept. And this is despite the fact that we are speaking of the very same risk. In each case, *the risk* is the risk of neurapraxia.

Of course, we have not yet examined the Court's genuine argument, which is contained in the following passage:

> [T]he ultimately persuasive force of that proposition [ie, the adoption of the separatist approach] lies not in its intuitive attraction but in recognition of the distinct nature of the material risks about which Dr Kam failed to warn Mr Wallace and in relating Mr Wallace's acceptance of the risk that came home to the policy underlying Dr Kam's duty to warn Mr Wallace of all material risks.[48]

This argument commits precisely the same error. It is true that the risks of which the plaintiff ought to have been informed were distinct. They were separate risks. But the issue is whether the plaintiff's ability to recover is to be determined in accordance with his attitude to the risk of neurapraxia where we imagine that he

[47] In other words, though his awareness of the risk of paralysis was sufficient for him to refuse consent, and thus though his awareness of the risk of neurapraxia was not necessary for that refusal, his awareness of the latter risk remains causally relevant. It is part of what led him to refuse to consent. Here we see yet another problem with the but-for test, which seems to suggest that the hypothetical plaintiff's attitude to the risk of neurapraxia cannot in this case have been causative, as it was not a necessary condition of his decision not to have the operation. That is because, in these circumstances, his decision is overdetermined. But the notion that the plaintiff's attitude was not causative is absurd. Consider also this example. The fact that my wife is beautiful was not a necessary condition for my marrying her—I would have married her anyway—but it was certainly one of the reasons I married her in fact, despite it not being a but-for cause of our marriage. There are, of course, many similar problems with the but-for test. For analysis, see A Beever, *Rediscovering the Law of Negligence* (Oxford, Hart Publishing, 2007) 415–17.

[48] *Wallace v Kam* (n 27) [32].

remains unaware of the risk of paralysis (the separatist approach) or in accordance with the plaintiff's attitude to the risk of neurapraxia where we imagine that he is aware of all of the risks of which he ought to have been informed (the cumulative approach). The Court simply adopted the separatist approach without providing an argument in favour of doing so.

Moreover, as we have seen, the Court tells us that 'the policy underlying Dr Kam's duty to warn Mr Wallace of all material risks' is the concern that patients be given sufficient information for them to make informed choices as to whether to undergo medical procedures.[49] That 'policy' does not support the separatist view. On the contrary, when people make decisions of this kind, indeed of any kind, they characteristically make them as it were cumulatively, taking into account all that they know about the risks, benefits, costs and so on.

The claim is not that the separatist approach is never appropriate. It is appropriate when the risks relate to separate *procedures* so that the patient must consent separately to each procedure. Beyond that, however, even given the loss model, it ought almost never to be applied. The default approach ought to be the cumulative as that reflects the way in which decisions are ordinarily made.

VI. Why Negligence?

This section examines purported rationales for the disclosure rule. The first thing that must be said in this context is that even purported rationales are remarkably difficult to come by. Take, for instance, the following passage from Mason CJ, Brennan, Dawson, Toohey and McHugh JJ's judgment in *Rogers v Whitaker*, which is frequently taken to be central:

> In this context, nothing is to be gained by reiterating the expressions used in American authorities, such as 'the patient's right of self-determination' or even the oft-used and somewhat amorphous phrase 'informed consent'. The right of self-determination is an expression which is, perhaps, suitable to cases where the issue is whether a person has agreed to the general surgical procedure or treatment, but is of little assistance in the balancing process that is involved in the determination of whether there has been a breach of the duty of disclosure. Likewise, the phrase 'informed consent' is apt to mislead as it suggests a test of the validity of a patient's consent. Moreover, consent is relevant to actions framed in trespass, not in negligence. Anglo-Australian law has rightly taken the view that an allegation that the risks inherent in a medical procedure have not been disclosed to the patient can only found an action in negligence and not in trespass; the consent necessary to negative the offence of battery is satisfied by the patient being advised in broad terms of the nature of the procedure to be performed.[50]

[49] ibid [8].

[50] *Rogers v Whitaker* (n 1) 490 (citations omitted).

This passage assumes that the disclosure rule is justified. It does nothing to argue for it. The first sentence merely sets out what is meant to be shown. The second sentence speaks of a 'balancing process' that must be used in this context. The expectation is that this process is elucidated elsewhere in the judgment. That expectation, however, is not met. This is the one and only time that the judges speak of balancing in their judgment. The third sentence correctly alleges that informed consent is an issue regarding the validity of the patient's consent, but it dismisses the relevance of this concern here because it assumes without argument that this validity is not the central issue. The penultimate sentence assumes that the disclosure rule is justified. The last sentence does no more than assert that 'Anglo-Australian law has rightly' adopted the disclosure rule and then describes that rule. In short, there is no argument here. This may be the central passage on this theme in Australian law, but that only demonstrates again the need for reform in this area.

However, it seems possible to say that, apart from the influence of the loss model, there are at least seven reasons it might be thought that negligence rather than battery is the appropriate action in these contexts. These are examined now.

A. Risk

The law of battery is concerned with intentional and unwanted touching. The law of negligence is about injuries caused by defendants taking unjustified risks. And the cases under discussion involve risk; they arise when the defendant has failed to inform the plaintiff about a relevant risk. This suggests that negligence is the proper action. Risk is the problem and so the proper response is in terms of the area of the law designed to deal with risk. But this argument is unsound.

First, the presence of risk is no contraindication to a claim in battery. Imagine that you and I are on a date when I think that *the moment* has arrived. Aware that I might be wrong, I nevertheless decide to take my chances and throw myself at you, attempting to perform deeds that need not be described here. In this case I am taking a risk and, assuming that my advances are unwanted,[51] it is a risk I should not have taken. But this does not mean that I commit only negligence and not battery. As we saw in Chapter 4, the same is true if I play Russian roulette with you and, unhappily for you, strike the chamber that contains the bullet. In fact, defendants in battery cases can always be described as taking some type of relevant risk—certainty, after all, is but one kind of risk—but that does not mean that actions for battery are unavailable.

Second, in a claim for negligence, the plaintiff's complaint is that the defendant behaved in a way that exposed her to an unreasonable level of risk of injury. But that is not what the cases under consideration are about. As the Court said in *Wallace v Kam*, they are about the right to choose, the right to control one's own

[51] Strictly: assuming that they are not immediately consented to.

body. The defendant must disclose the relevant risks to the patient so that the patient can make a properly informed decision as to whether to undergo the operation.[52] In *Wallace v Kam*, then, the plaintiff's complaint is not that the defendant exposed him to an unreasonable level of risk; it is that the defendant did not give him the information necessary to enable him to make a properly informed choice about the use of his body. It is just a detail that this information was about risk.

As we know, the defendant's failure to give the plaintiff this information was held to be negligent. But what does this mean? It does not mean that the defendant exposed the plaintiff to an unjustified risk of injury, which is what negligence means in the law of negligence. It means that the defendant should have but did not give the plaintiff the information that the plaintiff ought to have had (about risk, so it happens) so that the plaintiff could make a properly informed decision. The plaintiff was not complaining about any risk taken or created by the defendant. He was complaining about the fact that he was not able to make an informed decision about whether to undergo the operation when the defendant had a duty to give him the relevant information and the reason the defendant had that duty was to ensure that the plaintiff was able properly to make that decision.[53] It just happens that this information is about risk. But that is a detail. It is not central to the nature of the wrongdoing.

In these contexts, liability is not about risk. It does not fit the law of negligence. The liability is about the plaintiff's right to choose. It fits the tort of battery.

This can also be exposed by considering the following question: when did the wrong to the plaintiff occur? Given the disclosure rule's insistence that the law of negligence must be utilised in these contexts, the answer must be that the wrong is committed when the injury occurs. This is because liability for negligence requires damage. But that cannot be right. When a surgeon operates on me without my consent, I am wronged the moment I am touched. That is because I am touched in a way to which I have not consented, in violation of my right to control the use of my own body. The same is true when a surgeon operates on me without informing me of the risks about which I ought to have been informed. As the High Court of Australia maintained in *Wallace v Kam*, the duty of the defendant in these cases is 'founded on the underlying common law right of the patient to choose whether or not to undergo a proposed treatment' and 'the common law recognises not only the right of the patient to choose but the need for the patient to be adequately informed in order to be able to make that choice rationally'.[54] It follows from this position that when I am touched in the circumstances under consideration, I am touched in violation of my rights. The wrong occurs then and not when any injury develops.[55]

[52] *Wallace v Kam* (n 27) [8].
[53] ibid.
[54] ibid.
[55] Indeed, no injury may develop. But, according to the argument presented by the Court at this point, the argument I entirely endorse, I am still wronged. Thus, I of course mean to support the notion that liability in this area ought to be per se and not to require injury.

The claim that the plaintiff in *Wallace v Kam* 'should not be compensated for the materialisation of a risk he would have been prepared to accept'[56] involves a misconstrual of the nature of his complaint. He was not suing for the materialisation of any risk. He was suing because he was not given the information that he needed to make a properly informed decision concerning the operation (and that this resulted in injury).

B. Intention

A second argument maintains that the failure of the medical professional fits the law of negligence better than the law of battery. This is because battery is an intentional tort and the defendant does not have a relevant intention. Characteristically, the defendant does not intend to withhold information from the plaintiff, for instance. It is rather that the defendant does not consider carefully enough what information ought to be given and as a result gives the patient too little. That is negligence rather than intentional wrongdoing.[57]

In fact, however, there seems to be good reason to think that defendants in these cases are very frequently withholding information deliberately. That is clearly what occurred in *Montgomery*.[58] In *Sidaway*, it was recurrently claimed that defendants are right to do so. But let us put that aside. Even on the assumption that the failure to disclose is characteristically negligent rather than intentional, this does not support the disclosure rule.

The wrongful act is not the failure to disclose risk per se. If it were, then the wrong would be committed and an action would in principle be available even before the operation commences. The wrong is not the failure to disclose—it is operating on the patient having failed to disclose. And that is wrongful because, as the risk was not properly disclosed, the patient has been unable to make a properly informed choice as to whether to undergo the operation. This means that the wrongdoing is intentional in the sense necessary for the commission of a battery. Operating on the patient in the relevant circumstances is an intentional act to which the proper consent has not been given. The failure properly to inform the patient may not be intentional, but the touching of the plaintiff that occurs during the operation is.

C. Fault

A third argument is that battery implies a level of fault not normally exhibited by defendants in these circumstances.[59] However, as we have seen in Chapter 4,

[56] *Wallace v Kam* (n 27) [32].

[57] *cf* Somerville (n 2) 747–52, who appears to rely on a view of this kind.

[58] *Montgomery v Lanarkshire Health Board* (n 3) [13].

[59] eg, *Sidaway v Board of Governors of the Bethlem Royal Hospital* (n 15) 883; WE Peel and J Goudkamp, *Winfield and Jolowicz on Tort*, 19th edn (London, Sweet & Maxwell, 2013) 785–86.

though an 'intentional tort', the tort of battery does not require fault. This is evidenced by the fact that a surgeon who operates on a plaintiff without the plaintiff's consent commits a battery even if the surgeon possesses a sincere and reasonable belief that the plaintiff consented. The law requires the defendant to touch the plaintiff intentionally, but not that the absence of consent feature in the defendant's intentional state. To put this from the other side, even reasonable and sincere mistake is not a defence to a claim in battery. Thus, it is possible for a defendant without fault to be liable for committing a battery.

Though it is impossible to be certain, it is likely that the name of this tort is one of the main reasons why we have the disclosure rule. Particularly given its connection to the criminal law, 'battery' has connotations that do not readily apply to surgeons acting in what they consider to be the best interests of their patients. But we must not let words get the better of us. If the tort of battery were labelled instead the tort of touching another without proper consent or justification, then we may never have heard of the disclosure rule.

D. The Scope of the Plaintiff's Consent

A fourth argument—the standard argument found in the case law—holds that the disclosure rule is a consequence of the ordinary rules of the law of battery. It maintains that the defendant cannot be liable in battery because the plaintiff consented to the operation.[60] Again, however, this argument is unpersuasive.[61]

Imagine that I hold out my hand to greet you. You reach over and shake my hand unaware that I have applied contact poison to my ring. Did you consent to the handshake? In one sense, you did. You took my hand willingly. But in another sense, you did not. You did not consent to being touched with contact poison, a concomitant of this particular handshake. And that means that, in that way, our handshake constitutes a battery.[62]

Let us ask the question again: did you consent to the handshake? It is crucial to see that there is no single answer to this question. And it is just as important to see that this is not because there is something unusual about this case. It is no more than the immediate product of the aspectual character of human intentionality.[63] This is not the place to examine that notion in detail. The crucial

[60] *Chatterton v Gerson* (n 1) 442–43; *Hills v Potter* [1984] 1 WLR 641, 653; *Sidaway v Board of Governors of the Bethlem Royal Hospital* (n 15) 886–87; *Reibl v Hughes* (n 1) [9]–[13]; *Rogers v Whitaker* (n 1) 490.

[61] See also Somerville (n 2) 750–51; TK Feng, 'Failure of Medical Advice: Trespass or Negligence?' (1987) 7 *Legal Studies* 149.

[62] One possible reply is to argue that there is fraud or misrepresentation in this case. But why does fraud and misrepresentation vitiate consent? Surely it is because the presence of fraud or misrepresentation means that the victim is unable to control the use of her own body. It shows that, in fact, the apparent consent is not operative. It is not as if fraud or misrepresentation here is an independent wrong, so that, in our example, there is no battery, only a deceit. See also Somerville (n 2) 747–48.

[63] Here intentionality refers not to intentions, but rather to that property of the mind by which it is directed towards the world. For discussion, see especially JR Searle, *Intentionality: An Essay in the Philosophy of Mind* (Cambridge, Cambridge University Press, 1983).

point is that descriptions of objects and events are always aspectual—the Eiffel Tower is square when seen from above, but triangular when seen from the side, for instance. Seen under one aspect, our handshake was no more than a handshake. Viewed as such, the handshake was consensual. But the same interaction can also be interpreted as a poisoning. Seen under that aspect, it was not consensual. Was the handshake consensual, then? It depends under which aspect the handshake is viewed.

The correct way to deal with the aspectual character of human experience is to acknowledge it and adopt the appropriate aspect for the context. So, for instance, if I am asked by a friend to indicate the Eiffel Tower while ballooning over Paris and I do so by pointing and saying 'Look, it is that square structure below us there', you are being nothing but obtuse if you reply: 'The Eiffel tower isn't square, its triangular.' Importantly, what makes your claim obtuse is not that it is false. It is not false; it is true under one aspect. The claim is obtuse because that is not the *relevant* aspect—relevant, that is, to my interaction with my friend.

Unfortunately, the law frequently responds to aspect inappropriately, attempting to deal with the uncertainties generated by aspect by inventing legal rules. As it were, the law's response to our ballooning conversation would be to create a rule according to which we must adopt the overhead perspective when describing the Eiffel Tower. The problem, of course, is that this rule is inappropriate when dealing with the Eiffel Tower from the side.[64]

This discussion may at first seem esoteric. In fact, however, we have already witnessed an error of just this kind. Section V.C examined the High Court of Australia's insistence in *Wallace v Kam* that the plaintiff could not recover for the materialisation of the risk that he would have accepted: the risk of neurapraxia. The problem is that this risk can be viewed under two different aspects, under one of which the plaintiff would have accepted the risk, while under the other he would not have. As is not unusual, the Court insisted on one particular approach, the separatist, a decision that will now be taken to have laid down a precedent. The problem is that it was the wrong decision and has set what will often (but not always) be an inappropriate precedent. It is not rules that we need here but judgement informed by a proper understanding of the pertinent issues.

Consider also the decision in *Hegarty v Shine*,[65] which was first examined in Chapter 6. The parties had consensual sex, but the defendant had failed to reveal to the plaintiff that he had venereal disease, with which the plaintiff was infected. The Irish Court of Appeal held that no battery had been committed. However, the plaintiff ought to have succeeded, a fact that can be made clear by imagining that she sued on the basis not that the defendant had had sex with her without her consent, but that the defendant infected her with venereal disease without her consent.[66] Clearly, she did not consent to the transmission of the virus

[64] Examples are also analysed in A Beever, 'Agreements, Mistakes, and Contract Formation' (2009) 20 *King's Law Journal* 21, 45–50.

[65] *Hegarty v Shine* (1878) 14 Cox CC 145, 4 LR Ir 288 (CA).

[66] *cf R v Konzani* [2005] EWCA Crim 706, [2005] 2 Cr App R 14 (CA).

(or whatever microbe was involved), a transmission that occurred intentionally from the defendant's perspective.[67] Thus, under the aspect 'sexual intercourse per se'—perhaps I can be forgiven for not detailing it here—the plaintiff consented to the sexual activity. But under the aspect 'transmission of VD', the plaintiff did not consent to the activity. As Boyce J said on the Court of General Sessions of Delaware, in a case dealing with sexual relations between spouses:

> A wife in confiding her person to her husband does not consent to cruel treatment, or to infection with a loathsome disease. A husband, therefore, [having the sexually transmittable disease] inflicts on her physical abuse, and injury, resulting in great bodily harm; and he becomes ... guilty of an assault, and indeed, a completed battery.[68]

While on this theme, it is also significant to note how unhelpful the language of vitiated or mistaken consent is in this context—more deleterious consequences of the attempt to deal with the aspectual character of human intentionality by instituting legal rules. Again consider the case of the handshake. There can be no question that you consented to the handshake viewed as such, just as there can be no question that you did not consent to the handshake viewed as a poisoning. Thus, the reason I am liable for a battery is that I touched you without your consent when our interaction is viewed under the relevant aspect. This can be brought out by examining what we say in such circumstances. If asked 'Did you consent to what he did?', you would have to be very strange to answer: 'Yes I did, but that consent was mistaken or ought to be inoperative.' Rather, you will say: 'No. I did consent to a handshake, but not to *that*.' Note that this contains reference to the aspectual character of experience—'*that*' makes sense to us only because we see that my action can be described in different ways and that only some of these will be appropriate in the given contexts. And also note that we have no difficulty identifying the appropriate aspect. If I respond to you by saying 'But *that* was a handshake', all will recognise that my comment, though perfectly true, is obtuse, so much so that, though what I say is entirely accurate, I would have to be insane seriously to intend it.

How does this relate to the issue of patient consent? Let us return to *Wallace v Kam*. In that case, the plaintiff clearly gave genuine consent to the procedure *as described to him by the defendant*. The issue, however, is whether this description was an appropriate one; whether that description captured the procedure's appropriate aspect. We must ask whether the plaintiff consented to the operation fairly described.

The fundamental problem with the law at this point is that it has proceeded on the assumption that there is only one aspect under which the operation can correctly be viewed: that there is an interpretation of the event in question that is clearly available, uncontroversial and neutral as between the parties. There is no

[67] Here we must remember that intention in tort law does not mean purpose, but is much wider. For discussion, see A Beever, 'Transferred Malice in Tort Law?' (2009) 29 *Legal Studies* 400.

[68] *State v Lankford* 102 A 63 (Del 1917) [2]. See also *Crowell v Crowell* 105 SE 206 (NC 1920).

such thing. Consider, for example, the simplest case: a general practitioner administering a Band-Aid to cover a patient's lesion. There are endless ways in which this procedure could be described: treating a wound, applying a plaster, covering a lesion, showing care for the patient, using up surplus office supplies, getting rid of a hypochondriacal client and so on. All of these descriptions can be true. Under some of them, the plaintiff will have consented to the procedure, but under others the plaintiff will not have. The task, then, cannot be to pick out the uniquely correct description. There is none. The task is to adopt an *appropriate* description and ask whether the plaintiff consented to the procedure so described.

In line with the general argument of this book, this means adopting an interpretation that captures the dispute between the parties and is fair as between them.[69] Importantly, this does not mean automatically accepting that the description of the procedure given by the defendant to the plaintiff must have been the appropriate one. What is more, there is no justification for any rule that holds that it cannot be necessary to include an analysis of the risk associated with a medical procedure in order to describe that procedure appropriately. In fact, that rule, a consequence of the disclosure rule, is bizarre. Imagine an operation that carried a 0.99 risk of death. In those circumstances, it would be quite implausible to argue that the operation can appropriately be described without mentioning this risk or that a patient who had signed a consent form unaware of that risk had genuinely consented to the operation.

What was the operation in *Wallace v Kam*? If we define it as the medical procedure as described to the plaintiff by the defendant, then the plaintiff consented to it. But if we define it as that procedure with its attendant risks, then it is just as clear that the plaintiff did not consent to it. The issue, then, is which description is appropriate (not whether the plaintiff's consent was mistaken or should be vitiated). There is every reason to think that an appropriate description of the operation would include an analysis of at least the risk of paralysis. If one asked a medical professional to describe the procedure, she might well respond that it is a procedure carried out in such and such a way with the aim of achieving so and so and is accompanied by this and that risk.[70] That is likely to be how the procedure would be defined in a medical textbook. In fact, given the significance of the risk of paralysis—a one in 20 chance of 'permanent and catastrophic paralysis'[71]—I submit that it is implausible to suggest that an appropriate description of the operation could fail to mention it in this context. Under that aspect, the plaintiff did not consent to the operation.

Here we can see the disclosure rule chasing and biting its own tail. In *Wallace v Kam*, the Court accepted that it was wrong for the defendant not to inform the plaintiff of the risks. In line with the disclosure rule, it maintained that this showed

[69] See also Beever (n 47) 140–42. Note, then, that the position is not that the plaintiff should always succeed.

[70] See also Feng (n 61) 154–67.

[71] *Wallace v Kam* (n 27) [1].

that, pending proof of damage (which proved impossible), the defendant was guilty of negligence. However, the reason why the defendant needed to inform the plaintiff of these risks was because they were significant aspects of this operation. But if that were so, then how it is possible to conclude that the patient consented to the operation when he was not informed of significant aspects of it?

The disclosure rule determines that there was no battery in *Wallace v Kam*. I submit that this is no more appropriate than ruling that there was no battery in our handshake case or in *Hegarty v Shine*. In cases of the kind under examination, the courts have adopted an approach to interpreting the interaction between the parties that unfairly favours the defendant medical professional.

In related contexts, it appears that the courts appreciate this point. First, there is no equivalent of the disclosure rule outside of the medical context. Second, in Canada at least, it has been recognised that if an individual apparently consents to undergo medical research, the consent is operative only if she is aware of the attendant risks.[72] Here, the courts are not prepared to accept that the research must be rightly defined without taking into account the risks involved. There is no justification for treating medical operations differently.

E. The Standard for Determining Liability

In *Rogers v Whitaker*, the central issue for the High Court was to elucidate a test for determining when risk must be disclosed. The Court held that:

> [A] doctor has a duty to warn a patient of a material risk inherent in the proposed treatment; a risk is material if, in the circumstances of the particular case, a reasonable person in the patient's position, if warned of the risk, would be likely to attach significance to it or if the medical practitioner is or should reasonably be aware that the particular patient, if warned of the risk, would be likely to attach significance to it.[73]

Perhaps the idea here is that only the law of negligence is capable of conducting the balancing required in cases of this kind. However, that is not so.

The rule adopted by the Court in *Rogers v Whitaker*, a rule that is supported by the argument presented here, presents a picture consistent with the law of battery—indeed, with the law of trespass generally. As discussed in Chapter 6, it is not a battery to touch me in ways that are ordinarily regarded as acceptable without obtaining explicit consent—such as tapping me on the shoulder to gain my attention or gently pressing on my back with your hand in order to get by at a cocktail party—unless you have some reason to know that I do not consent to this behaviour. Similarly, it is not a trespass to my land to enter it in ways that are characteristically viewed as appropriate without obtaining consent—such as coming to knock on my front door or delivering mail to my letterbox—again unless you

[72] *Halushka v University of Saskatchewan* (1966) 53 DLR (2d) 436 (Sask CA).

[73] *Rogers v Whitaker* (n 1) 490. Gaudron J gave a separate concurring judgment.

have some reason to believe that I do not consent to this. And the rules enunciated in *Rogers v Whitaker* are the rules just examined as applied to the particular circumstances of patient consent to medical procedures. This, then, gives us more reason, not less, to think that the disclosure rule is a mistake and that battery is the appropriate action in these cases.

F. The Doctor/Patient Relationship

A further argument in favour of the disclosure rule maintains there is something special about the doctor/patient relationship that entails that liability for battery would not be appropriate in this context. The problem with this view is that it produces no support for the disclosure rule. Recall that this rule maintains that the failure to disclose risk sounds only in negligence. On the other hand, when the failure is of another kind, the ordinary approach applies, including, for example, holding that those who operate on patients without properly informing them of the nature or point of the procedure are liable for batteries. Thus, even if the peculiar nature of the doctor/patient relationship called for leniency towards doctors, it would not call specifically for the disclosure rule.

There is no doubt that the nature of the doctor/patient relationship must be taken into account when determining the doctor's duties, including her duty to inform the patient of risk, but that has nothing to do with the disclosure rule. We have not been asking: when has a doctor failed in her duty to disclose? We have been asking: what is the appropriate action when the doctor has failed in her duty to disclose? The character of the doctor/patient relationship is relevant to the first question, but not to the last. In short, the question is not whether the doctor has been guilty of wrongdoing—an important though different question. The question is, given that all accept that the doctor has been guilty of wrongdoing, how should that wrongdoing be classified?

G. Policy Arguments: Cost and Resource Allocation

A final argument focuses on the deleterious consequences of adopting the view advanced here for the providers and consumers of medical services. In the highly charged atmosphere of US medical malpractice litigation, it is understandable that some would not welcome an increase in liability. Similarly, finding surgeons liable for battery in the UK may have serious insurance implications for the National Health Service.[74] These arguments are, of course, important, but again they are not properly regarded as arguments for the disclosure rule. They maintain that liability in this area must be restricted. Perhaps that is right. But they do not show

[74] That itself, however, seems to be due to the misunderstandings uncovered in sections II and III in Ch 6.

that liability should be restricted because, in these circumstances, the plaintiff cannot have suffered a battery, but only negligence, and that is what the disclosure rule maintains. That rule presents itself as an implication of the principles of the law of tort, not as a policy-based exception to those principles.

Moreover, if we are to restrict liability in this way, we ought to make clear what is at stake. Those who support this restriction should say that patients' rights to control the use of their own bodies must be abridged in order to promote medical goals so that this view can be tested in the courts of public opinion. In our law courts, however, as we have seen, the clash between these values is occluded through the pretence that the right is, in fact, being respected. That is not acceptable.

I conclude that these reasons do not support the disclosure rule or show that negligence is the appropriate action in this context.

VII. Conclusion

Caught up in the loss model, to various degrees the courts have attempted to deal with the issue of informed consent to medical procedures through the law of negligence. That has been a mistake. The issue here is not injury, but the right of the patient to control the use of his own body. That calls for liability in the law of battery. We are dealing here not with injury or with loss prevention, but with control.

16

Conclusion

The law of tort is a remarkable creature. It is all but universally regarded as one of the bedrocks of the common law system. For this reason, it is taught as a foundational subject in most, perhaps all, law schools in and beyond the common law world. As such, it is hard to imagine a legally trained person unaware of that law's leading cases. How many Commonwealth lawyers have not heard of *Donoghue v Stevenson*[1] or American lawyers of *Palsgraf v Long Island Railroad Co*?[2] Moreover, no student of this law can avoid the impression that tort law deals with something of the utmost importance. The cases themselves are sufficient to reveal this. They present a kaleidoscope of snapshots of the human condition in conflict with itself, person to person, and the attempts to deal with the difficulties that arise. In this regard, tort law is perhaps the most human of all legal subjects.

And yet tort law is routinely disparaged by those who are closest to it. Much of it is in a state of disarray. Little of it fulfils the functions it is said to have. Because of this, in some jurisdictions, most notably that of my birth,[3] large chunks of it have been replaced by more or less successful—often less than more—statutory compensation schemes.

The famous 'Boring Figure' is an optical illusion that can appear as an ugly old woman looking towards us or a beautiful young woman looking away. Interpreted in the first way, the young woman's well-defined jaw appears as an enormous nostril, her elegant cheek as a protuberant nose and her delicate ear as a wrinkled eye. Now imagine that the drawing actually were only of the young woman and that you knew this, but that you were forced to listen to critics bemoaning the figure's grotesqueries, insisting that the woman was disfigured and in need of plastic surgery to remove her deformities. And, as if that were bad enough, imagine then needing to listen to a new bunch of critics, now determined to defend the figure's ugliness. That is my world.

Tort law is not the monstrosity staring at us in the face. It is the sophisticated and beautiful creature looking away.[4] Though not flawless, it is not the poor loss spreader or public policy enactor of our imaginations. Far more so than its more illustrious legal cousins, it is, at least potentially, the most important defender of human liberty that we have.

[1] *M'Alister (or Donoghue) (Pauper) v Stevenson* [1932] AC 562 (HL Sc).

[2] *Palsgraf v Long Island Railroad Co* 162 NE 99 (NY 1928).

[3] Accident Compensation Act 2001 (NZ).

[4] It must be remembered, however, that it is possible to be both beautiful and feckless and that beautiful young women are not always dedicated to serving one's welfare. See section III of Ch 1.

INDEX

Pages references in **bold** denote information found in tables.